ECOLOGY AND SPIRITUALITY

CW00820156

The publication of this book was supported by the Harmony Institute

 Prifysgol Cymru
Y Drindod Dewi Sant
University of Wales
Trinity Saint David

**Y Sefydliad Cytgord
The Harmony Institute**

ECOLOGY *and* SPIRITUALITY
A Brief Introduction

Jack Hunter

SOPHIA CENTRE PRESS
Ceredigion, Wales
2023

Ecology and Spirituality: A Brief Introduction
by Jack Hunter

Sophia Centre Press
University of Wales, Trinity St David
Ceredigion, Wales SA48 7ED, United Kingdom.
www.sophiacentrepress.com

Cover Design and typesetting: Jenn Zahrt
Cover Image: Max Ernst, 'La Joie de Vivre' (1936), © ADAGP, Paris
and DACS, London 2023

Publisher's Cataloging-in-Publication
(Provided by Cassidy Cataloguing Services, Inc.)
Names: Hunter, Jack, 1986- author.

Title: Ecology and spirituality : a brief introduction / Jack Hunter.
Description: Ceredigion, Wales : Sophia Centre Press, 2023. | Includes
                bibliographical references and index.
Identifiers: ISBN: 978-1-907767-23-4 (paperback) |
               978-1-907767-67-8 (ebook)
Subjects: LCSH: Ecology--Religious aspects. | Ecotheology. | Nature--
             Religious aspects. | Spirituality. | Environmental psychology.
             | Permaculture. | Environmental education.
Classification: LCC: BL65.E36 H86 2023 | DDC: 201/.77--dc23

For British Library Cataloguing in Publication Data,
A catalogue card for this book is available from the British Library.

Printed globally on demand by Lightning Source.

CONTENTS

ACKNOWLEDGEMENTS

Special thanks to Nick Campion, Bernadette Brady, Carole Taylor, Dawn Collins, Andy Letcher, Bettina Schmidt, Jenn Zahrt, David Luke, Freya Matthews, Patrick Curry, Renée E. Mazinegiizhigo-kwe Bédard, William Rowlandson, Rachael Ironside, Bron Taylor, Steve Jones, Julia Wright and the students on the MA in Ecology and Spirituality. Thanks to Les Lancaster, Bethany Butzer, Matt Colborn and Nick Boeving for facilitating such fascinating and wide-ranging discussions on the nature of consciousness. Big thanks and much love also to my family, who have to put up with my weird interests.

FOREWORD:
The Ecological and the Spiritual

Nicholas Campion

JACK HUNTER'S INTRODUCTION TO ECOLOGY AND SPIRITUALITY is a timely account of the scholarship and teaching we are currently pursuing at the University of Wales Trinity Saint David especially, for me, the exploration of the ancient and classical concept of Harmony, with a capital 'H', in relation to sustainability, a concept based on the premise of universal interconnectedness.[1] The question before us is how do we human beings live on our planet, knowing that we are an integral part of a single system of quite extraordinary complexity.

My own route into the complexity of the natural world has always been through simple observation: sit still, watch, and we can see some amazing phenomena. Anyone who has ever contemplated a solitary spider building a web, or a column of ants carrying food to their nest, will know that intelligence is spread throughout the animal world amongst creatures who have nothing resembling the brains that human beings, or most animals, possess. Once it was thought that only human beings have a thinking, reflective, consciousness, or what is sometimes called reason. This philosophy, or religious belief, if we like, is the essence of anthropocentrism, the doctrine, inherited from the creationist, monotheistic religions, that human beings are special, unique, and set clearly apart from the natural world. According to this world view, animals are purely reactive, unable to think or plan, and devoid of any sense of a past or future. The entire non-human animal world, it is believed, is governed by instinct, an ill-defined concept designed to explain how animals could act while having no capacity to think.[2] However, complex animal behaviour, from spiders creating webs and ants collecting food, to a pack of lions hunting an antelope over distances too great for them to maintain visual contact with each other, or a flock of birds forming astonishing patterns, such as the as yet unexplained murmurations of starlings, surely challenges the lingering belief that animals cannot think, collaborate, or plan.[3] Rather than concluding that they cannot think, though, it might be more profitable to find an alternative solution – that they think, but in ways we cannot comprehend. If one bee can learn from another how to access sugar-water, then we are surely in what, for standard models, is uncharted territory of animal cognition.[4] This is before we even come on to the recently much-publicised evidence for plant cognition, which is dramatically eroding the commonly accepted boundaries between plants and animals.[5] It is over a century-and-a-half since Charles Darwin effectively collapsed the notion that human beings are not part of the animal world and set us on a new path to understanding the complexities of the natural world: his great work, *The Origin of Species*, was published in 1859. It was in the wake of Darwin's work that Ernst Haeckel introduced the term 'Oecologie' in 1866.

Ecology is, arguably, the most important science of our times. The term science has various meanings so, to clarify, here I am talking about critical and evidence-based research with the aim of expanding our knowledge. Ecology may not have the dramatic profile of space technology, the massive social consequences of the computer revolution, or the likely hugely imminent and disruptive impact of artificial intelligence, but it is the only form of science which starts from the fundamental premise that all things are interconnected. This understanding is of huge consequences for our relationship with the physical environment, for it requires us to recognise profound interrelationships between the tiniest microscopic organisms and insects, larger animals, biological processes, plant life, geology and topography, mountains, valleys, deserts, forests, air, water, heat, light, cold, dark and seasons on both local and global levels, along with the rhythms, cycles, and pulses of time. We can look at small patches of ground or the whole planet, but ultimately everything exists in a relationship with everything else. And human beings are an intimate part of those relationships. Nothing is outside the system. Human beings as individuals are part of it, as are their thoughts, feelings, emotions, aspirations and actions.

In modern terms, adapted from the language of electromagnetism, everything is part of a field. Arne Naess, who formulated the principles of Deep Ecology in 1973, adopted the field metaphor when he described Deep Ecology's first principle as:

Rejection of the man-in-environment image in favour of the relational, total-field image. Organisms as knots in the biospherical nest or field of intrinsic relations.[6]

Everything, Naess concluded, is relational: nothing can be said to exist except in relation to everything else, a concept which now pervades anthropology. Phillipe Descola, for example, talks about human-animal-planet ecologies as 'an ecology of relations', or a relational ecology.[7] Andrew Benjamin proposes a 'relational ontology' in which we can only understand being – or existence – if we recognise that nothing exists in itself, only in relation to everything else.[8] Kenneth J. Gergen presents relationality as central to human experience and well-being.[9] Manuel da Landa explored the ways in which matter is central to existence, relating to, and acting on, each other, shaping the world as they do so. This model, termed the 'New Materialism' or 'New Materiality' has been taken up at the University of Wales Trinity Saint David, for example by Luci Attala in her work on water.[10]

Naess himself was deeply influenced by Albert Einstein and the concept of time and space as interdependent and in 1985 he met the physicist Øyvind Grøn, with whom he collaborated on an attempt to make the mathematics of relativity accessible to a general audience. Together, Naess and Grøn considered the consequences of Einstein's theory of relativity for vector fields. Using wind as an example, they wrote:

> When we are outdoors in the wind, the moving wind fills the region around us. There is a measurable velocity of the air everywhere in the region [...] The velocity [of the wind] has a magnitude and a direction. It is a vector. Thus, a velocity field is linked conceptually with every point of the region. These abstract vectors are everywhere. If one can think of God as omnipresent, then one might also be able to think of the factors as omnipresent. In such a region there is said to be a vector field.[11]

Every single thing, then, participates in a field, perhaps many fields, in which it connects with all other things in the field to the extent that it is impossible to be sure that a single thing actually exists. Einstein's influence pervades modern thought, encouraging ideas of interconnectedness across different disciplines and specialities. The French philosophers Gilles Deleuze and Félix Guattari came up with a version of interconnectedness rationalised by the rhizome, a plant which sends out horizontal roots which, in turn send out new shoots. The rhizome has no central trunk, which for Deleuze and Guattari signified that nothing has a real centre. This is how they put it:

> A rhizome ceaselessly establishes connections between semiotic chains [chains of meaning], organizations of power, and circumstances relative to the arts, sciences, and social struggles.[12]

Deleuze and Guattari take the rhizome as biological plant and make it a universal metaphor for human society and politics, arguing that there are neither centres nor hierarchies, only relationships which encompass everything. We may perceive hierarchies and centres of power in particular situations, and we may indeed need to deal with them in order to resolve social, economic and political issues, but, from a wider perspective, we are mistaken. When we see the totality of existence on our planet as a single thing, rather than many things, then everything, from the smallest and most transient, to the largest and, seemingly most permanent, is interdependent.

Such interdependence takes us to the somewhat problematic distinction made in post seventeenth-century western culture between things which are conscious and alive on the one hand, and things which are not, on the other. Modern biology holds that things which reproduce are alive, and things which don't are not, so stones, water, soil and air are therefore not alive. The conventional modern position added an additional layer, that only human beings are conscious. Safe to say, this was the dominant intellectual position in the West for most of the nineteenth and twentieth centuries.

Yet the dominant position in the West *until* the seventeenth century, and other cultures until they began to import western ideas, was quite the reverse, and held that there is no clear boundary between biologically reproducing organisms and those things that don't reproduce. Neither is there any part of the world which is not alive and therefore not part of the conscious universe. The standard manifesto of this world view is Plato's dialogue *Timaeus*, written around 350 BCE and available to western scholars, at least in part, without a break since then. One passage which every literate person in medieval and Renaissance Europe from the end of the Roman Empire up to the seventeenth century would have been familiar with is this:

> But we shall affirm that the Cosmos, more than aught else, resembles most closely that Living Creature of which all other living creatures, severally, and generally, are portions. For that Living Creature embraces, and contains within itself, all the intelligible Living Creatures, just as this

Universe contains us, and all the other visible living creatures that have been fashioned.[13]

The English translation may smack of that slightly old-fashioned style so often favoured by modern classical scholars, but the meaning is clear: the entire world is living and conscious. The post-seventeenth-century western distinctions between what is alive and what is not, and between what is conscious and what is not, is therefore a recent deviation from the standard view and increasingly looks like a failure of perception. The logic of ecology is so challenging because it takes us straight back to the previous way of thinking.

Perhaps it is time to turn to Timothy Morton, who Jack Hunter quotes extensively. Morton talks about the fundamental principle of ecology being to 'join the dots and see that everything is connected'.[14] But this is not enough, he says. What he calls *the* ecological thought has to do with:

> love, loss, despair, and compassion [...] capitalism and what might exist after capitalism [...] amazement, open-mindedness, and wonder [...] doubt, confusion, and scepticism [...] concepts of space and time [...] delight, beauty, ugliness, disgust, irony, and pain [...] consciousness and awareness [...] ideology and critique [...] reading and writing [...] race, class, gender [...] sexuality [...] ideas of self, and the weird paradoxes of subjectivity [...] society [... and] coexistence.[15]

Ecology, therefore, deals with everything: nothing is outside its remit. It is the ultimate interdisciplinary discipline.

This then takes us to the thorny question of spirituality, a word with particularly uncertain and ill-defined meanings. Jack Hunter deals with this ably and effectively in chapter 2. A common view is that spirituality is a kind of flexible, undogmatic and often individualistic version of religion. However, as scholars in the field know, many religions require a spiritual dimension. One solution to the problem of definition was proposed by Paul Heelas and Linda Woodhead and their colleagues, who acknowledged that the common usage of the terms religion and spirituality might overlap in that, for example, Christians can have a spiritual devotion to Christ. Yet, Heelas and Woodhead propose a distinction between the two concepts in which religions require obedience to a greater authority, while spirituality, as they write, 'sacralizes subjective life', subjectivity being the experience or perception that there is something greater and beyond material existence.[16] Of course, Heelas and Woodhead adopt the objective-subjective binary model in which the former refers to phenomena which are real, and the latter to those which are only thought to be real, a distinction which is constantly shifting in terms of western science as new research opens fresh understandings of the world, as evidenced by the latest findings in plant intelligence. It is also at odds with most spiritual traditions themselves. Is there something more in the natural world than physical matter? Actually, much of the latest science says there is. And is consciousness more than a biproduct of physical processes? Well, a substantial current of western philosophy, let alone the worldviews of non-western cultures, assumes that it is. The question of, and inquiry into, spirituality therefore becomes a logical extension of the need to comprehend humanity's place in the world, and therefore of our understanding of ecology. And this is why Jack Hunter's book is essential reading.

INTRODUCTION

From mycelial networks to mystical experiences, sacred geography to the ecological self, and non-human intelligence to indigenous cosmologies, this book serves as an introduction to key themes arising at the intersection of Ecology and Spirituality. Questions considered in these pages include: What is the relationship between nature and culture? Can there be a spiritual response to the ecological crisis currently facing our planet and, if so, what might it look like? What is the role of religion? What do paranormal and other extraordinary experiences tell us about the nature of the self and our relationship with the world around us? What is the role of traditional ecological knowledge in facing up to the challenges of a rapidly changing world? How do we study and make sense of this field, and what methods can we use to research it? These are just some of the questions explored by staff and students on the MA in Ecology and Spirituality, taught through the Sophia Centre for the Study of Cosmology in Culture, a teaching and research centre at the University of Wales Trinity Saint David, who I have had the privilege of working with since 2019.[1] This book has grown organically from seminars with students on the course, and seeks to draw together many of the different threads that interconnect the ecological and the spiritual.

For my part, I have been thinking increasingly about the issue of non-human consciousness over the past few years, and in particular about how human beings relate to and understand the natural world. My own journey into this territory began when I started work with a permaculture education project in 2016 – the *One School One Planet* project – which introduced me to the study of natural principles and ecological processes through the lens of permaculture design.[2] During conversations with permaculture practitioners I began to notice that they would occasionally talk about their observations of natural systems in almost animistic terms (see Chapter Five) – they might say things like 'the willow chose me', for example, as if some sort of communication had taken place between them and the plants they worked with.[3] I also noticed that a crucial factor in establishing this kind of animistic perspective was a process of active observation and interaction with natural systems – which is in fact the first of permaculture's twelve design principles (see Chapter Eleven). This resonated with elements of my own doctoral research on trance and physical mediumship in Bristol (which may at first glance seem worlds apart from the study of ecology), where I had argued that the emergence of spirit personalities in séances – another subtle form of non-human consciousness – requires a similarly detailed and active process of participatory observation and interaction.[4]

This line of inquiry was continued in 2019 with the publication of *Greening the Paranormal: Exploring the Ecology of Extraordinary Experience*,[5] which is a curated collection of essays from a multi-disciplinary cast of contributors examining the relationship between ecology and anomalistics (encompassing fields such as parapsychology and cryptozoology, as well as the study of religious and spiritual experiences). Each chapter approaches the subject from a different perspective (from the anthropological and indigenous to the parapsychological), and the book attempts to map out this area of intermingling research trajectories. Indeed, parts of my introduction to *Greening the Paranormal* have been woven into (and built upon in) this book. This book and *Greening the Paranormal* are, therefore, organically entangled with one another across time and space. It is also entangled with two other edited volumes – *Mattering the Invisible: Technologies, Bodies and the Realm of the Spectral*, which I co-edited with Dr. Diana Espirito Santo and *Folklore, People and Place: International Perspectives on Tourism and Tradition in Storied Places*, which I edited with Dr. Rachael Ironside.[6]

Both of these books have themes that intersect with those explored in these pages. Finally, since 2019 I have been developing and teaching the MA in Ecology and Spirituality as an online course taught through the Sophia Centre. This has given me the opportunity to think more deeply about many of the issues raised in these preliminary excursions with my colleagues and students, and to develop the ideas brought together in these pages.

This book might share some similarities with other tomes exploring the meeting points of the religious, the spiritual and the ecological – and there are numerous excellent books on this and related subjects out there, many of which will be referred to in the pages that follow.[7] But while this is the case, it is also true that this book seeks to push beyond established models and standard conversations in the study of religion and ecology. This book aims to enable the exploration of *new* possibilities in the study of this relationship, as well as providing suggestions for practical participation in subtle activism. In this sense, this book represents what I would call an 'ontologically flooded' introduction to ecology and spirituality. This essentially involves an appreciation of as wide a range of contributing factors as possible – some of which might even challenge the dominant ontological frameworks – or theories of the nature of being – of the 'popular western scientific worldview'. While many academic studies of the intersection of ecology and spirituality operate from an ontologically and phenomenologically bracketed social-facts approach (that is that we can study all manner of extraordinary beliefs about the world, so long as we acknowledge that they are *just beliefs*), this study embraces and explores other ontological possibilities. Evidence and implications from parapsychological research, for example, are taken into consideration, perspectives from traditional and indigenous worldviews are presented alongside new discoveries in the biological sciences, and discussions about telepathy, fairies, gnomes and monsters are all to be found between these covers. Hopefully, their relevance will become clear as we get deeper into our conversation. Taken together, these different strands suggest that when it comes to thinking about spirits of place (or other forms of non-human intelligence) and the often profound sense of connection felt with them by human beings, we are not *just* talking about beliefs, but something much more complex, and much more *real*.

This book can be thought of as a primer, or foundation course, for students of the emerging field of research at the intersections of ecology and spirituality. The first chapter introduces the science of ecology and the role of culture in interpreting ecological systems. It is important to note from the outset that this conversation is rooted in the earth and its processes. Chapter Two then examines the concept of spirituality from a variety of sociological, psychological and phenomenological perspectives. Chapter Three gives a survey of the many crises currently facing the world's ecosystems, and considers some of the political, activist and philosophical responses to them. It is these crises that give real meaning and value to the conversations presented in this book. The next chapter moves into phenomenological territory and considers the connection between nature mysticism and Green Religion. In the fifth chapter the non-human is the focus of attention, with discussions centering around the natural history of mind and intelligence. Chapter Six – 'Fairies at the Bottom of the Garden' – surveys some of the different ways that human beings conceptualise non-human intelligences and engage with them through cultural practices such as gardening. Chapter Seven seeks to explore the convergence of the anthropology of consciousness, Deep Ecology and parapsychology in the concept of the ecological self. Chapter Eight is a survey of ideas and perspectives on Sacred Geography, exploring the nature of the sacred and its relation to space and place. The next chapter gives an overview of perspectives on traditional ecological knowledge systems from around the world and the role they might play in dealing with the unfolding ecological crisis. Chapter Ten takes a deep dive into 'Organic Ontologies', exploring how organismic models of reality might provide better orientations within the cosmos than popular mechanistic models. The final chapter then considers how broader cultural attitudes towards the living natural world can be influenced through education and outdoor learning.

Every effort has been made to make this book as comprehensive and concise as possible, given its small size, and any omissions or errors are my own. It is also hoped that the bibliography included at the end of the book will be useful for those just beginning to navigate these waters, as well as for those who have already dipped their toes.

CHAPTER ONE:
What is Ecology?

To begin, this first chapter introduces ecology as a field of scientific research and lays out some of its essential concepts, before moving on to consider some of the different ways in which ecology and culture interact. It is the grounding of ecology in the interconnected physical and biological processes of nature that gives the field its vitality, and it is also what makes its relationship to spirituality – a concept often associated with the immaterial and non-physical (see Chapter Two) – all the more interesting, so it is worth taking some time to unpack.

Origins

The term 'ecology' is derived from the Greek words *oikos*, meaning house, or home, and *logos*, meaning to reason, plan or study. Ecology is, therefore, in a very literal sense, concerned with the 'study of our home' – *with where we live*. It is also clear from its etymological roots that the word has a relationship to other familiar terms, such as *economy* – which refers to planning the movement of goods into, out of, and between households.[1] This association raises interesting questions about the different ways that we understand and manage our homes in relation to the world around us, and the various impacts of the decisions we make within the household on the wider environment. But the word ecology has also come to mean much more than this – expanding outward from the household to encompass the wider natural environment, and indeed the planet as a whole – the study of our home, with a capital H.

As a concerted and systematic effort to document and understand the natural world, ecology can be traced back at least as far as Aristotle's pioneering classifications of animals and other natural phenomena in the fourth century BCE, along with his student Theophrastus' classifications of plants.[2] It is also clear that an understanding of ecological principles would have been essential for our much earlier ancestors. Hunter-gatherer societies, even today, are fully dependent for their survival on having an intimate knowledge and understanding of the flora, fauna and natural cycles and processes that surround and sustain them.[3] These indigenous modes of ecological understanding are often referred to as systems of 'Traditional Ecological Knowledge' (TEK), understood as systems of knowledge built up over thousands of years of engagement with particular environmental niches[4] (see Chapter Nine). Ecology is therefore something that human beings have likely always done, in one form or another. We have always tried to make sense of the world around us, and to position ourselves within it through detailed observation and modelling of the natural environment.

As a 'scientific discipline', however, ecology is still a relative spring chicken compared to other fields of inquiry, such as chemistry, physics and even psychology. It gradually emerged as a sub-field of biology in the nineteenth century, but did not become established in university departments in its own right until the middle decades of the twentieth. The honorary title of 'father' of ecology is often given to the controversial German zoologist Ernst Haeckel (1834–1919), who introduced the term 'Oecologie' into biological discourse in 1866. Haeckel's contribution to the biological sciences was immense – ranging from the discovery and naming of thousands of hitherto unknown species, through to the pioneering use of scientific illustration in natural history.[5] His reputation is unfortunately tarred, however, by his promotion of social Darwinism, which applies natural selection to human society, and eugenics, which he saw as socio-cultural extensions of biological evolutionary principles.[6] Dark and disturbing strands such as these continue to run through attempts to interpret and employ ecological observations and theories for social and cultural purposes. It is also clear that although Haeckel was a brilliant biologist, and a pioneering one in many regards, he was far from an ecologist in the modern sense of the term, failing to fully grasp the complexity of the interconnected systems that 'modern' ecology reveals.[7]

Scientific Ecology

Ecology eventually crystallised as a distinctive field of research – establishing what might be termed 'Scientific Ecological Knowledge' (SEK) – in the 1960s and 1970s. As ecological insights began to percolate through into the popular consciousness they also became woven into various different cultural and counter-cultural currents (some of which will be explored later). A major player in both the professionalisation and popularisation of ecology in the 1960s was the biologist Eugene Odum (1913–2002). He was particularly influential in broadening the appeal of ecology as a field of study, primarily through his best-selling textbooks, including *Fundamentals of Ecology,* first published in 1956 and still in print today. Odum argued that as a science ecology is concerned with understanding the relationships between living organisms and their environments, but he also emphasised the extent to which human beings are themselves embedded within this complexity as an active part of nature, rather than separate from it. Indeed, Odum saw ecology as a bridge between the natural and social sciences, defining it as the 'the study of the structure and function of nature', crucially adding that 'mankind is a part of nature.'[8]

Broadly speaking, though, ecology is a positivistic science in the sense that it relies on empirical and quantitative research methods that align it with other so-called 'hard science' disciplines in the academy, rather than with the 'soft' social sciences. Similarly, there is little room in 'mainstream' ecological science for what might be termed the 'spiritual' – biology and ecology generally adopt a materialist metaphysics, though there are exceptions (see Chapter Ten).[9]

Nevertheless, the big picture of the natural world that ecological science reveals, as well as the implications for our behaviour that go along with it, have a much wider relevance and public appeal, and is often incorporated into 'spiritual' worldviews.[10]

Cultural Ecologies

An important distinction to make at this juncture is between ecological models created by human beings, which are cultural, and the actual natural world and its processes. Different cultural systems have their own idiosyncratic interpretations and elaborations of ecological principles, which in turn lead to different modes of behaviour in the world. In the 1960s, the anthropologist Charles O. Frake (1930–2021) sought to highlight these cultural models of ecology as a valid field for ethnographic research, exploring how they are informed by and impact upon ecological systems. From this perspective cultural ecologies may be understood as interfaces between human beings and the natural world, shaping the way that we interact with and behave in the ecological environment. Frake explains that while scientific ecology entails the 'study of the workings of ecosystems' and the 'behavioral interdependences of different kinds of organisms with respect to one another and to their non-biotic environment', the field of cultural ecology is concerned with the study of 'the role of culture as a dynamic component of any ecosystem of which [humans are] a part.'[11] Cultures, therefore, contribute to the ecosystem – and are in fact a part of it. The anthropologist Roy Rappaport (1926–1997) explains that:

> Nature is seen by humans through a screen of beliefs, knowledge, and purposes, and it is in terms of their images of nature, rather than of the 'actual structure' of nature, that they act. Yet it is upon nature itself that they do act, and it is nature itself that acts upon them, nurturing or destroying them.[12]

The cultural models we use to frame our interactions with nature must therefore be central to any effort at trying to address human environmental behaviour. It is also possible to talk about popular culture ecologies, which shape and inform the ways that we interact with natural systems in the contemporary media-oriented world. For example, the ways in which ecology and ecological themes are represented in films and on television, or in different contexts, such as in New Age and other popular spiritualities.[13] The influence of mycorrhizal networks – the so-called 'Wood Wide Web' – on the popular imagination, and so also on popular culture more generally, is a particularly strong example of an emerging pop culture ecology, with a potential for wide-reaching socio-cultural effects.[14] The fascination with fungi and mycelium has been stoked by writers such as Terence McKenna (1946–2000), Paul Stamets, and more recently by Peter Wohlleben, Merlin Sheldrake and Aliya Whiteley,[15] and others. The mycelium has recently also entered into the realm of video games, TV and film.[16] Before moving on to consider some of the ways in which scientific ecology has been interpreted and applied by different cultural groups, however, I first want to unpack some of its key scientific principles and ideas.

Ecosystems

One of the most influential concepts to emerge from ecological science is the notion of the 'ecosystem.' Like many other scientific terms – such as 'quantum', for example – the idea of the 'ecosystem' rapidly osmosed into other fields of research, as well as into popular culture. Because of this the term is often employed in a variety of different ways and frequently with different inflections of meaning that may be far removed from its original intended usage – the 'media ecosystem,' the 'digital advertising ecosystem,' and so on. Its technical meaning in ecological science, however, is quite specific. Eugene Odum, for example, defined the concept of the ecosystem as referring to:

> A unit of biological organization made up of all of the organisms in a given area [...] interacting with the physical environment so that a flow of energy leads to characteristic trophic structure and material cycles within the system.[17]

The systematic study of living organisms embedded in their environmental contexts has revealed an image of the natural world as consisting of a complex network of relationships and cycles – interconnected systems. Not only are there interactions between living organisms – such as predator-prey relations, for example – but there are also interactions between living organisms and what are often considered to be non-living components of the environment – sunlight, energy, gases, minerals, water and so on. From the perspective of the ecosystem *everything* is connected in a very real way – from the smallest bacterium and mineral to the largest mammals, trees and mountains – all bound together through continuous cycles of exchange. These interactions include the transfer of energy and nutrients through 'food chains,' which in turn form networks known as 'food webs' that connect the disparate elements of ecosystems into a whole.[18] This has come to be known as the 'systems view.'[19]

Plants (whether we are talking about flowers, shrubs, trees, mosses, phytoplankton, or any of the other varied forms of plant life), are referred to as 'primary producers' – they capture energy from the sun by the process of photosynthesis, creating energy rich sugars that enter into the food chain when consumed by herbivores – referred to as 'secondary consumers' – who in turn may be consumed by predators ('tertiary consumers'). Thus the sun's energy is gradually distributed amongst the biological organisms in an ecosystem, steadily decreasing in content as it moves higher up the food chain. Energy and nutrients are also constantly being cycled around this system through processes of growth and decay.

Energy and nutrients collected and stored by trees, plants and other living organisms over the course of their lifetimes are eventually released back into the wider system at death through the slow action of decomposers such as bacteria and fungi.[20]

Distinctive ecosystems develop in, and are adapted to particular geographical and environmental niches, so that we can talk of, for example, saltwater ecosystems, freshwater ecosystems, desert ecosystems, woodland ecosystems, and so on, all of which have their own distinctive features and characteristics, with specially adapted flora and fauna. That is not to say that they are entirely separate systems, however, because they are all connected by biological, geological, atmospheric and other processes to the extent that the destruction of one ecosystem can have a domino effect on another.[21] Groups of ecosystems that share similar environmental characteristics are referred to as *biomes*.[22] The sum total of the living organisms on Earth – including plants, animals, bacteria, fungi and more – is referred to as the *biosphere* (the totality of the Earth's many diverse biomes), which is in constant interaction with the atmosphere, hydrosphere and lithosphere. Remarkably, the biosphere has been shown to extend from about 0.5km below the floor of the ocean, right up to about 6.5 km above the Earth's surface.[23] It is a complex and seething meshwork of interconnected ecosystems that hugs the planet like a blanket.

Succession

An interesting and important feature of ecosystems is their apparent tendency to move toward increased complexity and diversity through a process known as 'succession,' first described by the biologist and botanist Frederic Clements (1874–1945). In 1928 Clements published an influential paper outlining his argument that plant communities – such as forests – can be thought of as holistic living organisms in their own right, functioning like complex physical bodies made up of many interconnected parts.[24] This would prove to be a major point of contention within the emerging field of ecology, which will be explored later in this chapter. Somewhat more recently, Eugene Odum provided a very specific, and much less controversial, definition of the term as referring to three key parameters. He writes that succession is:

10

(i) [...] an orderly process of community development that is reasonably directional [...] (ii) It results from modification of the physical environment by the community; that is, succession is community-controlled even though the physical environment determines the pattern, the rate of change, and often sets limits as to how far development can go. (iii) It culminates in a stabilized ecosystem [with] maximum biomass [...] and symbiotic function between organisms [...][25]

Each stage in the process of succession is referred to as a *sere*, and with each successive sere the plant community tends to become more biodiverse, and so more complex. Beginning with an area of land devoid of any plants – a bare rock surface, for example – specially adapted hardy plants (known as pioneer species) colonise the ground, establishing themselves in any small cracks that they might find. This is the beginning of the process of transforming the environment to make it capable of supporting other subsequent species.[26] They break up the soil, changing its structure to allow more air and water into the ground, making it easier for less hardy plants to become established. The organisms that make up an ecosystem are, therefore, active in changing and shaping local environmental conditions to suit their own needs, as well as the needs of other species.

From this perspective, *co-operation* between species seems to be essential to ecosystem development (though we cannot ignore the very real role of competition either). Indeed, organisms often work mutually within a system – where one species acts as a host for another, for example in the case of the remora fish (*Remora remora*), which feeds on the parasites of sharks in exchange for their protection – and sometimes symbiotically with one another – where two organisms live an entirely interconnected life, as in the case of mycorrhizal fungi in the root systems of trees – to create optimum conditions for biodiversity. The evolutionary biologist Lynn Margulis (1938–2011) suggested that symbiosis and collaboration are in fact fundamental organic principles driving evolution.[27] This observation, much like Frederic Clements' understanding of succession as a communal process, seems to run counter to the mainstream reductionist Darwinian concept of competition – 'survival of the fittest' – as the sole driver of evolutionary change and adaptation, and is a point of contention amongst ecologists who often tend towards one or the other interpretation.[28]

Keystone Species and Trophic Cascades

The complexity and biodiversity of ecological systems is maintained through a combination of interconnected processes and factors. Keystone species, for example, are species that have a large and important effect on their natural environment even though there may be relatively few of them in the ecosystem – apex predators, such as wolves, for instance. The concept was developed and introduced into ecology by the biologist Robert T. Paine (1933–2016) in the 1960s. Just like the keystone in a bridge, if a keystone species is removed the ecosystem will collapse from the top down. The standard view in ecology had been that ecosystems are maintained from the bottom up – in other words, that ecosystems are built on a foundation of plants (the primary producers), at the bottom of the food chain. In a simple field study Paine revealed that this might not be the full story. He set about to investigate what would happen if he removed ochre starfish – one by one – from a single rock-pool on the shore of Makah Bay, Washington. The removal of the apex predator from the rock-pool ecosystem resulted in a proliferation of mussels, which in turn consumed all of the algae in the pool, thus removing the ecosystem of its primary producer and so eventually culminating in a sterile rock-pool, devoid of life. Paine's findings suggested that ecosystems are also maintained by predators at the top of the food chain, just as much as it is supported by primary producers (plants). The role of the predators in the system is to keep the number of herbivores in check so that the primary producers are not overwhelmed.[29]

Paine referred to this movement of energy and modulation of ecosystems as a 'trophic cascade.' This is the notion that species at, or near, the top of the food chain directly and indirectly regulate the species and population sizes in the rest of the community lower down, which is contrary the common sense view of ecosystems as regulated from the primary producers upward. It means that biodiversity depends on predators just as much as it does on primary producers bringing energy into the system. The biologist Michael Pace and colleagues explain that:

> Reciprocal predator-prey effects [...] alter the abundance, biomass or productivity of a population community or trophic level across more than one link in a food web [...] Trophic cascades often originate from top predators, such as wolves, but are not necessarily restricted to starting only in the upper reaches of the food web.[30]

The classic example of the capacity of trophic cascades to transform ecosystems is the case of the eradication, and eventual re-introduction, of wolves in Yellowstone National Park. In 1995, after seventy years of near-extinction as a result of over-hunting, wolves were re-introduced into the Yellowstone National Park with remarkable consequences. In the absence of predatory wolves, large populations of red deer had resulted in overgrazing around streams and rivers (just as Paine's model would suggest), which in turn had negatively affected the stability of riverbanks causing them to meander randomly through the landscape. When the wolves returned, red deer numbers fell into decline through predation and, as a consequence, trees along riverbanks were able to flourish again. The root systems of the newly established trees helped to re-stabilise the riverbanks, while their branches and leaves served to shade and cool the water, providing cover for fish and creating new habitats for insects and birds. The effects of the re-introduction of wolves into Yellowstone National Park were seen right the way through the ecosystem, encouraging much higher levels of biodiversity through the creation of new niches and habitats for exploitation by other species.[31]

Michael Pace and colleagues point out that trophic cascades such as this occur in all manner of diverse ecosystems: 'from the inside of insects to the open ocean [...] in streams, lakes and the marine intertidal zone [...] fields, soils [and] forests.'[32] Trophic cascades, therefore, appear to be universal characteristics of ecosystem dynamics at the micro and macro levels, and go a long way towards demonstrating that harmony in nature is a dynamic process that is never fully in balance. Ecosystem stability is a constantly fluctuating ebb and flow that arises through complex interactions between organisms and between organisms and the environment. What balance there is in ecosystems, therefore, comes from both the 'bottom up' – from the plants, as primary producers and the foundation of ecosystems – and from the 'top down' – through the activities of higher predators and their cascading influence on species lower down the food chain. This effect, which is well documented, resonates with ideas about ecological harmony arising through biodiversity and complexity within ecological systems – diminished ecosystems, with reduced biodiversity, are unstable and prone to collapse, while complex systems have greater stability.[33]

Cultures Within Ecological Science

It is probably already clear that ecological principles derived from the scientific observation of natural systems are not free from value judgements, and may be understood and interpreted according to different theoretical, ethical and political frameworks. Just as there are ongoing debates in the field of quantum physics over how best to understand and interpret the observation of weird natural phenomena at the subatomic scale,[34] so too are there different and competing interpretations within the science of ecology.[35] These differing interpretations can be understood in terms of the philosopher of science Thomas Kuhn's (1922–1996) notion of 'paradigms,' which he defined as 'accepted examples of scientific practice' including 'law, theory, application, and instrumentation.' These accepted theories and practices 'provide models from which spring particular coherent traditions of research.'[36] The differences between distinctive interpretations of the raw ecological data – between different 'traditions of research' within ecology – are illustrated through key debates in ecological science, which have been present since the discipline's emergence, and continue to this day.

Holism-Reductionism Debate

In a paper on the sociology of ecological science, the sociologists John Bellamy Foster and Brett Clark delineate a tension early in the development of the field between those researchers who adopted an organicist, holistic and teleological interpretation of ecosystem development, and those who assumed a materialist, mechanistic, systems view (see Chapter Ten). This has come to be known as the 'holism-reductionism' debate, or sometimes the 'emergentism-reductionism' debate.[37] There are similar debates in many disciplines, such as between macro and micro perspectives in sociology, for example. As an illustration of an emergentist and holistic approach in the history of ecology, Foster and Clark refer to the work of Frederic Clements, whose notion of succession is discussed above. For Clements, the direction of succession was always moving towards increased biodiversity and complexity, and as such was indicative of a teleological drive in nature. Clements' model saw the 'climax community' as a single living organism. Foster and Clark explain that:

> Clements provided an idealist, teleological ontology of vegetation that viewed a 'biotic community' as a 'complex organism' that developed

through a process called 'succession' to a 'climax formation.' He therefore presented it as an organism or 'superorganism' with its own life history, which followed predetermined, teleological paths aimed at the overall harmony and stability of the superorganism.[38]

From this perspective, succession is the cumulative endeavour of a community of living organisms towards increased diversity, interconnectivity and stability within the ecosystem. It is the natural process by which super-organisms – such as climax forest systems – grow to maturity. Understood through the lens of Clements' organic emergentism, ecosystem development is a communal process, with different elements working together for the mutual benefit of the whole, supporting Margulis' symbiotic hypothesis. This has been a particularly controversial idea amongst Western biologists.[39] Biology is a field which by and large adopts a reductionist approach. The controversy is especially evident in debates over what has come to be known as the 'Gaia hypothesis.'

Complexity-Stability Debate

Just as there have long been debates between holists and reductionists in ecology, so too have there been disagreements between ecologists who suggest that ecosystems become *more resilient* to change the *greater* the diversity of species they contain, and those who suggest that *simpler* ecosystems are more resilient. This is known as the 'complexity-stability debate.'[40] Researchers in the 1950s, such as Eugene Odum, who assumed a broadly organicist view of ecology, had argued that greater connections for energy transfer within an ecosystem resulted in that system being less susceptible to the loss of any single species, or to unexpected climate fluctuations. In this scenario, if an element is removed from a food web it can be compensated for by redirecting energy flows, or by drawing energy from other parts of the system, so it makes sense to see an adaptive benefit in having a highly biodiverse, more complex ecosystem.[41] With this principle in mind, then, from the holist/organicist perspective ecosystems were understood to develop towards increased complexity and increased biodiversity, leading to a greater number of energy pathways within the system. This is known as the 'insurance hypothesis.'[42]

By the 1970s, however, this view was increasingly challenged by a new generation of researchers who held that ecosystems with *fewer* elements

15

were more resilient. Basing their models on mechanistic Newtonian physics, they argued that the more elements a system contains the more chaotic it becomes, and so the more likely it is to collapse. From this perspective simpler ecosystems were thought to be more resilient to change, while larger more complex systems were thought to be less so.[43] Here, again, we see the re-emergence of the holism-reductionism debate. Those who hold that greater biodiversity in a system leads to greater resilience are adopting an holistic perspective that emphasises complexity and reciprocal interconnections between organisms, while those adopting a reductionist view rather focus in on the micro-level, and emphasise a mechanistic simplicity. In reality, however, the truth is likely somewhere in between these two strong positions.

Gaia

The 'Gaia hypothesis' is essentially a logical extension of the principle of succession to the whole Earth system. The Gaia hypothesis, developed by James Lovelock and Lynn Margulis in the 1970s, suggests that planet Earth itself is an active living organism – a great whole composed of multiple inter-related parts working together to maintain a global equilibrium.[44] Lovelock and Margulis defined Gaia simply as the 'notion of the biosphere as an active adaptive control system able to maintain the Earth in homeostasis.'[45] The idea that the planet is a self-regulating system is not new in the history of science – there have been other proponents of the homeostatic Earth, such as James Hutton (1726–1797), who argued in the eighteenth century that atmospheric gases were regulated by planetary geological processes and that the Earth was an enormous living being.[46] But it would be another 150 years before the idea would be taken seriously (though not uncontroversially) in scientific circles. Lovelock's own discovery in the 1950s that the Earth's atmosphere was a single interconnected system, provided the empirical foundations that would make the scientific community take note of Gaia. His electron capture device, for example, made it possible to detect minute particles in the air, such as human-made chlorofluorocarbons (CFCs). In a series of independent research voyages Lovelock found ubiquitous evidence of CFCs in the atmosphere right around the world.[47] This was clear evidence of both the holistic nature of the Earth's atmospheric system and the impact of human beings upon this system. Later it was found that CFCs were contributing to the hole in the Ozone layer, and it was as a consequence of Lovelock's research that they were eventually banned in the 1980s, offering the Ozone layer an opportunity to repair itself.

In the 1960s Lovelock was tasked by NASA to come up with a method for detecting life on other planets. NASA was convinced that the best way to find extraterrestrial life was to send robotic probes to scout for evidence, but Lovelock came up with a simpler solution – life could be detected remotely (and much more cheaply) by long-range analysis of the composition of planetary atmospheres, which act as biomarkers. Lovelock emphasised an active relationship between planetary atmospheres and biological life – atmospheres rich in oxygen (like the Earth's), for example, would be a marker for the presence of organic life, because abundant oxygen is a by-product of photosynthesis.[48] It is the combination of Margulis' understanding of the role of symbiosis and co-operation in nature, combined with Lovelock's appreciation of the intimate relationship between organic life and non-organic processes that provides the framework for the Gaia hypothesis.

Following the suggestion of his friend and neighbour, the author William Golding (1911–1993), Lovelock named the Earth's self-regulating system 'Gaia' – borrowing the name from the ancient Greek Earth Goddess. This framing of the earth's systems and processes in the language of myth and religion, however, has led to some considerable backlash against Gaia in the popular and professional scientific literature. In his 1982 book *The Extended Phenotype*, for example, the outspoken atheist and evolutionary biologist Richard Dawkins argued against the Gaia hypothesis on the grounds that it seems to present a top-down teleological explanation for global homeostasis (in other words, that it is, in some sense, purposefully directed by the biota). He writes:

> A network of relationships there may be, but it is made up of small, self interested components. Entities that pay the costs of furthering the well being of the ecosystem as a whole will tend to reproduce themselves less successfully than rivals that exploit their public-spirited colleagues, and contribute nothing to the general welfare.[49]

Dawkins' Neo-darwinian understanding of life processes leaves no room for the kind of cross-species co-operation implied by the Gaia hypothesis, Margulis' symbiosis, or Clements' organicist model of succession. There is no communal goal-oriented activity in nature, just the perpetual competition of individuals fighting for survival – as Dawkins puts it, *The Selfish Gene* is the sole driver of evolution. At its core the holism-reductionism debate, of which this is an expression, represents a clash of paradigms – between blind mechanism and teleological organicism (see the discussion in Chapter Ten). Such disagreements are characteristic of debates in ecology (as well as most other fields) and are unlikely to ever be fully resolved. Adopting a spectrum, rather than binary, approach to these differences, the earth scientist James Kirchner makes a distinction between 'strong' and 'weak' forms of Gaia, and argues that there are in-fact several different formulations of the 'Gaia Hypothesis' between these extremes. Indeed he goes so far as to develop a taxonomy of different Gaia hypotheses:

> *Influential Gaia.* The weakest of the hypotheses […] asserts that the biota has a substantial influence over certain aspects of the abiotic world, such as the temperature and composition of the atmosphere […] *Coevolutionary Gaia* […] asserts that the biota influences the abiotic environment, and that the environment in turn influences the evolution of the biota […] *Homeostatic Gaia* […] asserts that the biota influences the abiotic world, and does so in a way that is stabilising […] feedback loops […] *Teleological Gaia* […] holds that the atmosphere is left in homeostasis, not just by the biosphere, but by and for (in some sense) the biosphere […] *Optimizing Gaia* […] holds that the biota manipulates its physical environment for the purpose of creating biologically favourable, or even optimal, conditions for itself […].[50]

Those who adopt the 'Gaia Hypothesis,' then, will assume a position within – or between – these various categories. If asked about his own position in relation to Gaia, Kirchner explains that he would align himself with the 'weak' hypothesis, but goes on to add a caveat that this does not mean that he believes that 'the biota is part of a global cybernetic control system, the purpose of which is to create biologically optimal conditions,' arguing that this 'is another matter entirely.'[51] For many ecologists and biologists the strong Gaia hypothesis is a step too far. The geographer Richard Huggett has highlighted a similar competition between the terms 'biosphere,' 'ecosphere' and 'Gaia.' Each term comes pre-loaded with conceptual baggage, which can render the terms more or less useful for different purposes, though apparently there is no scientific use for the concept of 'Gaia.' He explains that referring to the earth system as Gaia is best avoided:

> [...] because Gaia is an emotive word with a gamut of confusing undertones and overtones. Gaian terminology can be unscientific [...] A purely mechanistic world is characterless compared with the world of gods and goddesses, and of superorganisms with superphysiologies and (presumably) superanatomies [...].[52]

Huggett's own preference is for the 'ecosphere,' which he considers to be the 'most appropriate term for all situations where living things and their supporting environment are taken as a whole,' because it avoids the connotations that go along with labels such as Gaia – in particular the implication that Gaia might be a self-directed intelligence of some sort.[53] James Kirchner describes the perceived threat to scientific rationalism of this kind of thinking:

> Because many people do not understand the risks of treating poetic statements as scientific propositions, the public at large thinks that scientists are busy trying to figure out whether the earth really is 'alive.' I don't think that perception helps any of us.[54]

From this perspective, it is actually *dangerous* for the public to think that scientists are seriously considering whether or not the Earth is a living organism.

Gaian Spirituality

The historian of religion Bron Taylor also distinguishes between different cultural formulations of the Gaia hypothesis. He outlines four dominant frameworks adopted by what he calls Dark Green Religionists (see Chapter 4), and suggests that different interpretations of the Gaia hypothesis run through these various strands.

	Animism	*Gaian Earth Religion*
Supernaturalism	Spiritual Animism	Gaian Spirituality
Naturalism	Naturalistic Animism	Gaian Naturalism

In this context Taylor explains that Gaia is understood as referring to a perception of 'the biosphere (universe or cosmos) [as] alive or conscious, or at least by metaphor and analogy [resembling] organisms with their many interdependent parts.'[55] Taylor points out that the perspective of the Earth as a single homeostatic system is frequently interpreted as either supernatural or spiritual in nature (as a teleological Gaian consciousness, organism or Goddess), or entirely naturalistically (as global homeostasis maintained through physical-material systems and processes). Stephan Harding's formulation of the Gaia Hypothesis is representative of Taylor's category of 'Naturalistic Animism.' His book *Animate Earth*, for example:

> [...] explores how Gaian science can help us develop a sense of connectedness with the 'more-than-human' world. His work is based on the integration of rational scientific analysis with our intuition, sensing and feeling and replaces the cold, objectifying language of science with a way of speaking of our planet as a sentient, living being. The book is a contemporary attempt to rediscover *anima Mundi* (the soul of the world).[56]

Animism will be explored at length in Chapters Six and Eight, but it is interesting to note that Gaian and Animistic interpretations of ecology can be complimentary, and that Taylor's categories are not necessarily discrete, but often merge and overlap with one another. In contrast to these differing 'spiritual' interpretations of Gaia, the sociologists Timothy Lenton and Bruno Latour's (1947–2022) notion of 'Gaia 2.0' is much less concerned with revealing the animate principles of nature, or with considering whether or not there is a consciousness or intelligence driving global ecology. They opt instead for a very pragmatic approach that sees *human beings* as contributing an element of self-awareness and directionality to the Earth system. They explain that:

> [...] deliberate self-regulation—from personal action to global geoengineering schemes—is either happening or imminently possible. Making such conscious choices to operate within Gaia constitutes a fundamental new state of Gaia, which we term Gaia 2.0 [...] By emphasizing the agency of lifeforms and their ability to set goals, Gaia 2.0 may be an effective framework for fostering global sustainability.[57]

In essence this approach sidesteps the debate over whether there is an inherent teleology in the nature of Gaia – arguing instead that *we* are the teleological component of the global system, and as such its survival (and our own) depends on *our* choice of action.

Summary

The debates outlined above, and the controversies that arise from them, demonstrate that there can be (and are) many different interpretations of the 'facts' of ecology – scientific and non-scientific. We can think of these interpretations as 'cultural ecologies.' There are also different interpretations of ecological facts within the science of ecology, which could be understood as Kuhnian paradigms. Cultural models and understandings of ecosystems and ecosystem functioning influence the way that human beings behave in and towards the world, and are therefore an important area of study. It is also clear from this that there is scope for cultural responses to the ecological crisis our planet is currently undergoing, as our cultural models provide the framework for out engagement with the actual world (see discussion of different responses in Chapter Three).

CHAPTER TWO:
What is Spirituality?

The term 'spirituality' exerts a certain seductiveness [...] It is often used as if we all knew what it means. And yet the uses are so various that there seems to be a question mark set against any such assumption, for often there is not even a family resemblance between the various uses we come across.
—Margaret Chatterjee[1]

'Spirituality' is a concept that is widely used, but in many different ways. Like the category of 'religion' it has been the subject of long, and on-going, debates. This chapter gives an overview of some of the different scholarly perspectives on spirituality with the aim of trying to develop a nuanced understanding and an inclusive, though specific, definition.

Spiritus, Spirituality and Materiality

The etymological root of the word 'spirit,' and by extension 'spirituality,' is the Latin Spiritus, meaning 'breath.' The implication is that the 'spirit,' or 'soul' is a sort of life-giving essence that animates the physical body, and presumably departs at death, when we cease to breathe. From this starting point, spirituality might be concerned with different ways of accessing or cultivating the inner sense of this life-giving flow. The role of the breath and air in the concept of spirit might even represent a connection between the ecological and the spiritual, and to processes beyond the human. There are also associations in the Western world between the spirit/breath and notions of the immaterial and non-corporeal – like the air that we inhale (and which also gives us life) the spirit is invisible, subtle and cannot be grasped or dissected like a physical body. From this perspective, spirituality is often held to be concerned with subtle, hidden, non-physical dimensions, rather than with the 'mundane' world of everyday matter. This divorce of the spirit from the physical in many Western philosophical traditions was reinforced in the seventeenth century by the philosopher and natural scientist René Descartes' (1596–1650) famous segregation of mind and matter into two distinct domains, or substances. In the Cartesian model, matter was the domain of rational scientific enquiry, while mind, or the soul, was portioned off for religion.[2] The anthropologist Jan Platvoet argues that this opposition of mind and matter has become central to Western ways of thinking about the world, and about spirituality in particular, and suggests that evidence for its foundational influence can be found in the number of different ways that Western scholarship duplicates the dichotomy in different terms:

> One is 'the material' versus 'the spiritual,' another the 'physical' versus the 'metaphysical,' a third 'the empirical' (world) versus 'the meta-empirical' (realm), and a fourth, the 'seen' versus the 'unseen.' A fifth, finally, is the testable world, which is taken as the (one and only) object of research of the sciences, versus the meta-testable realm(s) postulated by religious beliefs (and by certain kinds of metaphysical philosophy).[3]

Platvoet goes on to explain, however, that this binary mode of conceiving of the world – of seeking to divide and distinguish in order to understand – is anything but universal amongst human cultures. Many indigenous cosmologies, for example, collapse dualistic categories and binary schemes such as these, effectively blurring any kind of neat distinction between the 'sacred' and the 'profane,' or the 'spiritual' and the 'material' (see discussion of the sacred in Chapter Eight and of indigenous worldviews in Chapter Nine). As an illustration Platvoet points to Ghanaian Akan spirituality, which he suggests expresses an entirely different ontological and cosmological framework for understanding the world:

> [...] for the Akan, their spirituality implied no opposition at all to the material, the empirical, the touchable and the testable. On the contrary, Akan believers postulated several kinds and degrees of materiality for the spiritual and thereby integrated the spiritual into their own physical world. Actually, the dichotomous categories 'spiritual' versus 'material' and so on were completely absent from Akan minds and language.[4]

Spirituality, then, is not exclusively or necessarily concerned with the invisible, the immaterial, the metaphysical, or the untouchable, but may be very much grounded in the empirical world – in matter and the everyday things that surround us, and in daily rituals and routines. Spirituality does not necessarily take the form of silent contemplation, meditation or prayer (though of course it can do), but may also be expressed through gardening, crafts, cookery, dance, and so on. The spiritual may also be embodied in rocks, trees, animals, rivers, dolls, cups, and many other very *material* things.

Sociological or Phenomenological?

It is possible to study spirituality from a number of different perspectives. In the social sciences there is a tendency towards either a sociological or phenomenological approach. Sociological approaches focus on how spirituality is understood and practiced, and the social functions it performs within those frameworks. Sociological approaches frequently adopt an *etic* position, attempting to understand spirituality from an outsider perspective, or through particular theoretical lenses. Phenomenological approaches, by contrast, move towards an *emic* understanding – in terms of the different ways that people experience spirituality from the insider's point of view. Of course, there is scope for overlap between these different approaches, and they are very often complimentary, but it is worthwhile keeping the distinction in mind when considering research on spirituality. This chapter will focus on sociological perspectives and the insights that they might reveal, because we will have the opportunity to explore the phenomenological (experiential) dimension in greater detail later on in the book (in particular in Chapters Four, Six and Seven). Before returning to the issue of defining 'spirituality' the next couple of sections will consider some differing perspectives on religion, which often frame discussions of spirituality.

Religion and the Social Sciences: Common Disciplinary Ancestors

It is important to point out here that anthropology and religious studies (as well as other social scientific disciplines, such as sociology and psychology) share many of the same founding figures and impulses.[5] Think of the scholarly shadows cast by the likes of Durkheim, Tylor, James, Weber, Freud and so on. One of Émile Durkheim's (1858–1917) most influential contributions to the study of religion, for example, was his observation that religion acts like a kind of 'social glue' that binds members of society together under a common set of beliefs and practices.[6] The anthropologist E.B. Tylor (1832–1917) saw all religions as manifestations of a far older way of perceiving the world – something he termed *animism*, or the belief in spiritual beings, and which he considered to be irrationally derived from misperceptions.[7] William James (1842–1910) emphasised the importance of

24

religious experience for understanding religion, while Max Weber (1864–1920) charted the decline of religion in the Western world with the advent of modern science and industry, and Sigmund Freud (1856–1939) shone a light on the unconscious psychological drives underlying the religious impulse.[8] The writings of these scholars have been adopted as foundational texts by anthropologists, sociologists and scholars of religious studies (amongst other disciplines).

Social and Psychological Functions of Religion

As previously noted, it was Durkheim who suggested that religion performs the vital function of maintaining social cohesion. The idea that religion might perform 'social functions' was hugely influential in anthropology. The twentieth century anthropologist Bronislaw Malinowski (1884–1942) also drew attention to the psychological functions of 'religion' – and magic in particular – in the everyday lives of the Trobriand Islanders of Papua New Guinea. Malinowski was a pioneer of *participant observation*, an ethnographic research method that has since become the bedrock of anthropology.[9] Through participating (more or less successfully) in the lives of his fieldwork informants, Malinowski came to realise that the Trobriand Islanders' complex systems of hunting and gardening magic were not simply systems of belief (i.e., made up fantasies with no basis in reality), but rather were practical techniques that served to reduce stress and anxiety during dangerous or unpredictable activities, such as when fishing in the open ocean or planting crops during periods of unpredictable weather patterns. From this perspective, religion – and by extension spirituality – is eminently *practical* – it does something, performs a function, and is much more than 'just' a system of beliefs, ideas and concepts. But crucially, according to the dominant view, it is not what it says it is – religion is a system of *erroneous beliefs*, rather than spiritual truths.

Ritual

Ritual has been an important focus for anthropologists since the emergence of the discipline in the nineteenth century. This is partly because ritual is very often (but not always) a public expression of religion, making it a much easier aspect of religious belief and practice for anthropologists to observe in the field. But ritual also provides a glimpse into the deep structures that scaffold and sustain religions and societies, and give structure to peoples' spiritual lives and experiences. The anthropologist Fiona Bowie writes of the importance of ritual in human society, explaining how rituals:

> [...] channel and express emotions, guide and reinforce forms of behaviour, support or subvert the status quo, bring about change, or restore harmony and balance [...] The succession of a culture's most deeply held values from one generation to another may be facilitated by means of ritual.[10]

Victor Turner (1920–1983), building on the earlier work of the Belgian ethnographer Arnold van Gennep (1873–1957), also emphasised the importance of ritual, and especially of 'Rites of Passage,' in many societies.[11] According to van Gennep and Turner, there is a distinct three-part process found in most rituals, which includes a *separation* from normal life, followed by a *liminal period* of anti-structure, finally culminating with a *re-aggregation* of the individual into society as a changed person with a new social status.[12] Rituals of this sort form a common thread that links many religious and spiritual traditions around the world – think of *bar* and *bat mitzvahs* in Judaism, which demarcate the transition from childhood to adulthood, wedding ceremonies across the board, and funerals, which structure and make sense of the transition from life to death through particular cultural, religious and spiritual frameworks. Many anthropologists have also expanded the notion of ritual to include secular activities as well, such as football matches or graduation ceremonies, which may perform similar social and psychological functions to religious rituals.[13]

Lived Religion and Rationality

One of the major contributions of anthropology to our understanding of religion is its emphasis on the centrality of 'lived religion' – the realisation that religion is not simply a system of beliefs, doctrines and dogmas, but rather is a *mode of living in and understanding the world*. E. E. Evans-Pritchard's (1902–1973) classic book *Witchcraft Oracles and Magic Among the Azande* explores how the Azande of Sudan employ cultural ideas about magic and witchcraft to make sense of their roles and positions in an unpredictable world. One of Evans-Pritchard's key observations was that magical, or religious, knowledge often goes hand-in-hand with practical,

26

scientific and technological knowledge (as Malinowski had recognised with the Trobriand Islanders), and furthermore that Azande notions of witchcraft cannot be reduced to the dominant natural/supernatural dichotomy found in most Western cultures. He writes:

> To us supernatural means very much the same as abnormal or extraordinary. Azande certainly have no conception of the 'natural' as we understand it, and therefore neither of the 'supernatural' as we understand it [...] It is a normal, and not an abnormal happening [...] belief in witchcraft is quite consistent with human responsibility and a rational appreciation of nature.[14]

Anthropological case studies such as these go a long way towards demonstrating that in studying religion, or spirituality, we are not dealing with 'irrational' ideas about the world, but rather with alternative ways of making sense of it, even if they begin from very different ontological starting points to Western science.

Top-Down and Vernacular Religion

Sociology has a long-standing tradition of research into religion that goes right back to the discipline's beginnings in the mid-nineteenth century. Auguste Comte (1798–1857), widely credited as the founder of sociology, for example, saw religion (much as later anthropologists would come to see it) as a primitive stage in the development of rational – read 'European' – thought.[15] Émile Durkheim, whose elaboration of sociology is the true ancestor of the discipline today, also wrote extensively on religion arguing that it functions as a sort of social-glue, helping to bind society together under a common set of norms, values and symbols.[16] Sociologists have frequently understood religion in this way – as a 'social institution,' with roles, hierarchies, rituals and symbols, that performs a function from the top-down. Karl Marx (1818–1883), for instance, famously interpreted religion as the 'opium of the masses' – serving the top-down function of re-enforcing the capitalist economic system by luring the working classes into a 'false consciousness'.[17] From these 'macro' perspectives religion is frequently conceived as an external, though nevertheless socially constructed, force that exerts its influence on the individual from the top-down.

There is also an element of religion that is deeply personal – an inner experience that these top-down perspectives do not quite seem to grasp. Similarly, it is clear that religion also exists and operates outside of the formal structures of organised institutions – in communities and households, at sacred sites, and in private thoughts and actions. This is sometimes referred to as 'vernacular religion,' which Marion Bowman defines as '"religion" as it is played out on a day-to-day basis in the life of the individual'.[18] The category of vernacular religion opens up scope for the sociological investigation of a range of religious activities that would otherwise go unnoticed by top-down emphases. The sociologists Navtej Purewal and Virinder Kalwa, for example, point out that the vernacular religion approach can reveal hidden elements of the religious lives of everyday, and often overlooked, people in India:

> [...] spiritual rituals and events performed, largely by women are either conveniently overlooked by religious authorities or seen as contentious by more rigid perspectives on religious belonging [...] [W]omen's participation and worship at spiritual sites draws our attention to the continuum of practices that run between life-course rituals and acts of spiritual embodiment and worship, making it difficult to maintain [...] distinctions between cultural and religious practices [...].[19]

Shifting focus away from the top-down view of religion as a set of ideal doctrines and social institutions, and turning to examine the beliefs, practices and experiences of everyday people reveals a much more diverse and nuanced perspective on religion. The sociologist Jeff Astley, for instance, coined the term 'ordinary theology' to refer to the personal beliefs and ideas of church congregants, defining it as the 'theology and theologising of [those] who have received little or no theological education of a scholarly, academic or systematic kind.'[20] These ordinary theologies often take on a much more heterodox nature than the official teachings of the church, for example belief that it is possible to communicate with dead relatives – as well as other paranormal beliefs – that do not have an official place in church doctrines, but that are nevertheless widespread and relatively common.[21] Ordinary theologies, then, may incorporate elements from official religious doctrines combined with other cultural and sub-cultural ideas, as well as drawing on personal experience to form an individual 'spiritual' perspective, but within a wider religious context.

From Religion to Spirituality

The sociologists Paul Heelas and Linda Woodhead have noted a relatively recent shift in the religious landscape of Western societies. They write that 'survey after survey shows that increasing numbers of people now refer to themselves as spiritual' rather than religious, and argue that what they call a 'subjective turn' has taken place in Western societies.[22] They propose the terms 'life as' and 'subjective life' to highlight the distinction between these two kinds of religio-spirituality. For instance, those who adopt a 'life as' attitude will often emphasise a transcendent source of authority (such as God or the Bible), to which individuals must conform at the expense of cultivating their own subjective sense of the spiritual. This would be characterised as 'living as a Christian,' or 'living as a Muslim,' for example. They argue that this form of religion is most likely to be in decline in the West, in line with trends noted by secularisation theorists. 'Subjective life,' on the other hand, places a much greater emphasis on the cultivation of inner sources of significance and authority – this form of spirituality may be much more 'self' focussed, and would also include many belief systems and practices promoting self-development, personal growth, and health and wellbeing. Heelas and Woodhead argue that this form of spirituality is most likely to be growing in Western societies, which increasingly emphasise the importance of cultivating a unique and individual self-identity.[23]

Of course, as with all such scholarly distinctions, the real word is rarely quite so black and white. Graham Harvey, for instance, suggests that there are obvious points of overlap between 'life as' and 'subjective life' approaches to spirituality. People who adopt a normative religion or spiritual practice will still, nevertheless, have their own subjective point of view, and their own unique orientation to the world, and may understand doctrine as spiritual guidance.[24] In recent years there have been several innovative scholarly perspectives that have directly challenged any kind of simple distinction between 'life as' and 'subjective life.' As we have already seen with the concept of 'ordinary theology' the subjective lives of mainstream religious congregants often have a profound impact on interpretations of doctrine (such as through the influence of personal extraordinary experiences).[25] There are also many currents within mainstream religious traditions that seek to foster a personal sense of the spiritual and a direct relationship with the divine within an orthodox framework (see the discussion of mysticism in Chapter Four).

Religious Experience and the Extraordinary

More recent work in anthropology has reminded the field of the extraordinary dimension of religion – the element of *religious experience* that motivates many religious and spiritual believers. The renewed emphasis on experience in anthropology goes hand-in-hand with the discipline's concern for lived religion, and how religion is understood from an insider (or *emic*) perspective. The work of Edith Turner (1922–2016) is a particularly good case in point. While fully engaging in the *Ihamba* healing ceremony of the Ndembu in Zambia, Turner had an extraordinary experience that seemed to accord well with the beliefs of her informants. She explains:

> I *saw* with my own eyes a giant thing emerging out of the flesh of her back. This thing was a large gray blob about six inches across, a deep gray opaque thing emerging as a sphere.[26]

The experiences of anthropologists like Edith Turner remind us that if we want to truly understand what religion and ritual are, then we need to learn 'to see as the Natives see,' and to appreciate that much of what people believe is drawn from their own personal experiences.[27] Indeed paranormal and other extraordinary experiences are widely reported across a range of demographic sectors, and are a very important source of people's spiritual beliefs and orientations.[28]

Alternative and Popular Culture Spiritualities

Sociologists have argued that the shift towards the subjective in Western society has led to a proliferation of new forms of spirituality. These have occasionally been referred to as 'alternative spiritualities,' or may be classified as 'New Age,' or as New Religious Movements (NRMs). Marion Bowman identifies ten core features of these emergent forms of spirituality, including:

1. The Personal Quest – search for meaning.

2. 'Mix and Match' Spirituality – incorporation of diverse beliefs and practices.

3. Remythologising – old myths are reinterpreted, new myths are created.

4. Healing – a concern for healing and well-being.

30

5. The Golden Age and 'Noble Savages' – e.g. Celts, Indigenous traditions.

6. Hidden Wisdom – e.g. theosophy, channeling, ley lines.

7. Past Lives and Reincarnation – incorporation of metaphysical beliefs.

8. Interconnectedness – all life exists in an interconnected web.

9. Sacred Landscapes – belief that certain locations are 'power centres,' e.g. Glastonbury.

10. Pilgrimage – travelling with purpose to connect with people and place.[29]

With the increasing complexity of an ever-more globalised world, and spurred into overdrive by the proliferation of digital and social media, these new forms of spirituality have spiralled out in radical new directions. The sociologist Adam Possamai, for example, has suggested that religion and spirituality are moving into a new phase in our post-modern post-industrial world – they are blending into and merging with mass media and popular culture. He calls these 'Hyper-real religions,' which are defined as 'innovative religions and spiritualities that mix elements of religious tradition with popular culture.'[30] Examples include Matrixism, Jediism and Dudeism, all of which derive their inspirations and philosophical underpinnings from Hollywood movies (*The Matrix, Star Wars* and *The Big Lebowski* respectively). Bron Taylor has also written extensively about the eco-spirituality inherent in James Cameron's 2009 movie *Avatar* and its sequels, for example.[31] Although these new expressions of spirituality may seem to be unique consequences of twenty-first century media technology, in truth spiritualities have always drawn from – and fed into – popular culture for their vitality and public appeal.[32]

Indigenous Traditions

Hyper-real religions and alternative spiritualities may be forging new traditions in post-industrial digital societies, but indigenous cultures are the living embodiment of beliefs and traditions that have spanned hundreds, if not thousands of years, of oral retelling and ritual re-enactment. Although they may have adapted and changed over the centuries – often unwillingly – indigenous societies are the keepers of very ancient traditions. Furthermore, while the hyper-real religions and 'pick and mix' spiritualities discussed above thrive and proliferate in online digital spaces, indigenous spiritualities are often deeply rooted in particular 'bioregions' or ancestral territories.[33] They are grounded in a physical place, and accordingly are also expressed through bodily engagement with the environment and the ancestors that constitute it – the plants, rocks, mountains, rivers, animals, spirits and so on. As has already been noted in the context of Akan spirituality, indigenous traditions often collapse the etic categories of Western sociologists completely. John Grim explains that what:

> [..] is immediately apparent in traditional native religions is that both narratives of spiritual experiences and religious practices transmit extraordinary encounters with spiritual realms that are not separated from ordinary life [...].[34]

Everyday activities, such as hunting, gardening, cooking and so on, may also simultaneously be interactions – dialogues and negotiations – with the spirit world. John Grim suggests that if we 'want to talk about indigenous religious traditions it is necessary to situate them within their lived communities, or lifeways'.[35] Spirituality, then, from an indigenous perspective might be conceived as an orientation and a mode of interaction with, and in, the world – it is a framework for establishing and maintaining good relationships (see Chapters Five and Nine).

Moving Beyond the World Religions Paradigm

There has been an emphasis in recent years on moving the study of religion away from the so-called 'World Religions Paradigm,'[36] referring to the tendency to focus primarily on the world's major faith denominations – usually consisting of: Christianity, Islam, Judaism, Buddhism, Sikhism and Hinduism – the 'big six.' The World Religions Paradigm has been problematic, not least because of its tendency to ignore smaller religious denominations, and new religious movements, as well as indigenous traditions.[37] A recent alternative proposition has been to shift toward an emphasis on the concept of 'worldviews' in teaching about religion. The concept of worldview can be traced back to nineteenth century German phenomenology (and the notion of *Weltanschauung*). The religious studies scholars Van de Kooij, Ruyter and Miedema have argued that the concept of worldview might be a more suitably inclusive framework for teaching and learning about religious and non-religious worldviews within the education system.[38]

Personal Religion and Orientation to the World

The philosopher and pioneering psychologist William James was primarily concerned with the phenomenology of religious experience, rather than with the doctrines or social functions of organised religions. He considered 'religious experience' to be the essence of religion – its primary motivator and source of vitality. James' ideas about the nature of religious experience will be discussed in greater detail in Chapter Four, but in his book *The Varieties of Religious Experience*, he also introduces the concept of 'personal religion,' which he defines as:

> [...] the feelings, acts, and experiences of individual[s] in their solitude, so far as they apprehend themselves to stand in relation to whatever they may consider the divine [...].[39]

Personal religion is a very useful starting place for developing an encompassing understanding of spirituality, and for finding a bridge between the various different approaches outlined above. James' idea might include many different modes of standing 'in relation to the divine,' from strict adherence to religious doctrines, right through to perspectives such as atheism, for example, which is a rejection of the idea of the divine. It can even accommodate the recent emergence of the category of non-religion. All of these might be understood as different 'personal religions,' or spiritual orientations. A similar idea is expressed in the notion of 'personal mythologies,' which have been an important concept in certain forms of psychodynamic and humanistic psychotherapy since the 1950s. The psychologist Stanley Krippner gives a very useful definition of the idea, which begins to clarify precisely how spiritual orientations translate into behaviour in the world:

> [...] each individual has a notion of how the universe works and of his or her place in it and connection to it. One's personal mythology includes all the interacting and sometimes conflicting thoughts and feelings a person

harbors about the world, both consciously and unconsciously. These myths shape the actions individuals take and the interpretations they give to their experiences [...].[40]

These personal mythologies may be equivalent to what Nick Campion has called 'personal cosmologies,' which he defines as the 'ways in which human beings locate themselves in relation to the cosmos, seen as the totality of everything.'[41] We each foster and develop our own personal narratives and models of the world which help us to navigate our way through it. These personal models might draw from cultural traditions, but are also influenced by personal experience, so that while there may be an overarching cultural or spiritual framework providing categories and concepts, each individual will nevertheless understand the world from their own unique perspective.[42] In their research on children's spiritual perspectives, the religious experience researchers David Hay (1935–2014) and Rebecca Nye came to an understanding of spirituality that resonates with the idea of spirituality as a mode of cosmological orientation. They explain that in their view:

> [...] spirituality is the potential to be much more deeply aware of ourselves and our intimate relationship with everything that is not ourselves [...].[43]

Understood in this way, spirituality is our mode of orientation in the world – similar to the notion of 'worldview' – the way in which we anchor and position ourselves in the cosmos, and understand our place and role within it. It need not be concerned with the metaphysical, immaterial or supernatural (though it could be), but might very much be a part of everyday life in a variety of different spheres. Spiritual orientations may draw from centuries old traditions, or they may take their starting points from new cultural and technological innovations. Regardless of the particularities of any individual spiritual or cosmological orientation, it is quite clear to see their role in mediating human relationships with the world around them.

Summary

It should have become clear over the preceding pages that spirituality is a kaleidoscopic category, that is very difficult to pin down explicitly. It shares this characteristic with the concept of religion, which scholars have been debating for centuries. Part of the problem arises from attempting to define something in objective terms that is, for the most part, a subjectively held perspective. This has led to a proliferation of different definitions and approaches that are not quite able to fully encapsulate what spirituality is and means to people who live it. As the scholar of religious studies Doug Oman reminds us:

> To some extent, a varied repertoire of definitions can reflect a healthy and rich diversity of scholarly approaches. Beyond a certain point, however, multiple definitions may undermine professional communication and scientific and scholarly progress.[44]

The solution suggested in this chapter is to consider spirituality in terms of our subjective orientation to the world – to look at what a spirituality is in general, rather than focussing on any particular manifestation or cultural form. Spirituality, then, from this perspective, is concerned with how we orient ourselves in the world, how we understand our place in the cosmos and the narratives, concepts, categories and symbols that we use to make sense of it. With this understanding of spirituality it becomes clear to see how important our spiritualities are – they *matter* – because they have a very real impact on the ways that we behave, and so also on the living environment around us – human and non-human.

CHAPTER THREE:
The Ecological Crisis

It is the shocking facts of the ecological crisis that really give value and significance to the conversations presented in this book. *If* it is possible to develop effective responses to the crisis, then a very real difference can be made, but we will only be able to formulate a response if we know the full extent of the problem, and the kinds of responses that have already been proposed and implemented.

Ecological Crisis

We are living in a time of unprecedented ecological change. The past ten years have been the hottest since records began in 1850, and global atmospheric greenhouse gas levels continue to rise in spite of international efforts to curb emissions. Ice sheets are melting at never before seen rates, leading to rising sea levels around the world. Climates are shifting and habitats are being lost. Up to as many as 60% of animal species have been driven to extinction in the last half-century, according to the World Wildlife Fund.[1] The plant world is not faring much better. A recent longitudinal study published in the journal *Nature* reveals that we have been losing somewhere in the region of three species of seed-bearing plants every year since 1900.[2] When this is combined with the continued deforestation of vast swathes of the world's ancient woodland for agricultural purposes and to access hidden fossil fuel reserves, as well as with the wildfires that have been burning in Australia, California and the Amazon in recent years, we are presented with a very grim picture indeed. Something needs to be done – or rather something should have been done a long time ago – if we hope to prevent a catastrophic collapse of our surviving ecosystems. As the sociologist Bruno Latour puts it: 'we haven't lacked for warnings. The sirens have been blaring all along.'[3] With this sense of urgency in mind, this chapter will outline some the major symptoms of the ecological crisis, as well as some of its suggested natural, human and cultural causes. The final section of the chapter will then consider different responses to the crisis from various philosophical, ethical, spiritual and religious perspectives.

What kind of crisis is it?

There have been a range of different labels applied to what is currently happening to the global system. Climate change, global warming, environmental change, and ecological crisis. Each of these labels refers to a particular phenomenon, though they are often used interchangeably in popular discourse, and are certainly related.[4] The philosopher Timothy Morton has sought to encapsulate the complexity of these entangled crises with his notion of the 'hyperobject,' drawing on multi-dimensional geometry and imagery to emphasise the long-range and deeply interconnected processes that are affecting the Earth's ecology as a result of human activity. Plastic, for example – another of the symptoms of human ecological impact, like the CFCs that James Lovelock identified – is a hyperobject:

> Hyperobjects do not rot in our lifetimes. They do not burn without themselves burning (releasing radiation, dioxins, and so on). The ecological thought must think the future of these objects, these toxic things that appear almost more real than reality itself [...].[5]

The ecological crisis is not a single thing, it is rather a knotting of multi-dimensional and multi-faceted phenomena with butterfly effect-like implications simultaneously felt across vastly different contexts – from the melting ice-caps to the food that we buy and eat. It is biological and geological as much as it is psychological and cultural. Before getting into some of the psychological and social impacts and responses, it is first necessary to consider some of the physical facts of the matter.

Climate Not Weather: Long-Range Thinking

The term 'climate' refers to prevailing weather conditions averaged over a long period of time. For example, the climate of the Sahara desert is hot and dry, while Wales is moderate and wet, on average (though there may be occasional exceptions to the rule – particularly hot or cold days, or wet or dry seasons, for example). Weather refers to the short-term state of the atmosphere – whether it is raining or snowing on a particular day, or how high or low the air pressure and temperature are at a given moment. A record hot July one year, then, does not necessarily mean that the climate is changing, but record temperatures over multiple summers in a row might begin to suggest a long-term change in climate. Long-range observation is therefore essential for grasping global climate change. We can tell from ice core samples that the Earth's climate has always changed due to natural factors, such as atmospheric composition, volcanic activity, solar radiation, and so on.[6] All of these can affect long-term weather patterns, but they have always done so within relatively stable boundaries. We can also see that the Earth's climate and long-term weather patterns are changing in increasingly erratic ways as we move deeper into the twenty-first century, with progressively extreme weather events becoming the norm around the world and threatening traditional ways of life.[7]

Misplaced Carbon

A large part of the problem facing our planet is the influence of human beings on the carbon cycle, which we essentially syphon off, bypassing processes that have been ongoing for millions of years. It might be assumed that humans are unique amongst the many varied species that inhabit the Earth in that we have made large-scale changes to the global system over a relatively short amount of time, affecting in particular the planet's atmospheric conditions and constituents. We have removed woodlands, ploughed up soils, built vast mega-cities from tarmac and concrete and continue to burn coal, gas and oil dredged up from beneath the Earth's surface, releasing vast quantities of carbon into the atmosphere in the process. But humanity is not as unique is it would often like to think given that changes in atmospheric composition – specifically oxygen levels – brought about by the photosynthetic activity of Stromatolites in the primordial past made it possible for insects, fish, reptiles and mammals to evolve in the first place.[8] A key difference between the influence of stromatolites on the atmosphere and that of human beings, however, is that the former's activity created conditions for the proliferation of a huge variety of biological organisms, while the latter's has led to a catastrophic reduction of species and the destabilisation of the global climate system.

The United Nations *Emissions Gap Report 2022*, notes that total global greenhouse gas emissions 'averaged 54.4 gigatons of CO_2 equivalent (GtCO2e) between 2010 and 2019, and reached a high in 2019.'[9] Since the Industrial Revolution human activity has contributed vast quantities of carbon to the atmosphere, leading to devastating long-term unintended consequences. Quite early on certain scientists had started to think about the impact that the burning of fossil fuels might have on the planet. They realised that the fumes, smoke and smog would in some way change the atmosphere's composition, but were not sure how, or to what extent these changes might come about. In 1896, for example, the Swedish chemist Svante Arrhenius (1859–1927) was the first to suggest that man-made pollutants in the air would speed up the greenhouse effect, that is the atmosphere's natural warming influence on the planet.[10] Mistakenly, however, he thought this warming would be beneficial for future generations, failing to appreciate the complexity and interconnectivity of the global system, and how finely balanced it is. Today it is widely accepted that the damage caused by excess CO_2 in the atmosphere could be irreversible for at least 1,000 years.[11]

Soil Depletion

Carbon is also released from soils through ploughing and other agricultural activities. Soil may not be something that many of us think about on a day-to-day basis, but it is essential to our very existence. Indeed, attitudes towards soil might vary considerably from one person to the next, and from one context to another. While working on the *One School One Planet Project*, I was involved in a conversation about issues surrounding the targets laid out by the Paris Agreement with students in a rural mid-Wales high school (see discussion in Chapter Eleven). Several competing understandings of soil became apparent in this admittedly limited sample population:

- 'Soil means dirt, crops and ploughing a field.'
- 'Mud, dirt, filth, messy, worms, earth, wet, moist...'
- 'My family has an allotment so we use compost for our gardening. We have fresh vegetables and fruit.'
- 'Soil is literally my life because my family are farmers.'
- 'Soil is the ground/surface of the earth. It can be found almost everywhere and is in no short supply. It is one of the most common things used in farming and agriculture.'[12]

Perspectives varied from the wholly dismissive through to detailed understanding. Regardless of what we think of it, soil is essential for our survival and for the maintenance of healthy ecological functioning, and contrary to the opinion of the final respondent quoted above, is in fact in very short supply, and is a major agricultural problem globally, as David Pimentel and colleagues explain:

> Although erosion has occurred throughout the history of agriculture, it has intensified in recent years. Each year, 75 billion metric tons of soil are removed from the land by wind and water erosion, with most coming from agricultural land. The loss of soil degrades arable land and eventually renders it unproductive [...].[13]

In particular, it was the expansion of industrial farming practices during the twentieth century, with their emphasis on monocultural food-production systems – systems that are designed for the mass production of a single crop species, for example maize, potatoes, rape, and so on. In this agricultural system the ideal conditions for crops are manufactured for maximum yields of a single species, at the expense of others on the land.[14] These conditions are maintained by labour and fuel intensive practices, such as ploughing, fertilising and the use of pesticides and herbicides. The life sciences researcher Ken Norris points out that while this shift in farming practices undoubtedly contributed to 'poverty alleviation and improved food security globally [...] these benefits came at a cost to the environment [...].'[15]

Biodiversity Loss

In the 1980s there was a growing awareness of the rate at which species were being lost from ecosystems around the world, which spurred an increase in research and activism concerning conservation and loss of biodiversity in the 1990s and 2000s. New research on the role of keystone species and the importance of trophic cascades for ecological stability (see Chapter One), for example, found that loss of species could 'substantially alter the structure and functioning of whole ecosystems' in sudden and dramatic ways.[16] The biologist Bradley Cardinale and colleagues provide a useful summary of some of the key findings from the last three decades of research into biodiversity, which include:

> 1. [...] unequivocal evidence that biodiversity loss reduces the efficiency by which ecological communities capture biologically essential resources,

produce biomass, decompose and recycle biologically essential nutrients

2. [...] mounting evidence that biodiversity increases the stability of ecosystem functions through time [...]

3. [and that] Diverse communities are more productive because (a) they contain key species that have a large influence on productivity, and (b) differences in functional traits among organisms increase total resource capture [...].[17]

They go on to suggest, drawing on thirty years worth of ecological observation and research, that the effects of biodiversity loss 'might be sufficiently large to rival the impacts of many other global drivers of environmental change.'[18] Complex, biodiverse ecosystems are more resilient to change and help to store water, preventing flooding and run-off, as well as capturing carbon from the atmosphere and locking it up in the soil. If ecosystems are prevented from doing this then the consequences will be felt for a long time to come. It is the capacity of ecosystems to capture carbon, build soil through succession and prevent flooding that underlies and motivates the rewilding movement.[19]

The Anthropocene

The term 'anthropocene' has gained prominence over the past decade and is used in a variety of disciplinary settings – from the hard sciences to the social sciences – to refer to a new geological epoch that is dominated by the influence of humankind on the environment. There are continuing debates about what exactly the anthropocene is best characterised by, and when it can be said to have started. The palaeo-climatologist Andrew Glikson, for example, has suggested a three stage model of the anthropocene, beginning with the mastery of fire at least 1.8 million years ago (Early Anthropocene). This stage came to an end with the emergence of agriculture and urbanisation in the Neolithic some 6,000 years ago, culminating in a new era characterised by a relatively stable climate (Middle Anthropocene). This stable period in turn came to an end around 1750 CE with the birth of the Industrial Revolution, large scale burning of fossil fuels and its concomitant atmospheric carbon emissions (Late Anthropocene).[20]

As an interesting illustration of differing scholarly opinions on this matter, the environmental scientists Simon Lewis and Mark Maslin have suggested that the origins of the anthropocene can be dated, quite specifically, to either 1610 or 1963, and add that the year we choose might have an impact on the degree of our optimism for the future. If we opt for 1610, they suggest that it was:

> [...] colonialism, global trade and coal [that] brought about the Anthropocene. Broadly, this highlights social concerns, particularly the unequal power relationships between different groups of people, economic growth, the impacts of globalized trade, and our current reliance on fossil fuels. The onward effects of the arrival of Europeans in the Americas also highlights a long-term and large-scale example of human actions unleashing processes that are difficult to predict or manage [...] [This perspective] tells a story of an elite-driven technological development that threatens planet-wide destruction.[21]

If the anthropocene began in 1610, then we are already deep into a long-term process over which the majority of people have very little control. The power to make broad-reaching changes lies with an elite few, whose vested interests are so far removed from the real-world problems facing the majority. On the other hand, if we choose 1963 as our start-date for the anthropocene, a slightly more optimistic perspective becomes a possibility. Lewis and Maslin point out that 1963 was a pivotal year in global international relations, suggesting that 'the 1963 Partial Test Ban Treaty and later agreements highlight[ed] the ability of people to collectively successfully manage a major global threat to humans and the environment.'[22] The suggestion here is that, if we work together as a global international community, then we might just be able to rein in the anthropocene.

The historian Lynn White Jr. (1907–1987) famously and influentially put forward the suggestion that the roots of the current ecological crisis ultimately lie in religion, and religious ideas about the place of human beings in the cosmos. In particular, White Jr. argued that 'in its Western form Christianity is the most anthropocentric religion the world has seen.'[23] It is this anthropocentrism that White Jr. saw underlying Western society's fractured relationship with the natural world. Christianity justified the extraction and consumption of natural resources for the benefit of human beings with little regard for non-human life – '[...] no item in the physical creation had any purpose save to serve man's purposes.'[24] He goes on to further explain how the anthropocentrism at the heart of Christianity eventually came to (often violently) dominate over nature-based pre-Christian paganism, referring to this as the 'greatest psychic revolution in the history of our culture.'[25] He continues:

> In Antiquity every tree, every spring, every stream, every hill had its own *genius loci*, its guardian spirit. These spirits were accessible to [humans], but were very unlike [them]; centaurs, fauns, and mermaids show their ambivalence. Before one cut a tree, mined a mountain, or dammed a brook, it was important to placate the spirit in charge of that particular situation and to keep it placated. By destroying pagan animism, Christianity made it possible to exploit nature in a mood of indifference to the feelings of natural objects.[26]

It was this shift away from seeing the world as living and feeling, so White Jr. argued, that laid the foundations for the emergence of the capitalist and industrial approach to resource consumption, culminating in what we now call the anthropocene. Both capitalism and the industrial revolution were themselves embedded in a deeper religious worldview, which essentially set the scene for the proliferation of the capitalist extraction of resources and the degradation of ecological environments. Jason W. Moore explains that:

> [...] capitalism's environment-making revolution [was] greater than any watershed since the rise of agriculture and the first cities. While there is no question that environmental change accelerated sharply after 1850, and especially after 1945, it seems equally fruitless to explain these transformations without identifying how they fit into patterns of power, capital and nature established four centuries earlier.[27]

Once again, the roots of the anthropocene seem to run far deeper, and spread out much further, than any single explanatory cause seems to acknowledge. However we define the anthropocene – whether in terms of the negative impacts of humankind on the global system as a consequence of religion, capitalism, politics or industry, or based on our optimistic ability to come together across geographical, cultural and political divisions to make a collective difference – and however long ago it began, the philosopher Donna Harraway thinks that 'our job is to make the anthropocene as short/

thin as possible and to cultivate with each other in every way imaginable epochs to come that can replenish refuge.'[28]

The Chthulucene

But what might these epochs to come resemble? Harraway's suggested alternative to the anthropocene is the 'Chthulucene.' She explains that:

> [...] we need a name for the dynamic ongoing sym-chthonic forces and powers of which people are a part, within which ongoingness is at stake. Maybe, but only maybe, and only with intense commitment and collaborative work and play with other terrans, flourishing for rich multispecies assemblages that include people will be possible. I am calling all this the Chthulucene—past, present, and to come.[29]

She goes on to clarify that the Chthulucene is not named after the weird fiction writer H.P. Lovecraft's (1890–1937) 'racial-nightmare monster Cthulhu,' but instead evokes the chthonic, the earthy and the organic:

> [...] the diverse earth-wide tentacular powers and forces and collected things with names like Naga, Gaia, Tangaroa (burst from water-full Papa), Terra, Haniyasu-hime, Spider Woman, Pachamama, Oya, Gorgo, Raven, A'akuluujjusi, and many many more. 'My' Chthulucene, even burdened with its problematic Greek-ish tendrils, entangles myriad temporalities and spatialities and myriad intra-active entities-in-assemblages—including the more-than-human, other-than-human, inhuman, and human-as-humus.[30]

The Chthulucene – an antidote to the anthropocene – will be an epoch characterised by a radical re-engagement with the non-human (see the discussion in Chapter Five), and a concerted effort to shake away and re-evaluate the cultural and ontological blinkers that have characterised the anthropocene right into the present moment. The question is, then, how do we get to the Chthulucene? The final sections of this chapter will now turn to consider some of the possible responses to the ecological crisis, from the religious to the practical.

Social and Political Responses

There is a wide range of possible responses to the ecological crisis, reflective of its hyper-objective nature. Its immensity can make it seem distant and far removed from any given local context (but certainly not from all). As such, we can only experience parts of it – political, economic, philosophical, scientific, ecological, spiritual – sometimes in isolation, and sometimes in combination. Each part of the crisis is a node of the hyper-object, each with its own range of possible responses.

The origins of the environmental movement are often traced back to the publication of the marine biologist Rachel Carson's (1907–1964) *Silent Spring* in 1962.[31] The book raised public awareness about the negative impacts of human beings on the environment, by highlighting the detrimental effect of agricultural pesticides on biodiversity in the USA. The book galvanised the early environmental movement of the 1960s counterculture and gave it a voice and public face. Organisations such as Greenpeace, established in 1971, sought to build on the growing awareness of biodiversity loss to engage in spectacle-like forms of activism in order to bring the ecological crisis some much needed media attention.[32] The protests of Extinction Rebellion today are a continuation of this tradition.[33] The increased popular awareness of the environmental crisis that was beginning to become evident at this time also contributed to a proliferation of different socio-political and philosophical responses.

Today, there are many thousands of regenerative ecology projects all around the world working on a grass-roots level to restore local ecosystems on a place-by-place basis.[34] The Youth Strikes for Climate that have been taking place on every continent, inspired by Greta Thunberg's 'Skolstrejk för klimatet,' which started as a small protest in 2018 outside the Swedish parliament and continues to this day, are also raising awareness of our ecological crisis on a scale that has never been seen before, especially amongst the younger generations.[35] There are also promising signs of a growing ecological awareness from the top-down perspective, including the Paris Climate Accord, which was agreed in December 2015 and signed and ratified in April 2016 by 195 countries. This event was perhaps representative of Lewis and Maslin's more optimistic scenario of an anthropocene characterised by global co-operation. It was a major stepping stone in that the agreement represented an international scientific consensus on climate change – that it is real, that (certain) human beings bear the brunt of responsibility, and that we need to (and can) do something about it. The agreement is aimed at:

> [keeping] global temperature rise this century well below 2 degrees Celsius above pre-industrial levels and to pursue efforts to limit the temperature increase even further to 1.5 degrees Celsius. Additionally, the agreement aims to strengthen the ability of countries to deal with the impacts of climate change.[36]

The decarbonisation required by this agreement is a process that will involve radical social, cultural and economic transformations. These changes will (at least to begin with), be driven by the need to reduce carbon dioxide emissions by 50% in the next decade, followed by similar 50% reductions in the following two decades. It will entail a total transformation of the way we live our lives – food, energy, transport, culture and society. By 2050 we should be living in a carbon negative world if we hope to have even a 66% chance of avoiding run-away climate change.[37] Although it is true that no international agreement is ever going to solve the problems we face – we are talking about something much more than mere politics here – it is the overarching message of the Paris Agreement that is of greatest importance. In essence, the Paris Agreement calls on individual nations, communities, institutions and individuals to develop their own localised responses to climate change. In other words, it is up to us – in whatever capacity we can – to develop innovative new ways (or perhaps even return to some very old ways) of building resilient local communities, regenerating ecosystems, enhancing biodiversity, mitigating climate change and meeting the political targets and commitments of the Paris Agreement. So far it is not going well. To date the targets are not expected to be met on schedule.[38]

Religious Responses

If we follow Lynn White Jr.'s suggestion that the ecological crisis has its roots in the religious worldview implied by Christianity, then 'the remedy must also be essentially religious, whether we call it that or not.'[39] Since the 1980s there has been a growing awareness of anthropogenic climate change among the major world religions, as well as a rise of religiously motivated ecological restoration projects. Some have referred to this phenomenon as the 'Greening of Religion.'[40] In the build up to the United Nations Paris Climate Summit (COP21) in 2015, for example, statements were issued by representatives of the major world religions calling on members of their respective faith communities to take positive action on climate change.[41] Pope Francis, for instance, announced his first encyclical – *Laudato Si'* ('Praise be to you') – which is expressly concerned with issues of sustainable development, runaway consumerism, global warming and environmental destruction. In the encyclical, Pope Francis writes:

> I urgently appeal [...] for a new dialogue about how we are shaping the future of our planet. We need a conversation which includes everyone, since the environmental challenge we are undergoing, and its human roots, concern and affect us all.[42]

In his famous paper Lynn White Jr. suggested the figure of St. Francis of Assisi, who is widely regarded as the patron saint of ecologists, as a figurehead for a Christian response to the ecological crisis. Timothy Morton might argue, however, that Christianity is not quite ready to provide a solution to the problems it may have contributed to over the centuries:

> With its apocalyptic visions and thousand-year itches, Christianity isn't ready for hyper objects. Yet thinking about these materials does involve something like religion, because they transcend our personal death [...] Hyperobjects will outlast us all.[43]

But if Christianity does not contain all of the answers, then perhaps other traditions may have something to offer. A central connecting feature of many of the statements issued by representatives of the major faith denominations in response to the COP21 meeting was an emphasis on 'holistic, organic or relational images of the world,'[44] which highlight the fundamental interconnectedness of all life on Earth. The Hindu declaration on climate change, *Bumi Devi Yai Kah!*, for example, suggests that 'all elements of reality are organs of God's body [...] the entire universe is to be looked upon as the energy of the Lord,'[45] while the Islamic Declaration on Global Climate Change suggests that Allah 'has created the universe in all its diversity, richness and vitality: the stars, the sun and moon, the earth and all its communities of living beings. All these reflect and manifest the boundless glory and mercy of their Creator.'[46] Models of the universe such as these, which see the cosmos as a living system imbued with intelligence and agency, of which we are all a part, are valuable alternatives to the mainstream models of reductionist materialist science and capitalism, which have actively contributed to the collapse of our global ecosystems.[47] But while it is true that religion can provide useful frameworks for promoting environmental activism, the sociologist Randolph Haluza-DeLay suggests that 'religious perspectives and institutions can [also] be among the barriers to addressing significant issues such as climate change.' He explains that:

> It is unclear whether religious institutions are 'greening' any more or less effectively than other social sectors. Moving from environment in general to climate change in particular, the planetary scale of human-induced climate change can seem incomprehensible to millennium-old traditions.[48]

Deep Ecology

The Norwegian philosopher Arne Naess (1912–2009) pioneered a philosophical approach to ecology that has been particularly influential over the last fifty years. Naess made a distinction between what he called 'shallow ecology,' on the one hand, and 'deep ecology' on the other. *Shallow ecology* is focussed on quick fix solutions that maintain the status quo, such as through the implementation of renewable energy schemes, recycling, the roll out of electric cars, and so on. While these things are undoubtedly important, they nevertheless continue to maintain the same 'privileged' Western lifestyle, and the same philosophical approach to ecology – understood as a resource for human consumption – that has contributed to the crisis. *Deep ecology*, on the other hand, calls for a total transformation of our philosophy and relationship to the environment. In an influential 1973 paper Naess outlines seven key features of the Deep Ecology perspective as he conceived it:

(1) Rejection of the man-in-environment image in favour of the relational, total-field image [...]

(2) Biospherical egalitarianism —in principle [...]

(3) Principles of diversity and of symbiosis. Diversity enhances the potentialities of survival, the chances of new modes of life, the richness of forms. And the so-called struggle of life, and survival of the fittest, should be interpreted in the sense of ability to coexist and cooperate in complex relationships, rather than ability to kill, exploit, and suppress.

(4) Anti-class posture [...]

(5) Fight against pollution and resource depletion [...]

(6) Complexity, not complication [...]

(7) Local autonomy and decentralization [...][49]

Deep ecology, then, calls for a fundamental alteration of the philosophical underpinnings of our activities in the world, and a radical shift from anthropocentrism to what might be called 'ecocentrism' or 'biophilia,' a term coined by the evolutionary biologist Edward O. Wilson FRS.[50] A central feature of Naess' conceptualisation of Deep Ecology is the notion of 'intrinsic value,' the idea that nature has a value in itself regardless of its utilitarian value for humans. He explains that:

> The flourishing of human and nonhuman life on Earth has inherent value. The value of nonhuman life forms is independent of the usefulness of the nonhuman world for human purposes. [...] Abundance and diversity of life forms are values in themselves and contribute to the flourishing of human and nonhuman life on Earth [and] Humans have no right to reduce this abundance and diversity except to satisfy vital needs.[51]

Naess also proposed the notion of *ecosophy*, or a philosophy of place, which emerges naturally from participatory interaction with a particular location, rather than being super-imposed from an outside source. It is a philosophy that emerges from the land based in ecocentric principles. This naturally entails the possibility of multiple *ecosophies*, each emergent from its own particular niche. Further, Naess suggested the need to develop a greater sense of personal identification with the environment through the cultivation of what he called the 'ecological self' (see Chapter Seven).[52] The influence of Naess' formulation of the deep ecology concept was felt far beyond philosophical circles, and went on to establish a particularly strong foothold in psychology and psychotherapy.[53]

Ecopsychology and Green Psychology

The term 'ecospychology' was coined by the cultural theorist Theodore Roszak (1933–2011), though he himself credited the environmentalist Paul Shepard (1925–1996) as the first true ecopsychologist.[54] In his influential book *The Voice of the Earth*, Roszak defines ecopsychology's goal as being 'to awaken the inherent sense of environmental reciprocity that lies within the ecological unconscious [and] to heal the more fundamental alienation between the person and the natural environment.'[55] Furthermore, 'its goal is to bridge our culture's long-standing historical gulf between the psychological and the ecological, to see the needs of the planet and the person as a continuum.'[56] Clearly, then, ecopsychology is aimed at addressing a distinctively European sense of disconnection from nature – a sense that might not necessarily be found in indigenous traditions, for example (see Chapter Nine) – that manifests in a range of psychological disorders in which 'the ecological priorities of the planet are coming to be expressed through our most private spiritual travail.'[57] These ideas were developed and built upon by subsequent theorists such as the psychologist Ralph Metzner (1936–2019), who has been a major contributor to the establishment of a psychological approach to the ecological crisis. His preference was for the name 'green psychology,' rather than 'ecopsychology,' however, explaining that:

> [...] those of us in this field [...] do not mean to advocate [...] a new sub discipline of psychology [...] Rather we are talking about a fundamental re-envisioning of what psychology is [...] a revision that would take the ecological context of human life into account.[58]

Ecopsychology, or Green Psychology, is therefore different from other psychological sub-disciplines, such as environmental psychology, in that is is conceived as a whole new paradigm within which to conduct psychological research and carry out psychotherapy – that is, from an ecological orientation. Ecology provides the underlying ontology and framework for making sense of psychological disorders. Joanna Macy, for example, talks of the repression of ecological trauma associated with the ecological crisis and its impact on mental well-being in Western societies, writing:

> We block it out because it hurts, because it is frightening, and most of all because we do not understand it and consider it to be a dysfunction,

an aberration, a sign of personal weakness. As a society we are caught between a sense of impending apocalypse and the fear of acknowledging it. In this 'caught' place, our responses are blocked and confused.[59]

As part of a healing process centred around facing up to this deep seated ecological trauma, Macy and colleagues developed what they call 'The Council of All Beings,' a collective grieving ritual for the destruction of life on earth in which participants ceremonially embody the perspectives of different plant and animals species. John Seed, one of the co-creators with Macy of the Council, explains how:

> At each Council, we engage in several sensitising activities shifting us away from our usual cerebral mode. Guided visualisations [...] make our four-and-one-half billion-year journey present and vivid. Body movements accompanying the evolutionary recapitulation [...] tap into our knowledge of previous stages of evolution embedded in our neurological systems. The Council culminates in shedding our human identity and speaking from the perspective of another life-form.[60]

The radical embodiment of different species is aimed at destabilising our anthropocentric orientation to the world, encourages emotional identification with the non-human and facilitates in the development of the ecological self.

Problems in Ecopsychology: Colonialism and Anthropocentrism

Ecopsychology provides a radical ecological framework for addressing the relationship between the human and the non-human and the development of ecological consciousness, but it is not without its problems. Alysha Jones and David Segal, for example, argue that ecopsychology often unwittingly continues to perpetuate outdated colonial attitudes in its approach to the ecological crisis. They suggest that in order to make true progress ecopsycholgy must go through a process of what they call 'unsettling,' or decolonisation. They explain that:

> Unsettling the field is a process of revealing how ecopsychology reproduces and reinforces settler colonialism [...] By opening up this dialogue, we

[...] seek to make a critical contribution to the field of ecopsychology and, as non-Indigenous/settler practitioners, to encourage a discussion of accountability for those doing therapeutic land-based nature connection work as visitors on traditional Indigenous territories.[61]

There is a need, then, to take indigenous ecopsychologies seriously in this context. Indeed Roszak argues that all psychologies were once ecopsychologies. Another element that ecopsychology may wish to consider developing is its essentially anthropocentric orientation – geared, as much of mainstream psychology is, towards the promotion of human flourishing and addressing predominantly anthropic needs and concerns. But what about the non-human? The ecopsychologists Laura Sewall and Thomas Fleischner suggest that what is missing from ecopsychology is a much greater emphasis on the non-human, which could be remedied through an engagement with natural history. They explain that:

> Natural history—'a practice of intentional, focused attentiveness and receptivity to the more-than-human world, guided by honesty and accuracy' [...] is a pathway for digging ourselves out of a relentless hall of mirrors. It provides an accessible method for re-engagement with a richly patterned, textured, and animated world, and for becoming more ecologically informed human animals [...].[62]

This emphasis on natural history represents a shift away from the anthropocentric biases that have shaped much of the course of human development, which in Patrick Curry's terms 'demonstrate the malign influence of an exclusive human centredness instead of concern for the common good of life.'[63] The alternative proposed by this shift is 'ecocentrism,' a perspective that moves away from the hierarchical positioning of human beings at the top of the food-chain towards a more egalitarian view of life. Instead, Curry writes, we should begin:

> [...] from a recognition that all forms of life are enabled by, and completely dependent upon, the Earth. Human beings are [...] no exception [...] The well-being of the Earth – the integrity of its processes, places and organisms, human or otherwise – is thus of paramount importance. And in the web of life that has thus arisen, we are interdependent with countless

other creatures, from flora to micro-organisms to fellow mammals. We are literally all in this together, and all want to flourish, and none want to suffer.[64]

We will return to a more thorough discussion of the non-human, and its relation to the human, in Chapter Five, and to a conversation about the implications of indigenous worldviews in Chapter Nine.

Summary

As Timothy Morton suggests, the ecological crisis is a hyperobject – vast and interconnected with consequences that are simultaneously unfurling in different regions, and different ways, all around the world – from flooding and droughts, to soil erosion, biodiversity loss, loss of food security, rising energy costs, and so on. The crisis is predominantly anthropogenic – resulting from excessive human extractive and industrial activity, hence the new geological epoch in which we find ourselves living – the *anthropocene*. Debates continue concerning when exactly the anthropocene began, but perhaps more importantly, as Donna Harraway points out, we must develop ways of getting out of it as quickly as possible. The crisis has inspired numerous socio-political responses from grassroots activism all the way through to international governmental agreements and interventions. There have been religious responses, and psychological responses, but as of yet little has been able to have the effect that is required to bring about the kind of radical ecological transformation of society and culture implied by the notion of deep ecology.

CHAPTER FOUR:
Nature Mysticism and Green Religion

This chapter introduces mysticism, with a particular emphasis on mystical experiences that are spontaneously induced in the context of natural environments. Key theoretical perspectives on nature mysticism are considered, and examples of nature-mystical experiences selected from the archives of the Alister Hardy Religious Experience Research Centre (RERC) are presented and discussed, including their defining characteristics and effects on experiencers. These give valuable insights into elements of the phenomenology of nature mysticism and spiritual orientations more generally, and suggest the powerful capacity of extraordinary experiences to transform philosophical outlooks.[1]

Mysticism and Mystical Experience

As with many of the concepts discussed in this book, there is no single standard definition of mysticism and mystical experience, rather there are many different definitions and theoretical and theological orientations towards it.[2] Nevertheless, scholars have identified some common characteristics of mystical experiences that seem to recur relatively frequently across a variety of different experiential reports. William James, for example, included the following qualities as definitive of mystical experiences. They are, he writes:

- *Ineffable*—such experiences cannot adequately be put into words.
- *Noetic*—they impart knowledge, often of God or the ultimate reality.
- *Transient*—they are short-lived and temporary.
- *Passive*—they feel like they are coming from outside of the experiencer, beyond their control.[3]

Adding to James, the scholar of religious experience Caroline Franks Davis has highlighted four of the most commonly reported characteristics of mystical experience, including: 1) The sense of having apprehended an ultimate reality, 2) the sense of freedom from the limitations of time, space and the individual, 3) a sense of 'oneness,' and 4) feelings of bliss or serenity.[4]

These phenomenological characteristics may be interpreted in different ways depending on the historical contexts and cultural traditions within which they occur, as transpersonal psychologist Brian Les Lancaster explains:

> [...] discussions of the highest mystical states have invariably drawn on an understanding of God and other transcendent concepts, such as levels of the soul. As far as explanation is concerned, the distinctive features of mystical experiences are *explained* to the satisfaction of those [having the experience] by suggesting that they arise through union with God, or with the 'Absolute.' More than this the mystical state is placed in the context of a shared and meaningful system of thought [...].[5]

But mystical experiences are not necessarily confined to theistic interpretations. R.C. Zaehner (1913–1974), for example, discerned three distinctive forms of mystical experience including 'theistic' experiences of communion with a personal God, 'monistic' experiences involving the experiential realisation of the oneness and unity of the cosmos, and 'nature' or 'panenhenic' experiences of union with nature.[6] The next section will turn to nature mysticism, beginning with a case study example.

Nature Mysticism

In some respects it is quite surprising that Sir Alister Hardy (1896–1985), the founder of the Religious Experience Research Centre, was a biologist. We might expect such a centre to have been established by a psychologist, sociologist or anthropologist, perhaps, or some other researcher from the 'soft' social sciences, but not from the so-called 'hard sciences' (though admittedly biology is the softest and squishiest of the hard sciences). Indeed, Hardy started his academic career as a marine ecologist, and in that field is most widely known for his contributions to the study of plankton and their many fundamental connections to other parts of marine ecosystems. Hardy is also credited with the invention of the Continuous Plankton Recorder (CPR), used for documenting plankton levels in the ocean, and his research is still the benchmark for current work in this area.[7] Following his retirement in 1969, after a string of prestigious university posts, and in order to pursue another of his life-long fascinations, Hardy established the Religious Experience Research Unit (RERU) at Manchester College,

Oxford, and began the process of collecting, documenting and analysing contemporary reports of religious and spiritual experience through national questionnaire surveys. Today the archive is housed at the University of Wales Trinity Saint David, Lampeter campus (with the new name of 'Religious Experience Research Centre'), and contains over 6,000 first-hand accounts of religious experiences submitted by the general public.[8]

In other ways, however, Hardy's dual interests are quite unsurprising. The historian of religion Bron Taylor, for instance, has convincingly shown how a form of spirituality, which he terms 'Dark Green Religion,' quite often arises from participatory interaction with the natural world, whether that be as a scientist, as an ecological activist, or in the pursuit of other activities in the great outdoors, such as hunting, hiking, surfing or gardening. Taylor explains that this form of spirituality, which emerges from the land itself, is 'generally deep ecological, biocentric, or ecocentric, considering all species to be intrinsically valuable [...] apart from their usefulness to human beings.'[9] Hardy's fascination with religious experience co-evolved alongside, and was informed by, his curiosity about the natural world. In his autobiographical notes, Hardy recalls having powerful and transformative experiences in nature during his childhood years, which would go on to have a significant impact on the later unfurling of his life and work. He explains how as a student he would occasionally slip into reveries while observing the behaviour of butterflies, or would now and then experience moments of ecstasy while walking along the banks of the river near his school in Oundle, Nottinghamshire. He writes:

> There is no doubt that as a boy I was becoming what might be described as a nature mystic. Somehow, I felt the presence of something which was beyond and yet in a way part of all the things that thrilled me – the wildflowers, and indeed the insects too. I will now record something [that] I have never told anyone before, but now that I am in my 88th year I think I can admit it. Just occasionally when I was sure that no one could see me, I became so overcome with the glory of the natural scene, that for a moment or two I fell on my knees in prayer – not prayer asking for anything, but thanking God, who felt very real to me, for the glories of his Kingdom and for allowing me to feel them. It was always by the running waterside that I did this, perhaps in front of a great foam of meadowsweet or purple loosestrife.[10]

Many (though by no means all) of those who Taylor gathers together in his book *Dark Green Religion* came to their respective moral, ethical and spiritual positions through what could be described as peak, mystical, religious or even paranormal experiences in nature.[11] Aldo Leopold (1887–1948), for example, widely regarded as the father of modern wildlife conservation, experienced a radical transformation of perspective following an encounter with a wolf he had shot while working as a wilderness warden. Leopold had been responsible for culling wolves and bears in national parks in the USA, a task he had not thought twice about until he eventually came face to face with one of his victims. He relates:

> We reached the old wolf in time to watch a fierce green fire dying in her eyes. I realized then, and have known ever since, that there was something new to me in those eyes – something known only to her and to the mountain. I was young then, and full of trigger-itch; I thought that because fewer wolves meant more deer, that no wolves would mean hunters' paradise. But after seeing the green fire die, I sensed that neither the wolf nor the mountain agreed with such a view.[12]

Leopold's cognitive shift – from an anthropocentric to an eco-centric perspective – reflects one of the criteria that William James set out for identifying a genuine religious experience – that it should produce 'moral fruits' in the experiencer.[13] A connection between transformative religious and mystical experience and the natural world has long been recognised in the scholarly literature on religion and religious experience. The philosopher and scholar of mysticism Walter T. Stace (1886–1967) identified nature mysticism as one of the two fundamental forms of mystical experience more generally. He suggested that nature-mystical experiences be referred to as 'extrovertive' – as distinct from the much more interior 'introvertive' mystical experiences occasioned by dedicated meditation, prayer or other contemplative practices. Extrovertive experiences, by contrast, are often triggered by and 'transfigure' the *external* physical environment, frequently inducing a sense of the underlying unity of the natural world:

> The extrovertive mystic with his physical senses continues to perceive the same world of trees and hills and tables and chairs as the rest of us. But he sees these objects transfigured in such manner that the Unity shines through

them [...] the extrovertive experience is sensory-intellectual in so far as it still perceives physical objects but is nonsensuous and nonintellectual in so far as it perceives them as 'all one.'[14]

The RERC archive contains numerous accounts of extraordinary and transcendent experiences apparently induced as a consequence of bodily and psychological immersion in vibrant ecological systems. In his pioneering study of the reports contained in the archive, *The Spiritual Nature of Man*, Hardy identified 'natural beauty' as one of the most common triggers of religious experiences, marginally more common than religious worship – clearly suggestive of an important correlation between the perception of natural environments and extraordinary experiences.[15] More recently, Paul Marshall has conducted an extensive study of the relationship between mystical experiences and the environment. In the preface to his book on the subject, *Mystical Encounters with the Natural World*, Marshall explains the value in taking a renewed look at extrovertive mystical experiences:

> Apart from their significance as life-transforming events, the experiences are of considerable theoretical interest. They have been important in the modern study of mysticism, constituting one of the major types of mystical experience recognised by scholars [...] and they promise to be important in the future development of the field [...] The experiences provide an important test case for evaluating explanations [...] Extrovertive experience is also of interest for the stimulus it could give to the study of mind [...] Are there non-sensory forms of contact with the world? Does mind exist beyond the brain?[16]

We could also add the pressing need to respond to the ecological crisis to the list of reasons for taking a renewed look at extrovertive mystical experiences. As discussed in the previous chapter, many commentators have suggested that the ecological crisis has its roots in the perceived disconnect between humans and our natural environment, a separation that has emerged, especially in the Western world, over the last two hundred years.[17] Nature mysticism, by contrast, presents a parallel image of the human being as fundamentally embedded in nature. Moreover, it is an image and conviction that is born out of direct personal experiences in mystical states of consciousness. Such experiences seem to have a profound impact on the outlook and subsequent behaviour of experiencers,[18] and as such should be of interest when considering ways of establishing a sense of connection to nature more widely.

Phenomenology and Ecology

The next section will turn to explore some of the key phenomenological features of extrovertive experiences, and consider the ways in which they might resonate with ecological functions and processes. Extrovertive experiences in natural settings, as Stace pointed out, are often associated with a sense of unity and oneness in nature – a trait that links extrovertive experiences to other classical mystical-type experiences cultivated in many of the world's mystical traditions.[19] Take, for example, the following accounts of extrovertive experiences from the RERC archive, which are fairly characteristic of nature-mystical experiences in general:

> As I watched, suddenly the whole countryside changed and everything in it, without exception, simply glowed with numinous light – it seemed no longer to be lit by the sun but by its own internal radiance. Sunlight was not reflected from it, but I myself and everything else seemed to have become light – which now inter-penetrated and shone through our previously dense physical forms [...] The whole scene shone with an extraordinary golden glow, which included the sky and the atmosphere itself.[20]

> As we conversed the situation became unreal. The plants and shrubs and the three pine trees in a copse [...] became unreal. And yet they were more real than I had ever seen them in the 3 1/2 years I had lived there. Instead of merging into a general familiar pattern, each item of plant, shrub and tree, stood out singularly, vivid, vibrant [...] The whole area became something on its own, apart from the rest. The whole area became something I had never seen before. I became filled with a feeling of elation and well-being such as I have never before or since experienced [...] I felt that I had seen Nature as it really is.[21]

> My mother and I were walking on a stretch of land [...] known locally as 'the moors.' As the sun declined and the slight chill of evening came on, a pearly mist formed over the ground [...] Here and there just the

very tallest harebells appeared above the mist. I had a great love of these exquisitely formed flowers, and stood lost in wonder at the sight. Suddenly I seemed to see the mist as a shimmering gossamer tissue and the harebells, appearing here and there, seemed to shine with a brilliant fire. Somehow I understood that this was the living tissue of life itself, in which that which we call consciousness was embedded, appearing here and there as a shining focus of energy in the more diffused whole. In that moment I knew that I had my own special place, as had all other things, animate and so-called inanimate, and that we were all part of this universal tissue which was both fragile yet immensely strong, and utterly good and beneficent. The vision has never left me. It is as clear today as fifty years ago, and with it the same intense feeling of love of the world and the certainty of ultimate good. It gave me then a strong, clear sense of identity which has withstood many vicissitudes, and an affinity with plants, birds, animals, even insects, and people too, which has often been commented upon.[22]

In all of these examples it is the features of the landscape – the trees, plants and animals – that first seem to trigger the experience, and which are then transformed in the experiencer's perception to reveal subtle details of interconnection, oneness and unity. These experiences may be brief occurrences, but they leave a lasting impression on the lives of those who have them.

Animistic Mysticism

Religious experiences in nature may also take the form of a 'sudden flash' of animistic insight. Graham Harvey defines animism as the recognition that 'the world is full of persons, only some of whom are human, and that life is always lived in relationship with others.'[23] Animism implies a personal cosmos consisting of multiple perspectives (see Chapter Five). The following experience, took place in April 1917, during the traumatic events of the First World War, while the author was serving in the army, and gives a vivid impression of a what it might be like to experience an animate and personalised cosmos:

While spending an afternoon hour alone in my hilltop wood, a mood of depression had come down. We were due to move in a few days [...] After supper in the mess I felt restless. I wondered if the full moon shining down from a cloudless sky had anything to do with my mood. A walk by the canal might make it easier to sleep. I walked eastward for about two miles along the towpath and then turned about. The nearer I drew to the village, the more alive the surroundings seemed to become. It was as if something which had been dormant when I was in the wood were coming alive. I must have drifted into an exalted state. The moon, when I looked up at it, seemed to have become personalised and observant, as if it were aware of my presence on the towpath. A sweet scent pervaded the air. Early shoots were breaking from the sticky buds of the balsam poplars which bordered the canal; their pleasant resinous odour conveyed good-will. The slowly moving waters of the canal, which was winding its unhurried way from the battlefields to the sea, acquired a 'numen' which endorsed the intimations of the burgeoning trees. The river conveyed that it had seen me before in other places and knew something about me. It was now concerned with my return to the village [...] A feeling that I was being absorbed into the living surroundings gained in intensity and was working up to a climax. Something was going to happen. Then it happened. The experience lasted, I should say, about thirty seconds and seemed to come out of the sky in which were resounding majestic harmonies. The thought, 'that is the music of the spheres' was immediately followed by a glimpse of luminous bodies – meteors or stars – circulating in predestined courses emitting both light and music.[24]

In the above experience a conversation is initiated between the experiencer and the river, the moon and the trees, who all take on personal – relatable – characteristics. These multiple voices seem to contribute to the mounting intensity of the experience, culminating with a symphonic mystical harmonising of the many diverse voices of nature into a whole conceived as 'the music of the spheres.'

Other accounts further demonstrate an overlap between religious experience and elements of animistic and shamanistic modes of perception, especially in relation to the issue of interspecies communication. The following account from the RERC archive suggests a form of therapeutic communication between humans and Elm trees:

Some 12 years ago I used to have four tall Elm Trees on our garden lawn; they grew forming a square. I was strongly drawn to these trees and used to stroke the trunks and talk to them especially when I felt depressed or ill. I always felt their response through a strong vibration through my hands then through my whole body. This convinced me that I am One with All Beings; the same life force which flows through my body flows through all vegetation, animals, birds, fish, minerals, under the ground or sea, even the very stones we walk on. Every animate and inanimate thing is held together with atoms which are of the whole 'Divine Being'.[25]

Unity and Diversity

Extrovertive experiences, then, seem to reveal an image of the world as *both* fundamentally 'unitary and interconnected' *and* 'diverse, complex and multiple.' This both/and understanding of the natural world is also echoed in the structure and functioning of ecological systems – which are both holistic and multiplex in nature. The plant biologist Frederic Clements, as already noted in the first chapter, thought of ecosystems as large-scale organisms in their own right, consisting of a multitude of smaller interconnected organisms (plants, animals, and so on). From Clements' perspective, natural systems may be thought of as harmonic wholes consisting of multiple component parts.[26] Clements' realisation was arrived at through scientific observation of physical ecological processes, but simultaneously resonates with the phenomenological characteristics of the kind of nature mystical experiences described above.

Extrovertive experiences might therefore be understood as instances when the experiencer no longer perceives a separation between themselves and the ecosystem that surrounds them, becoming simultaneously aware of the diversity and interconnectivity of life, as well as its underlying unity and their nested position with it. In these moments, when experience is in harmony with ecological reality, we might say that the experiencer has entered into a state of 'ecological consciousness,' or that they have developed a sudden awareness of what Arne Naess called the 'ecological self' (see Chapter Seven).

The Numinous

With these extraordinary extrovertive experiences we are moving into territory that the German theologian Rudolf Otto (1869–1937) called *numinous* – referring to the non-dogmatic, non-rational, experiential, essence of religion. Famously, Otto made a distinction between two polarities of the numinous – the *mysterium fascinans* – the element of the numinous experience that is fascinating, beautiful, and draws us in – and the *mysterium tremendum* – the terrifying, repulsive and yet awe-inspiring end of the numinous spectrum. The accounts of mystical experiences recounted above would certainly fall into the category of the *mysterium fascinans* with their wonderful transfigurations of natural landscapes, but many people also report darker and/or stranger experiences that, in the Western idiom, are often referred to as 'paranormal,' but that nevertheless share important characteristics with other forms of mystical and religious experience.[27] Otto describes the many forms that the numinous may take:

> The feeling of it may at times come sweeping like a gentle tide, pervading the mind with a tranquil mood of deepest worship [...] It may burst in sudden eruption up from the depths of the soul with spasms and convulsions, or lead to the strangest excitements, to intoxicated frenzy, to transport, and to ecstasy. It has its wild and demonic forms and can sink to an almost gristly horror and shuddering [...] It may become the hushed, trembling, and speechless humility of the creature in the presence of [...] that which is a mystery inexpressible [...].[28]

Examples of such stranger, though undoubtedly related, numinous experiences can be found in their multitudes in the folklorist Simon Young's *Fairy Census 2014–2017*.[29] The census collects together 500 contemporary self-submitted accounts of encounters with fairies collected between November 2014 and November 2017 (see Chapter Six for more on fairies and their relationship with gardens). Suffice to say that such experiences share similarities with the RERC experiences recounted above. See for example the following fairy encounters:

> I was sitting underneath the willow tree in the back garden and felt an electrical tingle. Turning to look over my shoulder I saw five small figures, very human like but much smaller [...] They were dressed in brown to dark green clothes – somewhat like tights with sturdy boots and smock like tops, their faces were more angular than human faces and very sun weathered in appearance. We looked at each other for a short period of time – there was an unspoken exchange of understanding (very hard to articulate) and then they marched off underneath a bush.[30]

[...] one afternoon in May, I was sitting out in my garden. The rhododendrons were in flower and it was a hot bright sunny day. I was very comfortable and content to listen to the birds and just relax. Unexpectedly I became aware of the golden outline of a figure down at the bottom of my garden. I say outline because it was not solid, but looked as though just its outline had been drawn with golden ink. The figure shimmered and had tall wings, but mostly it was transparent, like a rough sketch. It was about three foot tall and rose up in the air a little way before descending; it did this several times. Then I saw a second winged figure, very much smaller. This was also golden, but I remember seeing a flash of blue and green. My first thought was that it was a dragonfly, but on closer observation I saw that it flew quite differently and its shape was not that of an insect but a small human-like figure.[31]

Are fairy experiences such as these another form of extrovertive 'pan-enhenic' nature mysticism?

Extraordinary Effects: Ecological Consciousness

It is commonly reported that the kinds of ecstatic and paranormal experiences collected in the RERC archives, and in documents such as the *Fairy Census*, as well as other forms of extraordinary experiences,[32] often give rise to a shift in philosophical perspective, a renewed sense of vision of the Earth, and an enhanced sense of connection to the natural world, both physically and spiritually.[33] The Harvard psychiatrist John Mack's (1929–2004) work on the alien abduction phenomenon, for example, highlighted the frequent centrality of the eco-crisis theme in many of the abduction experience narratives he collected. Summarising the prevalence of ecological themes in accounts of apparent abduction by aliens, Mack writes that:

It seems impossible to avoid the observation that the alien abduction phenomenon is occurring in the context of a planetary ecological crisis that is reaching critical proportions and that information about this situation is often powerfully conveyed by the alien beings to the experiencers.[34]

Individuals who claim to have had contact with extra-terrestrial intelligences, it seems, may go on to develop a closer sense of connection to their terrestrial ecology, and to develop a new sense of their place in the cosmos following their experience. Again, this echoes William James' emphasis on the 'moral fruits' of religious experience. Similarly, the psychologists Kenneth Ring and Evelyn Valarino have noted parallel effects amongst Near-Death Experiencers, who often develop a 'heightened sensitivity to the ecological health of the planet' following their experience.[35] Changing patterns of behaviour and worldview have also been noted in the aftermath of other forms of extraordinary experience, for example Matthias Forstmann and Christina Sagioglou have found that 'lifetime experience with psychedelics in particular may [...] contribute to people's pro-environmental behavior by changing their self-construal in terms of an incorporation of the natural world.'[36] The psychical researcher Peter McCue also notes the environmental sub-theme that seems to run through many different paranormal experiences. He writes:

> It could be that 'aliens' (whatever their true nature) prefer to give warnings rather than intervene directly to protect the environment. But if that's the case, it seems that their message so far has been very ineffective.[37]

At face value, then, there appears to be a connection between anomalous and extraordinary experiences of various kinds and the development of a sense of ecological consciousness, even if it does not always translate into practical action on behalf of the environment. The connection certainly warrants further investigation, however, especially in this time of ecological collapse and climate change. The ecofeminist philosopher Val Plumwood (1939–2008) reported a similar transformation of consciousness and perspective that followed in the wake of a particularly intense, and highly extraordinary experience in the terrifying grip of a crocodile's death twist. Plumwood survived the ordeal, and went on to write about it in great and evocative detail, but what is of particular interest here is the way that the experience – much like the paranormal and religious experiences discussed above – shifted her perspective from an anthropocentric to an ecocentric point of view:

> Before the encounter, it was as if I saw the whole universe as framed by my own narrative, as though the two were joined perfectly and seamlessly together. As my own narrative and the larger story were ripped apart,

I glimpsed a shockingly indifferent world in which I had no more significance than any other edible being. The thought, *This can't be happening to me, I'm a human being. I am more than just food!* was one component of my terminal incredulity. It was a shocking reduction, from a complex human being to a mere piece of meat [...] Large predators like lions and crocodiles present an important test for us. An ecosystem's ability to support large predators is a mark of its ecological integrity. Crocodiles and other creatures that can take human life also present a test of our acceptance of our ecological identity. When they're allowed to live freely, these creatures indicate our preparedness to coexist with the otherness of the earth, and to recognize ourselves in mutual, ecological terms, as part of the food chain, eaten as well as eater.[38]

Mystical, religious and paranormal experiences may also perform the same (or similar) functions as Plumwood's terrifying crocodile encounter – in the case of alien abduction experiences, or other forms of entity encounter, for example, the experiencer is reminded that they are part of a much larger 'invisible ecosystem,'[39] and that human beings are not at the top of the food chain.[40] This may also go some way towards explaining why there can also be positive effects (such as an enhanced sense of nature connection and pro-environmental behaviour), as a result of what are often very negative and frightening experiences (such as crocodile attacks and alien abductions), as well as from positive experiences (such as interactions with entities on psychedelics, or experiences of mystical union with nature, for example).

Ecological consciousness, then, may be thought of more as a remembering of our already deep embededdness in ecological systems – a remembering brought about when the blinkers of our cultural models slip aside during extraordinary experiences that dissolve our cultural assumptions – rather than necessarily as a byproduct, emergent property, or a pre-condition of extraordinary experiences. Extraordinary experiences of all different types appear to remind us of something that our cultural models have convinced us to ignore – our relationship with the world (see the discussion about the ecological self in Chapter Seven).

Future Directions for Research

One possible line of enquiry for future research in this direction could be to conduct ethnographic research on spirituality and religious experience amongst practitioners of ecological regeneration. As an in-road into this arena, I conducted a limited informal online survey of permaculture practitioners to uncover possible connections between practical engagement with ecology and extraordinary experience. This is not the place to go into a full examination of what the survey found, but suffice to say here that the perceived connections between permaculture – a design process inspired by observations of natural systems (see Chapter Eleven) – and extraordinary experience recounted by my survey respondents point towards an interesting correlation between *interacting* with the natural world (whether through observation of ecosystems, the practical tending of gardens, and so on) and *extraordinary experiences* (feelings of connectedness to nature, communication with plants and animals, and so on).[41] Here are a few sample responses from my survey informants when asked what they thought the connection between permaculture and extraordinary experience might be, from their own point of view, just to give a sense of the kinds of perspectives reported:

'To me permies [permaculture practitioners] are close to reality and so is [the] paranormal. [It is an] awareness of life and being outside our personal selves.'

'You wake up to greater things when you deliberately work with the planet.'

'Care. Care for the inclusion of all beings.'

'If by "paranormal" you mean being connected with our environments, plants, animals, winds and mountains I think [Permaculture] can be a gateway for many – because to design, we have to observe.'

'Perhaps openness to exploring, learning and hoping to understand things beyond our current knowledge?'

'Within a purely materialistic plane, Ecology (from which Permaculture seems to derive its main perspectives) is a science which shows us the patterns and connections between things that we might not otherwise perceive. My perspective of mystical experience is that they often provide that same broad connected perspective of the spiritual.'

'The tending of a life filled space means the ability to see into things further – with the time spent tending there [are] often moments of connection that can be more rewarding than with humans. This allows a space for the unusual [...] to be seen.'

'Permaculture is an attempt to bring into conscious awareness the connections with the natural world that we largely ignore.'[42]

Through fostering a closer relationship with our ecology – by engaging in community gardening projects, or other forms of hands-on participation with the living world – we may open ourselves up to extraordinary experiences of connection, thus reinforcing our desire to interact with the natural world, creating a feed-back effect. The work of the agroecology researcher Maria Botelho and colleagues would seem to support this suggestion. In their study of Brazilian agroforestry (which is a combination of agriculture and forestry techniques to promote biodiversity while also generating large sustainable crop yields) they found that:

> [...] through the adoption and collaborative development of the agroforestry system, farmers have begun to conduct intense observations of the environment in relation to plants, animals, water, and soil and to shape and renew the use of traditional knowledge in their production methods. Furthermore, because the farmers now verbalize their reflections and exchange their observations and knowledge with others, they are internalizing the idea that a profound change is occurring in their conceptions of nature. This process is similar to the process that deep ecologists describe as a metaphysical reconfiguration of the self and the ecosystem.[43]

Active observation, interaction and engagement with ecological systems, through the lens of agroforestry, provided the means for these Brazilian communities to reconnect with their ancestral traditions and to re-establish an experiential sense of spiritual connection and belonging to the land.

Summary

One of the most exciting, and potentially important, aspects of this line of research – of trying to understand the spiritual and experiential motivations of those engaged in ecological regeneration – is the potential for practical application to real-world problems. Climate change, ecological collapse, species loss, pollution, and so on, are among the biggest problems facing contemporary societies. They are also most commonly thought of as problems for the 'hard sciences' to tackle, usually with technology. The 'soft' and social sciences, on the other hand, are often thought to have little to offer in terms of practical responses. But, if we can learn more about the role of human interaction with the natural world in the modulation of extraordinary experiences – which themselves, as a feedback loop, also seem to lead to a desire to re-engage with nature – then perhaps we can develop novel new approaches to rebuilding a more sustainable relationship with our natural environment – a relationship based on experiential and empathetic engagement with nature, rather than from the perspective of detatched objectivity. The 'soft' study of religious and other extraordinary experience may have an important role to play in shaping humanity's response to the ecological crisis. In this way we might begin to reverse some of the damage caused by our perceived detachment from nature and develop what Mark A. Schroll has called 'transpersonal ecosophical consciousness' – 'an ecstatic visionary philosophy of ecological harmony.'[44]

CHAPTER FIVE:
The Non-Human

This chapter aims to provide a brief introduction to the natural history of mind and consciousness. The variety and diversity of forms of life on Earth, and their concomitant mental worlds, provide a particularly rich context within which to consider the possibilities of other-than-human beings and all manner of different spirits of place. This chapter blends insights from contemporary scientific research on plant consciousness with perspectives from traditional animistic worldviews as well as from paranormal research to suggest an expanded view of the natural history of mind that is able to accommodate spirits and monsters alongside mushrooms and otters.

What is the non-human?

The answer may seem obvious – animals, plants, water, rocks and so on – everything that is not 'us.' But when approached critically the issue quickly becomes much less straightforward. There are, for example, parts of our own bodies that are technically 'non-human.' Indeed it has been found that human cells 'make up only 43% of the body's total cell count. The rest are microscopic colonists [...],' which include 'bacteria, viruses, fungi and archaea,' with the greatest concentration found in the 'dark murky depths of our oxygen-deprived bowels.'[1] It is also a widely known fact that the human body consists of 60–75% water.[2] We would seem to be more non-human than we are human, when considered from this perspective. Where, then, do we draw the line between the human and the non-human? Or is there a line?

Biomass and Biodiversity

The following is a fairly standard definition of the concept of 'biomass' as used in biology and ecology:

> Biomass refers to the mass of living organisms, including plants, animals, and microorganisms, or, from a biochemical perspective, cellulose, lignin, sugars, fats, and proteins. Biomass includes both the above- and below-ground tissues of plants, for example, leaves, twigs, branches, boles, as

well as roots of trees and rhizomes of grasses. Biomass is often reported as a mass per unit area (g m–2 or Mg ha–1) and usually as dry weight (water removed by drying). Unless otherwise specified, biomass usually includes only living material.[3]

Biomass is a crucial factor in the carbon cycle, capturing and storing carbon dioxide from the atmosphere through organic processes, such as photosynthesis in plants and trees. Indeed, it is the capacity of biomass to sequestrate carbon from the air that underlies global tree planting initiatives[4] – such as the United Nation's 'Plant for the Planet' billion tree campaign – which have been increasing in number in recent years.[5] In the United Kingdom, Woodland Carbon Code projects, which plant trees especially to capture carbon, are 'estimated to sequester 5.7 million tonnes of carbon dioxide over their lifetime.'[6] While this undoubtedly performs an important function, this attitude towards the use of trees nevertheless considers the value of woodland biomass in terms of its ability to rectify anthropogenic problems, rather than for the intrinsic vale of the trees themselves (see discussion of Deep Ecology in Chapter Three). The concept of biomass essentially reduces life on Earth to its constituent parts – to the weight of physical material produced through biological processes. This conceptual collapsing of life into a single seething mass of biochemical components is pure reductionism and ignores the true complexity and diversity of organisms and other forms of life that exist within that mélange, with little regard for their subtler aspects. This chapter seeks to move beyond biomass into the subtler dimensions of life.

Intelligence in Nature

The anthropologist Jeremy Narby points out that definitions of intelligence have tended to be highly anthropocentric – defined in terms of human capacities such as problem solving, tool use, symbolic thought, culture, and so on.[7] Research is increasingly demonstrating, however, that members of non-human species also possess similar attributes. These similarities are all the more impressive when found in species that are very distantly removed from us on the phylogenetic tree. Tool use (long regarded as a hallmark for the emergence of 'modern humans' in palaeoanthropology), for example, has been observed amongst a surprisingly diverse range of marine animals, including 'fish, cephalopods, mammals, crabs, urchins and possibly gastropods.'[8] Peter Godfrey-Smith's wonderful book *Other Minds* provides a fascinating insight into the evolution of mind and intelligence in cephalopods, associated with a broad spectrum of complex behaviours.[9] Observations such as these suggest that characteristic behaviours we have associated with intelligence in humans are much more widely distributed throughout nature than we have often wanted to admit.

Plant Minds

Recent developments in the study of plant intelligence are demonstrating that plants are much more than simply 'green objects' for human use. There has been a proliferation of research into plants and their subjective dimensions over the last twenty years. The pioneering plant consciousness researchers Stefano Mancuso and Alessandra Viola explain that:

> The study of plant intelligence points up a very interesting aspect of research on intelligence in general: how difficult it is for us humans to understand living systems that think differently from us. Indeed, we only seem able to appreciate intelligences very similar to ours.[10]

In spite of the dependence of the animal kingdom upon plant life on Earth – it is plants, after all, who draw down energy from the sun making it usable by animals, and who maintain stable atmospheric conditions for us to breath – humankind has had a tendency (at least in the dominant Western culture) to disregard plants as unconscious objects – devoid of subjectivity and personhood – which we have a right to dominate and bend to our will. In their book *Brilliant Green*, Mancuso and Viola call for a radical shift in the way that we think about plants. They argue that:

> [...] a compelling body of research shows that higher-order plants really are 'intelligent': able to receive signals from their environment, process the information, and devise solutions adaptive to their own survival.[11]

The plant behavioural ecologist Monica Gagliano's research has further demonstrated that plants are capable of both learning and remembering,[12] that they have the capacity to hear sounds,[13] and that they might also use sound for communication.[14] These findings have helped to solidify the newly emerging field of 'plant neurobiology,'[15] a field of research that was

72

(much as with parapsychology's relationship with academic psychology), considered 'fringe' research by mainstream biology, until recently that is. Indeed, plants exhibit all manner of behaviours that were previously assumed to be hallmarks of the so-called 'higher animals.' The forester and author Peter Wohlleben's hugely popular book *The Hidden Life of Trees*, for example, collects together evidence suggesting that trees are in fact social beings who – like humans – live in social communities. They look after their young and elderly by sharing out nutrients amongst themselves (even the stumps of long fallen trees have been observed to be supported with nutrients by the rest of the community), and communicate with one another through complex chemical signalling and mycorrhizal networks.[16] There are controversies over Peter Wohlleben's book and its implications, however, which highlight some of the key points of contention in this field of research:

> In parts of the book, Wohlleben's description of these ecological relationships is uncontroversial. Drawing on scientific literature dealing with plant physiology and ecology, he unveils some of the remarkable adaptations of trees and their dependence on other species for nutrition and reproduction [...] But to convey this difference between the planted forest and the natural forest, Wohlleben slips into language that is strongly anthropomorphic and teleological. Not only are trees like us in having an emotional and social life, but they seem capable of planning ahead to promote the optimum environment to guarantee their longevity [...][17]

As has already been noted, mainstream materialist science has a problem with the idea of teleology in nature,[18] but increasing numbers of scientific studies are beginning to push the envelope of our appreciation of non-human cognitive (and related) capacities, so that the idea of plants actively forming communities and manipulating the environment for their own (and others') benefit is not quite so improbable. Indeed, the more that is discovered the more probable it becomes. A recent study published in the *Journal of the Royal Society* by the computer scientist Andrew Adamatzky, for example, shows just how far these capacities might extend beyond our expectations by suggesting that fungi – amongst their many other remarkable capabilities – seem to be able to communicate with one another in a surprisingly similar manner to human beings – using a *language* made up of 'words.' By inserting electrodes 'into a substrate colonized by mycelium or directly into sporocarps,' Adamatzky and colleagues were able to record the 'electrical activity of ghost fungi (*Omphalotus nidiformis*), Enoki fungi (*Flammulina velutipes*), split gill fungi (*Schizophyllum commune*) and caterpillar fungi (*Cordyceps militaris*).' They found that:

> [...] distributions of lengths of spike trains, measured in a number of spikes, follow the distribution of word lengths in human languages. We found that the size of fungal lexicon can be up to 50 words; however, the core lexicon of most frequently used words does not exceed 15–20 words.[19]

With the capacity to learn, remember and communicate, plants and fungi clearly also possess an interior world of subjective consciousness. This is likely just the tip of the iceberg. Plants and fungi are expressions of mind amongst innumerable other modes and manifestations of consciousness. As the human world wakes up to the importance of plants, trees, and biodiversity more generally, for the immediate health of the global system, and new forest planting projects are initiated internationally to tackle the problems associated with climate change, it will soon become essential to realise that the process of re-greening and re-wilding is also, simultaneously, a process of re-minding and re-animating the environment. This will necessarily involve the creation of spaces for non-human minds to flourish. If we fail to recognise this going forward, and continue to treat plants simply as green objects for human consumption, then a truly ecological future will not be possible. The growing awareness of the sheer psychodiversity (the variety of forms of mind) expressed by life on Earth is immense, and opens up an important space in the scientific discourse for the consideration of other, perhaps even more subtle, manifestations of mind.

Paranormal Plant Minds

Monica Gagliano's recent and hugely popular book *Thus Spoke the Plant* documents and details how her own interactions with plant consciousness – initiated through dreams, ritual dieting and vision quests – have guided her mainstream scientific research on plant intelligence into novel, even revolutionary, new domains.[20] These communications hint at a future mode of scientific research in collaborative dialogue with plants, rather than treating them as agency-less research subjects, as has been the historical tendency. By incorporating her visionary interactions with plant intelligence as part of her research design process, Gagliano's work effectively blurs the distinctions between what we might call the paranormal, shamanism and the science of plant intelligence, and suggests that subtler modes of interaction with non-human consciousness might be possible through ritual and altered states of consciousness.

The findings emerging from Gagliano and her colleagues' envelope-pushing investigations also call for a re-appraisal of the controversial work of the polygrapher Cleve Backster (1924–2013), and his own studies of plant consciousness in the 1960s and 70s, which were largely dismissed by the mainstream at the time. Backster's interest began in 1966 when he first recorded polygraph (lie-detector) readings indicative of emotional arousal in house plants, which he noticed after watering a *dracaena massangeara* pot-plant in his office, to which he had attached electrodes and a galvanometer.[21] Backster was so intrigued by his findings that he went on to develop numerous other innovative experiments to test for further emotional states in plants, culminating in 1968 with the publication of a technical paper titled 'Evidence of Primary Perception in Plant Life' in the *International Journal of Parapsychology*.[22] In the paper Backster summarises his methods and findings, and presents what he calls his 'primary perception' hypothesis:

> The author proposes that there exists a yet undefined primary perception in plant life [...] and that this perception facility in plants can be shown to function independently of human involvement [...] this perception facility may be part of a primary sensory system capable of functioning at cell level.[23]

As if to make matters yet more complex, Backster also claimed that his experiments provided clear evidence of mind-to-mind (telepathic) communication between humans and plants. Backster's plants seemed to be able to react to his thoughts, emotions and intentions, often even before they had been expressed in the physical world. Peter Tompkins and Christopher Bird provided a thorough overview of the pioneering work of researchers at the borderlands of parapsychology and plant physiology in the 1960s and 70s in their book *The Secret Life of Plants*.[24] It would seem that the psi effects that have been documented in parapsychological laboratories since the 1950s are not limited to human beings, and may – like intelligence – be much more widely distributed throughout nature, providing opportunities for complex, subtle, interconnections within and between ecosystems and their constituent species. This may also go some way towards explaining how exactly plants are able to act with 'a kind of "swarm intelligence" that enables them to behave not as an individual but as a multitude.'[25]

Could it be possible that research in plant neurobiology, Monica Gagliano's experiments in plant memory and communication, the parapsychological polygraph experiments of Cleve Backster, and the long shamanistic traditions of experiential plant communication are all pointing towards a single truth? That plants are radically more conscious than we have given them credit for in materialist science. The seething mass of life referred to as biomass, then, is simultaneously a vast ocean of minds, thoughts and ideas.

Animism

'Animism' is by now a popular and widely used term. It derives from the Latin word *anima*, meaning 'soul' and was first employed as a scholarly category by the founding anthropologist Edward Burnett Tylor (1832–1917). Tylor used it to refer to the widespread, cross-cultural 'belief in spiritual beings.' His analysis of the ethnographic literature of the time had led him to understand animism as the very earliest expression of religious thought, from which all later branches of religion have ultimately stemmed. Tylor further reasoned that animism was essentially erroneous, with origins in the misinterpretation of dreams and other altered states of consciousness. He reasoned that:

> When the sleeper awakens from a dream, he believes he has really somehow been away, or that other people have come to him. As it is well known by experience that men's bodies do not go on these excursions, the natural explanation is that every man's living self or soul is his phantom or image, which can go out of his body and see and be seen itself in dreams.[26]

Influenced by Charles Darwin's (1809–1882) *On the Origin of Species*, first published in 1859,[27] Tylor's anthropology was closely wedded to a form of social evolutionism known as *developmentalism*, that was particularly popular during the latter half of the nineteenth century.[28] This view saw animism as a 'primitive' mentality, superseded by scientific rationalism, which if found in the present day was said to be a 'survival.' Embedded in the early conceptualisation of animism, then, were a range of colonial and Euro-centric biases and assumptions, which were actively used as a point of differentiation between the European, rationalist colonial worldview and the many indigenous worldviews found in the colonised territories. Professor of African Studies Harry Olúdáre Garuba (1958–2020), explained that:

> [...] animist understandings of the natural and social world functioned within discourses of colonial modernity as the aberration, the past-in-the-present, to be disciplined so as to create civilised worlds and subjects [...] In other words, animism has functioned as the metaphoric receptacle for everything that is a negation of the modern.[29]

Over the last two decades or so, however, animism as an etic category has been re-conceptualised in the academy as a feature of worldviews centred around notions of 'personhood,' 'relationship' and 'reciprocity' (see Chapter Nine). The religious studies scholar Graham Harvey, for instance, influentially re-defined animists as 'people who recognise that the world is full of persons, only some of whom are human, and that life is always lived in relationship with others.' He goes on to explain that:

> Animism is lived out in various ways that are all about learning to act respectfully (carefully and constructively) towards and among other persons. Persons are beings, rather than objects, who are animated and social towards others (even if they are not always sociable). Animism [...] is more accurately understood as being concerned with learning how to be a good person in respectful relationships with other persons [...][30]

Relationships, rather than notions of spirits, survivals and 'primitive mentality,' are now understood as central components of animistic cosmologies, constituting what have come to be referred to as 'relational ontologies' (see Chapter Ten).[31] As the Potowatomi botanist and philosopher Robin Wall Kimmerer explains, in order to live sustainably from an indigenous perspective it is necessary to live in good relationships with the other-than-human persons that make up the ecosystems that sustain us:

In such cultures, people have a responsibility not only to be grateful for the gifts provided by Mother Earth, they are also responsible for playing a positive and active role in the well-being of the land. They are called not to be passive consumers, but to sustain the land that sustains them.[32]

Theodore Roszak has suggested that animism's emphasis on the formation of 'right relationships' with other-than-human and non-human persons might have 'a proven ecological utility,' in that 'it disciplines the relationship of humans to their environment, imposing an ethical restraint upon exploitation and abuse.'[33] Animistic worldviews encourage us to participate in an 'intersubjective cosmos,'[34] in which we must take seriously the perspectives of other-than-human persons. The anthropologist Eduardo Viveiros de Castro has highlighted another important element of animist relational ontologies, which he has labelled 'perspectivism.' He explains that in Amerindian cosmological models the world is often thought to be 'inhabited by different sorts of subjects or persons, human and non-human, which apprehend reality from distinct points of view.' He elaborates:

> Typically [...] humans see humans as humans, animals as animals and spirits (if they see them) as spirits; however animals (predators) and spirits see humans and animals (as prey) to the same extent that animals (as prey) see humans as spirits or as animals (predators) [...] By the same token animals and spirits see themselves as humans: they perceive themselves as (or become) anthropomorphic beings when they are in their own houses or villages and they experience their own habits and characteristics as a form of culture [...] they see their food as human food [...] they see their bodily attributes as body decorations or cultural instruments, they see their social system as organised in the same way as human institutions are [...].[35]

From an animist, relational and perspectivist point-of-view, then, human beings inhabit a world of many minds, in which it should come as little surprise that plants, animals and other non-humans possess interior subjectivities.

Other-than-Human Persons and Ultraterrestrials

Any attempt at making sense of psychodiversity will also have to be inclusive of what are often referred to as 'other-than-human' persons in the anthropological literature. The concept was first used by the anthropologist Alfred Irving Hallowell (1892–1974) in the context of his research into Ojibwa cosmology and ontology, where animacy and personhood are acknowledged as fundamental properties of the cosmos, extending far beyond the human sphere. Kenneth Morrison explains that for the Ojibwa:

> [...] 'other-than-human persons' share with human beings powerful abilities, including intelligence, knowledge, wisdom, the ability to discern right from wrong, and also the ability to speak, and therefore to influence other persons. In Ojibwa thought, persons are not defined by human physical shape, and so the Ojibwa do not project anthropomorphic attributes onto the world.[36]

While the term non-human is frequently taken to include the biological lifeforms, geological processes, and other physical factors that constitute the living planet around us, the concept of the 'other-than-human' also expands out to consider what might be referred to as 'meta-empirical,' 'spiritual,' 'daimonic' or 'paranormal' forms of life and consciousness[37] – spirits and modalities of mind beyond what we can easily categorise, but no less a part of natural history than sparrows and blue whales.[38] This is the sense in which one of the founders of psychical research, the Cambridge classicist F.W.H. Myers (1843–1901), first coined the term 'supernormal' (which later mutated into 'paranormal'), in order to shift the dialogue around 'psychical phenomena' into the realm of the natural (see Chapter Seven). He explained how the 'word supernatural is open to grave objections' because 'it assumes that there is something outside nature. Now there is no reason to suppose that the psychical phenomena with which we deal are less a part of nature [...] they are above to norm [...] rather than outside [...] nature.'[39] Other-than-human persons, then, may be more paranormal than supernatural.

Pioneering paranormal researchers such as Charles Fort (1874–1932) and John Keel (1930–2009) – who followed in Myers' footsteps, spending their lives and careers investigating the anomalous – eventually came to consider the possibility that there might be a greater intelligence underlying the many diverse manifestations of paranormal phenomena that they documented.[40] John Keel wrote, for example, that:

It is quite possible – even probable – that the Earth is really a living organism, and that it in turn is a part of an even larger organism, that whole constellations are alive, transmitting and receiving energy to and from other celestial energy sources. Up and down the energy scale the whole macrocosm is functioning on levels of reality that will always be totally beyond our comprehension. We are a part of it all, just as the microbe swimming on the microscope slide is unknowingly a part of our dismal reality, and, like the microbe, we lack the perceptive equipment necessary to view the larger whole. Even if we could view it, we could not understand it.[41]

Keel's idea essentially represents a sort of paranormal Gaia-hypothesis, which in turn gave rise to another useful concept for considering the psychodiversity of our living planet – the notion of the *ultraterrestrial*. The idea emerged in response to the dominant view in UFOlogy that UFOs/ UAPs are *extra*-terrestrial in origin – coming from another planet in physical outer space.[42] Keel pointed out that many of the stranger UFO encounters did not seem to support this hypothesis, suggesting instead that they (along with other paranormal entities) might actually originate from the Earth – *ultra*- rather than *extra*- terrestrial – and have likely been here much longer than human-kind, existing on different frequencies of the electromagnetic spectrum:

At this moment you are surrounded by all kinds of energy, much of it manmade, vibrating on every frequency from the ultra high frequencies [to] the very low frequencies [...] There are other forms of energy tied in as well [forms of energy] on such high frequencies they cannot be detected with even the most sophisticated scientific instruments [...] If you could peer into this super spectrum, you would undoubtedly see some frightening things – strange shapes and eerie ghostlike forms moving through a sea of electrical energy like fish in some alien sea.[43]

These 'strange shapes and eerie ghostlike forms' are the *ultraterrestrials* – super natural beings native to the Earth. For Keel, then, the cosmos was very much alive – overflowing with life, in fact. The Earth is no exception – inhabited by beings on all manner of different frequencies, but no less indigenous or more alien to the planet than human beings. This is what Keel referred to as *Our Haunted Planet*.[44] There are resonances here with what agroecology researcher Julia Wright has called 'subtle ecologies,' which she characterises as ecological models in which 'a non-material dimension [is understood to exist alongside materially based ecological] systems.'[45] Sensitivity to, and awareness of, these frequently invisible ecosystems is often deeply ingrained in indigenous cosmologies.[46]

Living Stones

As has already been suggested, consciousness and personhood may extend much further into nature than just plants and other biological organisms, even into systems and structures that are frequently viewed as 'non-living,' such as rocks and stones. But, as noted above, not all cultural frameworks hold that rocks are 'non-living' or inanimate in the first place. Famously, Alfred Irving Hallowell gave the example of Ojibwa language, in which rocks are considered to be grammatically animate and are treated as 'persons' and 'relations,' rather than inanimate objects. Ojibwa words for rocks and stones, therefore, come with the implicit understanding that they possess the attribute of personhood. Similarly, terms such as 'mishoomis' (grandfathers), are used to refer both to genealogical ancestors (biological relations), as well as to the rocks themselves, who are also understood as relational persons. Given this linguistic animism, Hallowell once asked an old Ojibwa man 'Are all the stones we see about us here alive?' The old man reflected on the question and replied 'No! But some are.' The point here is that the Ojibwa 'do not perceive stones in general as animate any more than we do. The crucial test is experience.'[47] Ojibwa language and ontology essentially holds open the door for the *possibility* of interaction with animate rocks, so that in the event that an animate rock is encountered, it is not necessarily viewed as an 'anomaly,' but instead would be treated as a revered ancestor. Hallowell presents an account from his friend, and main informant, Chief William Berens (1865–1947), of an animate rock that would dispense medicine. He explains that Chief Berens:

> [...] had one of these [animate rocks], but it no longer possessed these attributes. It had contours that suggested eyes and mouth. When Yellow Legs, Chief Berens' great-grandfather, was a leader of the Midewiwin he used to tap the stone with a new knife. It would then open its mouth, Yellow Legs would insert his fingers and take out a small leather sack with medicine in it.[48]

Certain rocks, then, may present themselves in such a way as to invite our participation and engagement, seeking to establish relationships with human beings that stumble across them. Indeed, the dispensing of medicines for the benefit of humanity would appear to be a particularly beneficent act of good-will on behalf of the rock. An awareness of the personhood and agency of rocks and stones is not limited to the Ojibwa in North America, but can be found distributed throughout human cultures right across the globe. As an example of a parallel from a very different tradition, the American journalist Wirt Sikes (1836–1883), who travelled around Wales in the early twentieth century collecting fairy beliefs, explains that:

> In the tradition concerning Welsh stones, abundant personal attributes are accorded them, such as in nature only belong to animals. They were endowed with volition and with voice; they could travel from place to place without mortal aid; they would move uneasily when disturbed by human contact; they expanded and contracted at will; they clung to people who touched them with profane or guilty purpose; they possessed divers qualities which made them valuable to their possessors, such as the power of rendering them invisible, or of filling their pockets with gold.[49]

Rocks may also exhibit an inherent sacredness that is recognised by humans when they first encounter them. For example, the anthropologist Fabian Graham reports on an animistic deity called Shi Tou Gong – literally 'Respected Rock' – who is housed at the Zi Nan Gong temple in Taiwan. Graham explains: 'It was discovered 250 years ago after a devastating flood when they dug up a stone shaped like a human. It was assumed to possess a spirit, was robed and has been worshipped as a Money God ever since.'[50] Similarly, the anthropologist Holly Walters has documented 'the veneration of sacred fossil ammonites, called Shaligrams' in Nepal, noting that their veneration 'has been an integral part of ritual practice throughout South Asia', where they are understood as 'natural manifestations of the Hindu god Vishnu.' Walters explains that 'Shaligrams are called svarupa ("natural forms") and are therefore inherently sacred.'[51] Rocks are also a central feature of classical Chinese garden design, where their treatment carries the hallmarks of an animistic orientation to the world:

> As an ancient mentality, rock worship remains in Chinese legends, myths and is practiced in folk culture such as feng-shui, a traditional Chinese

practice used to harmonize people with their environment [...] In Chinese gardens rock worship mainly appears in two aspects: the adoration of rocks and use of rocks as [a] tool to drive evil factors away [...][52]

Similarly, Aguaruna Jivaro women in South America make use of magical gardening stones (known as *nantag*) specifically for protection against evil spirits while gardening. Gardens are understood as dangerous liminal places – a meeting place between cultivated human order and wild unpredictable nature (see Chapter Six) – where such spiritual protection is needed in order to carry out essential gardening activities.[53] Rocks with apotropaic functions are also found in European hag-stone traditions, where stones with holes running through them are hung or placed around doorways to ward off evil spirits.[54] In Estonia many traditional sacred sites feature rocks onto which wounded or injured limbs are placed for the purpose of healing.[55] But rocks are not *always* beneficent. A story from the village of Llanrhaeadr-ym-Mochnant, in Mid-Wales, illustrates the point quite nicely.

According to a local legend there was once a tall, pointed, stone pillar in the village of Llanrhaeadr-ym-Mochnant known as Careg-y-Big (The Bickering Stone). Every Sunday the people of the village would challenge each other to climb to the top of the stone and shout out that they were 'Captain of Careg-y-Big,' but only if they were able to reach the top. Unfortunately these competitions frequently turned violent, with full-blown skirmishes breaking out around the base of the pillar on a regular basis. It was not uncommon on a Monday morning for people to ask how many had been killed in Llanrhaeadr-ym-Mochnant on Sunday, trying to reach the coveted pinnacle of Careg-y-Big. Noticing that there was something unusual about the stone's unpleasant influence on the villagers, the parish priest employed the services of a local farmer from the nearby village of Penybont Llanerchemrys to get rid of the stone and its malevolent influence. The farmer used a team of large Oxen to remove the stone from the village, while the villagers were asleep, so as not to arouse them. When the farmer brought the stone to his farm, the animals began attacking one another. Realising the malevolent influence of the stone, the farmer hauled it to a deep pool in the river Tanat and threw it in, but its draw was too powerful and the farmer drowned after an attempt to retrieve the stone from the watery depths.[56] Why did the stone behave in this *monstrous* way towards humans?

Monsters

There has been an upsurge of academic interest in 'monsters' over the last twenty years, especially in the context of literary criticism, but also more recently spreading out like tentacles into other areas of the humanities and social sciences. Indeed, in 2020 *The Monster Theory Reader* was published,[57] which sought to consolidate the field of 'monster studies' through a corpus of key texts. Jeffrey Weinstock, the literary scholar spearheading the field, explains that monster studies aims to understand images of the monstrous as 'texts in need of interpretation,' from which we can 'tease out what such images and narratives say about their creators and cultures.'[58] In his chapter in the book, professor of Liberal Arts Anthony Lioi examines the image of the 'swamp dragon' – a common motif across folklore, popular culture and horror literature – which he suggests can serve as a catalyst for the emergence of an eco-centric cosmovision (echoing Donna Harraway's call for the replacement of the anthropocene with the Chthulucene). He writes:

> Serpentine alliances such as these might stand a chance of countering the logic of academic competition and harnessing the swamps of bureaucracy for our own ends. By thinking of ourselves in collective terms and working toward collective goals, by becoming a swamp dragon *en masse*, ecocritics might wield the influence we all hope for in the name of conservation and restoration, survival and flourishing.[59]

Arguing along similar lines, the transpersonal anthropologist Mark A. Schroll has pointed to the figure of the DC comic book hero Swamp Thing, whose 'superpower is to become one with Gaia,' as representative of an archetype for the emergence of an ecocentric worldview. Schroll explains that the monstrous figure of Swamp Thing – an ordinary human transformed into a green avatar of Gaia following an experimental accident – represents a 'twentieth century merging of science and nature that produces a rebirth of the Green Man' for the present day.[60] Simon Bacon also makes a similar point about the image of the vampire in his book *Eco-Vampires: The Undead and the Environment*. In particular, Bacon argues that Bram Stoker's (1846–1912) infamous Count Dracula – along with vampires more generally – can be understood as a force of nature, restoring ecological balance, holding back the push of modernity and threatening the destructive dominance of humanity over the natural world. Bacon explains that Vampires exist to remind us that:

> [...] the Earth is not ours to do with as we please. We must earn our place within its ecosystem. Vampires serve as a timely reminder to keep both the world and ourselves alive into the future, we do not need to accept the vampires but recognise them for the existential threat they are [...] and accept their challenge to be more at home in the world we live in.[61]

In this way, literary and cinematic encounters with vampires and other monsters can serve to remind us that we are a part of *this* world, not separate from it, and that human dominance is only perceived. The effect can be similar to the shift of perspective occasioned by other kinds of extraordinary experiences, from alien abductions to near death experiences discussed in the previous chapter.[62] Monsters in literature and culture remind us that there are strange things lurking just beyond the comforting threshold of human society – a super natural world that is radically alive and often radically other, with its own motivations and desires. The anthropologists Heather Swanson, Nils Bubandt and colleagues have gone further to suggest that:

> [...] ghosts and monsters [are] two points of departure for characters, agencies, and stories that challenge the double conceit of modern Man. Against the fable of Progress, ghosts guide us through haunted lives and landscapes. Against the conceit of the Individual, monsters highlight symbiosis, the enfolding of bodies within bodies in evolution and in every ecological niche [...] ghosts and monsters unsettle anthropos [...] from its presumed centre stage in the Anthropocene by highlighting the webs of histories and bodies from which all life, including human life, emerges. Rather than imagining phantasms outside of natural history, [these] monsters and ghosts [are] observable parts of the world.[63]

The ancient Greek figure of Pan, with his well-known half-human-half-goat form, is a good example of the 'monster' as mediator between human culture and wild nature. In the recent book *Pan: The Great God's Modern Return*,[64] Paul Robichaud presents a dedicated cultural history of the capricious god. Pan's mythical origins are traced back to the rugged hillsides of ancient Arcadia in Greece, where he was understood as the pastoral god of shepherds and goat herders. In his earliest representations Pan was associated with rural pastures, particularly with areas that might be understood as meeting places between the cultivated and the wild (much like Pan himself). Encounters with the god were traditionally thought to be terrifying, and indeed it is from such interactions that we have inherited the term 'panic.' In this sense, the figure of Pan is the perfect embodiment of what Rudolf Otto called the 'numinous' – an experience characterised by the dual features of awe and terror (see Chapter Four). Pan's dual nature was vividly portrayed in the author Kenneth Grahame's book *The Wind in the Willows*, in an extraordinary chapter entitled 'The Piper at the Gates of Dawn' (which is not included in certain editions of the book), in which Ratty and Mole come face-to-face with the caprine god on the riverbank while searching for their lost friend. He describes Mole's experience:

Then suddenly the mole felt a great Awe fall upon him, [...] he felt wonderfully at peace and happy – but, it was an awe that smote and held him, and, without seeing, he knew it could only mean that an august Presence was very, very near. [He] saw the backward sweep of the curved horns, gleaming in the glowing daylight; saw the stern, hooked nose between the kindly eyes [...] while the bearded mouth broke into a half-smile at the corners [...] All this he saw, for one moment, breathless and intense, vivid on the morning sky; and still, as he looked, he lived; and still, as he lived, he wondered. 'Rat!; he found breath to whisper, shaking. 'Are you afraid?' 'Afraid?' murmured the Rat, his eyes shining with unutterable love. 'Afraid! Of Him? O, never, never! And yet—and yet—O, Mole, I am afraid!'.[65]

Medieval and renaissance writers would go on to develop the Arcadian character of Pan, and emphasised the etymological similarity of the god's name to the Greek word 'pan,' meaning 'all.' This shift of emphasis gave the Great God another dual aspect as *both* half-human/half-animal *and* transcendent cosmic entity. Later, the Romantics would go on to embrace Pan for his wild sensuality, and his embodiment of an idyllic pagan past, where humans, nymphs and fauns frolicked in pastoral harmony.[66]

Psychodiversity Crisis

As explored in Chapter Three, the Earth's rich biodiversity is currently undergoing a radical upheaval. Up to as much as 60% of animal species have been driven to extinction in the last half-century, according to the World Wildlife Fund,[67] and the plant world is not faring much better.[68] But, as this chapter has suggested, the complexities of consciousness and intelligence that dominant science and culture have associated with humans (and possibly a hand-full of 'higher' animals), are in fact much more widely distributed throughout the natural world. The study of culture in nonhumans, for example, is a relatively recent field, but one with wide-reaching implications. Evidence of socially learned culture has been found amongst 'humans plus a handful of species of birds, one or two whales, and two species of fish,' for instance.[69] While bats have been found to possess 'different song cultures' between populations, and to 'chatter about food, sleep, sex and other bats.'[70] These subtle aspects of the Earth's biodiversity are frequently ignored. The behavioural ecologist Mirjam Knörnschild explains just how much of a threat the ecological crisis is to this subtle diversity of mind in nature:

> When you have pronounced cultural differences, losing populations is tragic because you're losing these animal cultures that have been built up over many years [...] they may hold local solutions to specific problems or unique mating preferences not found anywhere [else].[71]

In other words, the biodiversity crisis is much more than a crisis of biomass loss, it is a psychodiversity crisis in which we run this risk of losing innumerable forms of mind, intelligence and non-human culture.

Summary

The diversity of forms of mind and non-human consciousness in plants, animals and beyond all have implications for the interpretation of different ethnographic and ecological contexts, and an appreciation of this diversity of consciousness and different modalities of perception may go a long way in our interpretive and theoretical work. Can we, for example, apply approaches from the humanities to the nonhuman world? Can we have a nonhuman social science, or a non-humanities? Such an approach would also have to be inclusive of the wide variety of 'other-than-human' persons that inhabit this world with us, and with whom human beings have long sought to establish relationships. While the nonhuman is frequently taken to include the biological lifeforms, geological processes, and other physical factors that constitute the living planet around us, the concept of the 'other-than-human' also expands out to consider what might be referred to as 'meta-empirical,' 'spiritual,' 'daimonic,' 'paranormal' and 'ultraterrestrial' forms of life and consciousness – forms of life and consciousness that may be beyond what we can imagine, but no less a part of natural history than the oak trees and octopi. We should avoid the tendency to think of monsters as 'just' imaginary, they have much to tell us about our relationship with the living world. An inclusive study of consciousness will entail engagement with a wide range of different forms of sentience, mind and intelligence – human, nonhuman and everything in between. Traditional and indigenous perspectives may provide fruitful frameworks for engaging with nonhuman consciousness – not in terms of its constituent parts, but rather through the more holistic lens of personhood and relationship (see Chapter Nine).

CHAPTER SIX:
Fairies at the Bottom of the Garden

The previous chapter mapped out a vast conceptual space for considering non-human consciousness and intelligence as a feature of the natural world and for re-framing questions about spirits, monsters and other ultraterrestrials in the context of the natural history of mind. This chapter shifts focus slightly to consider some of the different ways that human beings have sought to conceptualise and interact with such non-human intelligences, in particular through the tending of outdoor garden spaces.

Gardens, Liminality and Spirits

The philosopher David E. Cooper has suggested that gardens can be thought of as 'hybrid' places – places where human culture and non-human nature meet – just as the fauns and monsters discussed in the previous chapter can be understood as 'hybrid' entities, part-human and part-animal.[1] From this perspective, gardens might be understood as liminal zones – spaces that exist between the domestic and the wild – where interactions with the non-human can take place, mediated through the lenses of human cultural frameworks. Gardens are not nature itself, but rather provide a structure through which human-nature interactions can take place. Nature does not necessarily need this structure (indeed nature likely does not perceive a boundary between itself and us, or between the garden and the surrounding fields), but perhaps human beings do (we should not forget, however, that we are also a part of nature, so the cultural systems that we create must also be natural in some sense). Human beings seem to create systems and structures to deal with all manner of our affairs. Like the structural anthropologist Claude Lévi-Strauss' (1908–2009) idea of human cultures bridging binary oppositions through symbolism, ritual acts and myths,[2] we may need a symbolic and ritual mode of bridging the perceived (cognitive) gap between nature and ourselves. Cultivating a garden is an excellent example of this kind of symbolic and ritualistic interaction with nature, of bridging the cultural binary between the human and the natural.

Gardens are also the ideal place to foster bio- and psychodiversity, as well as to engage in meaningful relationships with nature and the spiritual world. Indeed, there are long traditions around the world of understanding and using gardens as 'anterooms to the netherworld,' specifically as sites for ritual interaction with spiritual beings.[3] The garden historian Andrew Cunningham explains that gardens 'are spiritual places, and always have been, in both the Western and Eastern garden traditions.'[4] The ancient Greeks used sacred groves (*alsos*) to prepare for encounters with their gods, for example. As the sociologist and garden historian Michel Conan explains 'gardens and grottoes' or 'meadows' in the landscape, allowed for 'the presence of gods and invited encounters with them,' and 'permitted mortals to cross over the limits to the netherworld, something forbidden to most.'[5] While for the ancient Assyrians and Egyptians gardens were carefully laid-out ritual spaces designed to facilitate communion with the gods.[6] In traditional Japanese gardening the presence of invisible spirits called *kami* is acknowledged with the construction of 'compounds dedicated to spiritual entities and activities.'[7] Interestingly, the role of the garden as an ante-room for ritual interaction with spirits also came up during my own doctoral research at a Spiritualist home-circle in Bristol – all of the séances I attended took place in a wooden shed at the bottom of the circle-leader's garden.[8] Although it was not explicitly on my radar at the time (having only more recently become a focus of my research), I did subsequently reach out to the circle leader to ask her whether she thought the garden served any function in the séance procedure. Here is her response:

> [...] initially when the 'shed' was built and sitters left the house and walked to the shed I personally felt that it increased the 'fun' and 'adventure' elements [...] what we were about to do felt like a 'secret' [...] As we adjusted to the shed I would personally often sit out there with the door open and look out into the garden [...] which felt kind of 'spiritual' [...] like the 'shed' was natural [...] an integral part of nature. The same effect was recreated here when we moved house.[9]

Garden Magic

The twentieth century anthropologist Bronislaw Malinowski (1884–1942) famously documented and described the magical practices of the Trobriand Islanders in relation to their gardening activities in the so-called 'Coral Gardens.' Malinowksi used Trobriand gardening magic as an example of the way in which magic functions as a supplement to scientific and technological knowledge, rather than in place of it (as earlier intellectualist theorists – like Tylor and Frazer – had suggested). The later anthropologist Alfred Gell (1945–1997) summarised Malinowski's observations thus:

> Trobriand gardens were [...] arenas in which a magical scenario was played out, in the guise of productive activity. Yam-gardens were laid out with geometrical regularity [...] and were provided with complicated constructions described as 'magical prisms' at one corner, which attracted yam-growing power into the soil.[10]

Through the manipulation of subtle earth energies by magical means the Trobriand Islanders were seeking to work with natural-magical principles in order to ensure a good harvest. For Malinowski, this was understood primarily in etic psychological terms – as a coping strategy for dealing with the risk and unpredictability of gardening for subsistence, an important element in his psychological functionalist approach. From the emic perspective, however, the Islanders were engaging in a spiritual relationship with the land, negotiated through ritual and magical means. Similarly, the anthropologist Eric Keys explains that the gardens of the Kaqchikel Maya of Highland Guatamala perform a variety of material and non-material functions. Material functions include the deliberate production of essential plant crops for food, medicine and economic purposes, as well as providing valuable habitat to enhance biodiversity, while the non-material functions of garden spaces include 'ritual cleansing (in the tuj, or Maya sauna), seed blessing, spirit calling, and other religious activities.'[11]

The Aguaruna-Jivaro people of Ecuador and Peru create swidden gardens by clearing small patches of rainforest to cultivate manioc, sweet potato and other food crops. These gardens are predominantly cared for by women and so become the locus for a range of specialised activities, such as the exchange of essential horticultural and other knowledge between women – how to sing magical songs, cultivate crops, give birth, and so on. The anthropologists Michael F. Brown and Margaret Van Bolt also report that:

> [An] important characteristic of the garden is that it is the point of contact between women and certain kinds of spirits not commonly found elsewhere. The most important of these is Nugkui, a supernatural being who has been

variously identified as the 'earth mother' [...] and the 'feminine under-soil master of garden soil and pottery clay.' After Nugkui, the most important spirits with whom a woman has contact in her garden are those of the plants themselves, especially the spirits or souls of manioc.[12]

In this respect Aguaruna cosmology resembles other indigenous American traditions that understand the world through the lens of relational personhood and perspectivism (see Chapters Five, Nine and Ten). The Manioc, and all of the other plants and animals in the garden (as well as in the wider jungle) are understood as 'persons' – with their own lives, motivations, husbands, wives, and so on – and with whom reciprocal relationships must be established and maintained:

> To perform effectively as a gardener, she must acquire the knowledge necessary to meet the metaphysical as well as the physical needs of the cultivated plants, and at the same time protect herself from their potentially harmful powers.[13]

The metaphysical element is managed through three key ritual activities – 1) the singing of garden songs, 2) the use of magical gardening stones called *nantag*, and 3) through the maintenance of taboos, precautions and other ritual avoidances while performing gardening activities.

Fairies at the Bottom of the Garden

Many readers of this book are likely familiar with the idea that there are fairies at the bottom of the garden. It is something that we might tell young children, for example, encouraging them to go looking for the little-folk to keep them busy on a summer afternoon, while the grown-ups bask in the sunshine or try to get some gardening chores done. The notion might also conjure in our minds thoughts of the infamous Cottingley fairy photographs, taken in the 'beck' at the bottom of a Yorkshire garden by two young girls in the early 1920s, which were first popularised in *Strand Magazine* by Sir Arthur Conan Doyle (1859–1930) just over a century ago.[14] The cultural historian Nicola Brown has suggested that the phrase 'fairies at the bottom of the garden' and the Cottingley photographs have 'become welded together' in the popular imagination:

[...] the one seeming to encapsulate the other – its naïveté, or equally its faux-naïveté, its capacity to enchant, or to embarrass the viewer. The picture seems to ask the viewer to believe that there are 'fairies at the bottom of our garden' [...][15]

Regardless of the veracity of the Cottingley photographs (that is, whether they captured images of 'real' fairies and gnomes or not), the pictures, and the idea behind them, nevertheless represent a continuation of a long-standing popular belief that fairies – amongst other spirits and supernatural beings in the cross-cultural context – are associated with gardens, as well as with wild and semi-wild places. A seventeenth century manuscript housed in the Bodleian Library in Oxford, for example, contains a short treatise on the nature of fairies, and gives mention to the places they are said to inhabit:

> [...] they say they can enrich a man whom they effect [and] have power to hurt [and] kill whosoever [displeases] them, for which they came into any place w[h]ere they thought fairies use[d] to be, as gardens, meadows, w[h]ere green rings of [grass] were [...] which they call the fairie bord [...][16]

During the nineteenth century the association between fairies and gardens in particular was emphasised and elaborated by Spiritualists who were keen to encourage fairy presences in their own gardens. Sir Charles Isham (1819–1903), for example, an eccentric horticulturalist, landscape gardener and early member of the British National Association of Spiritualists, is widely credited with popularising garden gnomes in Britain following the creation of an epic display of busily mining gnomes in his rockery garden at Lamport Hall in Northamptonshire, which was first opened to the public in 1847.[17] For Isham, however, the small terracotta statues – which he had imported all the way from Germany – were not flights of fancy, but rather depictions of very real spiritual entities that he believed inhabited subterranean places. In a pamphlet that he wrote and published privately entitled *Notes on Gnomes and Remarks on Rock Gardens* in 1884, Isham explains that:

> Had Gnomes been imaginary creations, they would not have been admitted into the Lamport Rockery, but as there is any amount of evidence that they not only have been frequently heard, but are also occasionally seen

in and about certain mines, and in the cottages of miners [...] Seeing such things is no longer an indication of mental delusion, but rather EXTENSION OF FACULTY.[18]

Another eccentric Spiritualist, the lawyer, botanist and collector of microscopes Sir Frank Crisp (1843–1919) also took to gnomes in a big way when he constructed an enormous rockery at his gothic revival home, Friar Park in Oxfordshire, which he populated with diminutive miners and workmen, much as Charles Isham had done.[19] To begin with, garden gnome displays such as those at Lamport Hall and Friar Park were seen as symbols of elite social status – only to be found in the stately homes of wealthy aristocrats – but as time progressed the gnomes moved out from the rockeries and gardens of nineteenth century country estates and into the rapidly expanding number of sub-urban gardens in Britain during the twentieth century. This is a social trend that was later echoed in other parts of the world, such as New Zealand, for example.[20] Today garden gnomes are frequently viewed as 'tacky' – far removed from their original high status – and they have even been banned from the Royal Horticultural Society's prestigious Chelsea Flower Show.[21]

The Findhorn Foundation

The association between the little-folk and gardens also continues into more recent times. In the 1960s a group who claimed to be in communication with supernatural beings variously conceived as God, devas, fairies and elemental spirits established a garden at Findhorn on the eastern coast of Scotland. Led by Eileen Caddy (1917–2006), Peter Caddy (1917–1994) and Dorothy Maclean (1920–2020), the Findhorn garden developed into a highly productive plot producing vast quantities of fruit and (often oversized) vegetables, all in spite of being situated on relatively poor coastal growing land. The success and fertility of the Findhorn garden was attributed to guidance from the devas and elementals that the group claimed to be in communication with – who each had their own roles and functions in the garden:

> While the devas may be considered the 'architects' of plant forms, the nature spirits or elementals, such as gnomes and fairies, may be seen as

the 'craftsmen,' using the blueprint and energy channelled to them by the devas to build up the plant form.[22]

This spiritual component to horticultural practice draws inspiration from Biodynamic Farming, an approach devised by the influential anthroposophist Rudolf Steiner (1861–1925) and influenced by theosophy, which seeks to work with the elemental spirits of plants to promote abundant crops.[23] Despite being treated with scepticism by much of mainstream agricultural practice – which is rooted in an industrial model, petro-chemical fertilisers and pesticide use – Biodynamic farming systems have been shown to be highly effective,[24] and are popular methods of practice in the wine making world.[25] By working with the elementals, the Findhorn gardeners claimed that they were operating according to natural principles, which in turn led to an abundant and diverse garden. This is a good example of where the drive to establish and cultivate relationships with other-than-human beings results in an abundance of biodiversity – psychodiversity and biodiversity developing hand-in-hand. As Malinowski suggested in the case of the Trobriand Island manioc gardeners, the magico-spiritual dimension of the Findhorn Foundation's activities are complimentary to, rather than in opposition to, their practical horticultural knowledge.

Experiencing Fairies

More recently still, the transpersonal anthropologist Dennis Gaffin has noted a link between natural settings and real-life experiences with the fairy folk. He explains that:

> The locale of past and present fairy experience, in sightings or sensing fairy presence, is almost always in quiet, natural environments, away from the noise and the construction of populated areas.[26]

This suggestion is also supported by data from the wonderful resource that is the *Fairy Census, 2014–2017*.[27] As discussed in Chapter Four, the census is a collection of 500 contemporary self-submitted accounts of encounters with fairies. It is of particular interest to note that of these 500 accounts 97 experiences explicitly took place 'in the garden,' and a further 94 encounters took place 'in woodland' settings. Simon Young also makes the interesting observation that:

In adult fairy experiences in gardens and woods fairies are frequently connected to flowers and to trees. Interestingly, children see flower and plant fairies relatively rarely [...] despite spending more time in gardens.[28]

Seeing Gnomes in Gardens

In their traditional, broadly Northern European folkloric context, gnomes (and dwarfs) have most frequently been associated with rocks, caves, mines and other subterranean territories.[29] Gnomes, like their Cornish counterparts the Knockers, were said to knock loudly on cave walls to warn miners of impending disasters.[30] The garden historian Twigs Way, who has written the only history of garden gnomes, has suggested that Charles Isham likely first encountered gnomes in his 'extensive reading on folklore,' noting that he:

> [...] regularly holidayed in North Wales, where tales of little blacksmiths and gnomish miners echoed those on the continent. He soon began to collect stories of gnomes and 'mine fairies' from Wales, Dovedale (England), Germany, Bohemia, and Hungary.[31]

Given their traditional association with mines, caves and the deep places of the earth (reflected in Isham and Crisp's rockeries), it is curious that people should go on to claim experiences with 'real gnomes' in garden contexts, which are often far from the wild mountainous habitat of traditional dwarfs. Take the following example of an experience reported by a Mrs Rose of Southend-on-Sea, first recounted in Arthur Conan Doyle's 1921 book *The Coming of the Fairies*:[32]

> I see them constantly here in the shrubbery by the sea [...] the gnomes are like little old men, with little green caps, and their clothes are generally neutral green [...] I have seen the gnomes arranging a sort of moss bed for the fairies [...][33]

Gnomes, once dwellers in dark and inhospitable underground places, are now glimpsed amongst the shrubs and ornamental borders of suburban houses. Some contemporary garden encounters, however, do maintain something of the gnomes' ominous folkloric reputation. The following account recorded in the *Fairy Census*, for example, relates a particularly strange encounter with gnome-like beings in a garden setting in Canada, which clearly perpetuates the chthonic association of garden gnomes:

[...] a former teacher of French in that area, went to do gardening around the house. It was just after dinner, during a summer's day. Once ready to work the ground with gardening tools, she suddenly saw three small gnomes coming out of the ground, [staring] at her for maybe a second or two, then running out as fast as they appeared. The event lasts only a few seconds. However, she had time to notice the following details: they measured about thirty centimetres, they more or less look alike, seemed old with grey faces and grey clothing. She doesn't remember if they had caps or not. But their skin seemed from old-age persons. Very agile, they disappear[ed] [...] between her house and the next one.[34]

There is another intriguing entry in the *Fairy Census* in which gnome *statues* play a central role. The respondent begins their account by explaining how they had gone for a drive in the countryside with family and had stopped in a small village for a stroll. While walking the respondent heard 'a kind of sing-song "chanting" in [their] mind, which "sounded" like a multitude of very sweet, pleasing voices that were all speaking the same words almost simultaneously [...] "Don't you see us? We're all around you. We're all around you, don't you see us? Look – don't you see us?"' Later the voices seemed to guide the respondent to a particular location:

The voices said, 'We're here – come this way, walk this way. We're here,' and I looked to my left and saw another path through the woods [...] I turned left and walked down the path, still 'hearing' the voices, which, as I approached [...] came to a stop [...] rounding one of these curves, my eyes fell upon a grouping of four garden gnome statues on the front lawn of one of the homes. The statues were traditionally sculpted and done in what I would call a tasteful and 'realistic' manner; they weren't the kind of mass-produced cartoonish garden gnomes so prevalent today. The four gnomes were in sitting positions and arranged so that they were facing one another. When I saw them, it was like receiving a blow to the chest, though I realized instantaneously that they were statues. But seeing them at that moment seemed to 'identify' the source of the voices to me in a manner which I can only call profound, as if the statues were what I was meant to see [...] So I never 'saw' anything visually (other than the garden gnome statues), but I have, for some years now, come to the tentative conclusion that the 'voices' were 'fairy' voices.[35]

In the above account the garden gnome statues themselves – which are essentially decorative ornaments – seem to have served as a focal point for the experience. Indeed, the anthropologist Amy Whitehead has suggested that 'personhood' is an 'appropriate conceptual and methodological tool with which to frame theoretically' human interaction with 'other than human persons such as religious statues.'[36] As an interesting point of comparison, in an essay on the role of 'spirit houses' (*san phra phum*) – small brightly painted houses commonly found in Thai gardens and parks – the anthropologist of religion Martin Pearce explains how the small wooden spirit houses function to bring people into dialogue and relationship with subtle elements of place, serving as reminders of the presence of spirits. He describes how:

> [...] the ornate shrines which adorn many house compounds in contemporary urban Thailand tie into local understandings of the social character of places. It is suggested that the persistence of spirit houses can be partly understood through their roles as mediators of the phenomenological experience of certain places. Spirit houses are one part of a gathering process that imbues places with significant meaning. The shrines exemplify that culturally specific interactions and engagements with spirits associated with certain places influence how the phenomenological qualities of these places are constructed and experienced.[37]

Garden gnome statues, then, like Thai spirit houses, might – on occasion – also perform a similar function by making manifest, or drawing attention to, invisible presences in the garden – just as the garden gnome statues became the locus of the 'fairy voices' in the above account. In her recent edited book, *Subtle Agroecologies: Farming With the Hidden Half of Nature*,[38] agroecology researcher Julia Wright puts forward the concept of 'subtle agroecologies' to refer to this usually invisible element of the natural and horticultural environment. She explains that a subtle agroecology 'is not a farming [or gardening] system in itself, but [rather] super-imposes a non-material dimension upon existing, materially based agroecological farming systems.'[39] In a sense, then, the creation of garden gnome statues, and their placing within gardens, might represent a 'mattering' and personification of subtle ecological – or subtle-horticultural (particularly earth and soil based) – processes.⁴⁰ In his chapter in *Subtle Agroecologies,* the land whisperer Patrick MacManaway describes his own process of working with these subtle ecologies for land restoration purposes, including working with ostensible gnomes. He explains that:

> [...] we can work with the gnomes of the earth – all about soil structure and everything to do with supporting the entirety of soil ecology – they seem very able to work to create the ideal conditions for specific plants or indeed for specific animals grazing, or ourselves harvesting those plants [...] they need only to be lovingly asked for clear and specific help and support.⁴¹

As well as personifying natural processes, fairies, gnomes and other supernatural beings have also become emblems of the eco-protest movement. The ecologist and scholar of religion Andy Letcher has documented this phenomenon in the context of 1990s road protest communities, where protesters 'came to regard themselves as, or aided by, fairies or nature spirits in a just cause that pitted nature against artifice.'⁴²

Summary

When Victorian gentlemen like Charles Isham and Frank Crisp introduced statues of gnomes into the gardens of their stately homes they served a dual function – firstly as a horticultural spectacle and status symbol to establish new fashions, and secondly – perhaps most importantly – as an aid to re-enchantment. As Twigs Way suggests, 'belief in fairies was a part of Sir Charles's spiritualism,'⁴³ and as such the intention of his rockery gardens and gnome displays was to reveal the invisible workings of nature – which for him included a bustling world of busy subterranean gnomes. In this sense the gnomes came to represent a form of 'subtle ecology' that continues to play out today, at the Findhorn Foundation, for example. In ways that they were perhaps not fully aware of, Isham, Crisp and all of those who have followed in their footsteps by bringing statues of supernatural beings into their gardens, were working within long standing, cross-cultural traditions that have understood gardens and tended wild locations as meeting places for spirits and other supernatural entities. In this process gnomes underwent something of a transformation – or at least transportation – from ominous subterranean dwellers in mines and caves to (usually) friendly inhabitants of suburban garden soil and shrubberies. This shift also spilled over into real-life paranormal encounters with gnomes and gnome-like entities, even to the extent of statues of gnomes functioning as the focal-point for extraordinary experiences, perhaps even allowing for a particular kind of phenomenological engagement with place and subtle presences, as with Thai spirit houses. To finish, a feedback loop seems to emerge here: the experiences of miners hearing knocks in caves (sounds of the earth) gave rise to stories about gnomes (experience gives rise to culture). Images are made of the gnomes and adorn people's gardens, providing a visual template that also begins to appear in extraordinary experiences (culture gives rise to and shapes experience), and so the cycle continues.[44]

CHAPTER SEVEN
Parapsychology and the Ecological Self

This chapter draws together threads that link three fields of inquiry – anthropology, deep ecology, and parapsychology – and their respective perspectives on the nature of consciousness and the self (*see FIG. 1, below*). Research in these areas may be crucial for elucidating the processes that lead to a sense of connection to the natural world, which in turn can result in pro-environmental behaviour.[1] The development of the 'ecological self' may have very real benefits for the promotion and preservation of bio-psycho-diversity.

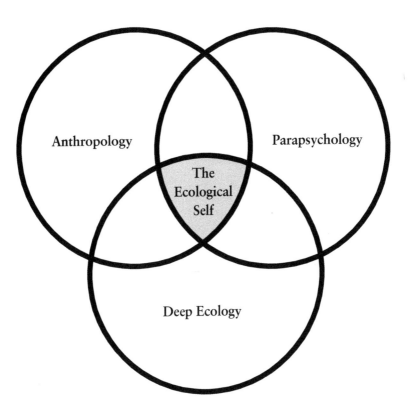

Fig. 1 Anthropology, Deep Ecology, Parapsychology and the Ecological Self

Different Modalities of Consciousness

In addition to the many different forms of non-human and other-than-human minds that may constitute and populate the natural world – from forms of baseline awareness through to the many varieties of animal, plant and fungal minds that are increasingly being revealed – it is also important to emphasise the diversity of forms of mind and perception *within* human (or any other species) populations. There has, of course, been a great deal of research on the role of various altered states of consciousness in human cultures around the world, as well as in the archaeological past. The anthropologist Charles Laughlin, for example, gives us the useful concepts of 'monophasic' and 'polyphasic' cultures to distinguish between differing socio-cultural attitudes towards altered states of consciousness. Monophasic cultures – such as most Euro-American societies – tend to 'skew the development of consciousness away from alternative states of consciousness and toward perceptual and cognitive processes oriented to the external world' – in other words, to our everyday, productive, waking states of consciousness. Polyphasic cultures, by contrast, tend to:

[...] value experiences had in the dream life, as well as those had in trance states, meditation states, drug- and ritual-driven visions, etc. These experiences are often conceived by the people as different aspects of reality, not unreality – indeed, the people rarely if ever make a distinction between experienced reality and extramental reality the way science does today. And their sense of identity incorporates memories of experiences had in dreams and other alternative states, as well as had in waking life.[2]

The monophasic attitude that has dominated much of Euro-American society has also tended to dominate interpretations of archaeological and ethnographic data – for example by emphasising the role of the 'productive' waking state of consciousness, necessary for meeting everyday survival needs, above other states of consciousness available to human beings. Much less attention, however, has been given to other forms of consciousness and perception in the archaeological record – of what might be called 'neurodiversity' – such as autistic spectrum disorders, dyslexia, dyspraxia and so on (although this is a growing field).[3] Key debates in this area centre around whether such conditions have an adaptive role and have shaped society and culture in positive directions,[4] or whether they are essentially maladaptive by-products of evolution.[5] Regardless of whether such states are 'adaptive' or not, perceptual differences, whether induced with consciousness altering techniques, as the product of environmental conditions (such as through sensory and oxygen deprivation in caves),[6] or as a result of conditions such as those on the autistic spectrum – are suggestive of the radical diversity of different states and modalities of consciousness. They are another expression of psychodiversity.

Gothic Psychology and the Ecological Unconscious

The Cambridge classicist F.W.H. Myers is perhaps best known as one of the founding members of the Society for Psychical Research (SPR), which was established in 1882 and is still active today.[7] This organisation was the first in the world to adopt a scientific approach in its investigations of 'that large group of debatable phenomena designated by such terms as mesmeric, psychical and Spiritualistic' – what we would today gather under the umbrella of the 'paranormal.'[8] In addition to co-founding this influential and pioneering society, Myers also made a unique contribution to the burgeoning field of psychology, offering a model of consciousness that was far ahead of its time. Drawing on his investigations into crisis apparitions (visions of loved ones that appear during moments of danger, or at the time of death), hysteria, automatic writing, hypnotism and spirit mediumship, amongst other varied abnormal psychological states and paranormal phenomena, Myers developed a model of the mind that consists of two separate, though interlinked, streams, which he referred to as the 'supra-liminal' and the 'sub-liminal mind.' He explains that:

> The 'conscious Self' of each of us, as we call it – the empirical, the supraliminal Self [...] does not comprise the whole of the consciousness [...] within us. There exists a far more comprehensive consciousness, a profounder faculty, which for the most part remains potential only so far as regards the life of earth, but from which the consciousness and the faculty of earth-life are mere selections [...][9]

The supra-liminal mind refers to those elements of our consciousness that we are fully aware of in our day-to-day waking state – our everyday stream of consciousness. The sub-liminal mind, by contrast, bubbles away just below the surface of our awareness, occasionally intruding above the threshold of consciousness in the form of extraordinary experiences of various kinds – from moments of inspiration to dreams, mystical reveries, apparitions and possession experiences. Myers explains his conception of the subliminal as follows:

> I propose to extend the meaning of the term, so as to make it cover *all* that takes place beneath the ordinary threshold [...] not only those faint stimulations whose very faintness keeps them submerged, but much else which psychology as yet scarcely recognises; sensations, thoughts, emotions, which may be strong, definite, and independent, but which, by the original constitution of our being, seldom emerge into that *supraliminal* current of consciousness which we habitually identify with *ourselves*.[10]

William James referred to Myers' work as a 'Gothic psychology,' because of its complex and multi-dimensional nature,[11] while Myers himself referred to it as 'multiplex.'[12] In an obituary published in the *Proceedings* of the SPR, James wrote evocatively of Myers' romanticist approach to the study of the mind. He explains that Myers' approach to psychology was:

> [...] like going from classic to Gothic architecture, where few outlines are pure and where uncouth forms lurk in the shadows. A mass of mental phenomena are now seen in the shrubbery beyond the parapet. Fantastic, ignoble, hardly human, or frankly nonhuman are some of these new candidates for psychological description [...] The world of the mind is shown as something infinitely more complex than was suspected; and whatever beauties it may still possess, it has lost at any rate the beauty of academic neatness [...] But despite the triumph of romanticism, psychologists as a rule have still some lingering prejudice in favour of the nobler simplicities.[13]

There are several points in this extract from James' obituary to Myers that resonate with the themes that have already been explored in this book. In particular, the notion that there are elements of the non-human even *within* human consciousness, that the mind extends out into nature much further than we have often given it credit for, and that whatever it is that we are dealing with it will best be understood by emphasising complexity, rather than reductionism.

Myers' model of the sub-liminal mind pre-dated the more widely known 'unconscious' of Sigmund Freud's psychodynamic model, as well as C.G. Jung's (1875–1961) notion of the 'collective unconscious.' Indeed, both Freud and Jung were influenced by the earlier writings of Myers and the work of the SPR. It is fair to say, however, that Myers' notion of the subliminal mind bears a closer resemblance to Jung's conception of the unconscious than Freud's. For Freud the unconscious mind was bounded within the individual, while for Jung the unconscious was understood to extend outwards – like a field – beyond the self. He wrote that 'a psychological truth is [...] just as good and respectable a thing as a physical truth [because] no one knows what "psyche" is, and one knows just as little how far into nature "psyche" extends'.[14]

Myers, and other *fin-de-siecle* psychological thinkers – including William James, Edmund Gurney (1847–1888) and Pierre Janet (1859–1947) – argued that consciousness is divisible – that it consists of many different parts, rather than being a single 'bounded' entity – an individual self. Where Myers and James differed from the likes of Janet, however, was in the extent to which they thought this capacity for the self to divide was normal and healthy. The historian of religious experience Ann Taves explains that for Janet all dissociative states were considered as evidence of pathology (a view that has come to dominate mainstream attitudes towards dissociative states in Western society), while for Myers and James certain dissociative states *could* be positive in the sense of giving access to gnosis, paranormal abilities and religious reveries.[15] From the perspective of Myers' gothic psychology, then, the divisible self is entirely natural and normal. He explains:

I regard each man as at once profoundly unitary and almost infinitely composite, as inheriting from earthly ancestors a multiplex and 'colonial' organism – polyzoic and perhaps polypsychic in an extreme degree; but also as ruling and unifying that organism by a soul or spirit absolutely beyond our present analysis – a soul which has originated in a spiritual or metetherial environment [...][16]

Anthropology – Porous and Plural Selves

Anthropologists have long suggested that there are widely diverging cultural differences when it comes to conceptualising the nature of the self. Despite the fantastic diversity of self-concepts across cultures, however, anthropologists have argued for the existence of two broad categories among them. On the one hand we have what has come to be known as the *individual self* – a conceptualisation of the self as independent, autonomous, and bounded by the limits of the physical body. The anthropologist Clifford Geertz (1926–2006) provided an influential definition of the individual self, describing it as:

> [...] a bounded, unique, more or less integrated motivational and cognitive universe, a dynamic center of awareness, emotion, judgment and action organized into a distinctive whole and set contrastively against other such wholes and against its social and natural background.[17]

This model of the self is often referred to as Western, and is taken to be broadly characteristic of a Euro-American post-industrial sense of self.[18] By contrast, there is the *dividual self*, considered to be made up of multiple constituent parts, or to be porous with permeable boundaries through which other selves or entities might come and go.[19] Take the following description of the sense of self in Japanese culture, for example:

> What it means to be a person [...] in the Japanese sense cannot be understood without reference to the individual's social ties: the particular, usually tight and limited human nexus to which he or she belongs, from which one derives identity, and to which one is totally committed.[20]

This model is often called non-Western, though this does not mean that dividual models of the self are absent in Western contexts; indeed there are many sub-cultural groups that embrace and deliberately foster dividual selfhood, even within Western societies. Mediumship development circles are one example,[21] as is the growing *Hearing Voices Network,* which seeks to de-stigmatise the phenomenon of voice hearing to create a 'a positive approach to voices and visions.'[22] Another interesting recent development is the acknowledgement of people who self-identify as *plural systems*. The historian of paranormal experiences Christopher Laursen, for example, recently discussed plural systems in the context of online *tulpa* communities, where community members aim to generate autonomous tulpas (thoughforms) through concentrated intention and interaction. Laursen explains that 'the term *plurality* or *plural system* is actively used in the community to normalise how one body can hold multiple identities – host and tulpa(s), the *system-mates*.'[23]

Laursen also documents the rise of *plural advocacy*, which seeks to de-pathologise mainstream perspectives on plural identities, which are often associated with conditions such as dissociative identity disorder (DID) and schizophrenia. Plural identities, especially when deliberately induced, are instead seen by self-designated plural systems as *healthy* ways of being in the world, leading to an improved sense of well-being.[24] My own research on trance mediumship development in the UK, and the 'spirit teams' associated with developing mediums, similarly suggests that mediumship development circles provide a safe space for behaviours that would otherwise be interpreted as pathological or abnormal.[25] Non-pathological modes of being that incorporate plural identities, or that extend beyond the usually assumed limits of the individual, are worthy of much greater attention. In particular, they may improve our understanding of how a sense of connection to the natural world is formed, and may bear some relevance to our understanding of the 'ecological self.'

Ecological Consciousness

The bounded, individualistic, model of the self that has dominated Western cultures for at least the last two hundred years – itself closely tied to the rise of scientific rationalism and materialism – has been linked by ecopsychologists to the ecological crisis the Earth is currently undergoing.[26] The bounded perspective on the self sees individuals as discrete islands of consciousness, disconnected from one another and from the rest of the world around us by the barrier of our skin. It is this atomistic way of thinking that – in spite of being scientifically outdated – can be said to have contributed to our growing sense of disconnection from the natural world, which in turn has contributed to ecological degradation through our exploitation of natural resources.[27] Perhaps a different model of mind, consciousness and self is required if we hope to reverse some of the damage that has been done and establish a renewed sense of identification with the natural world.

The Norwegian philosopher Arne Naess, founder of the deep ecology movement, developed the concept of the *ecological self,* which – I am suggesting here – could be conceived as another example of the expanded – or dividual – model of the self that emerges from Myers' gothic psychology.

Naess suggested that, through the process of what he called 'self-realisation,' human beings will ultimately move away from *egoic* (bounded, individual) conceptions of the self towards an ecological self, the boundaries of which are understood to be porous and to extend outwards into the natural world (which also extends *into* the self). Naess does not give an explicit definition of the ecological self, but he does offer a brief sentence, explaining that the 'ecological self of a person is that with which this person identifies.' He further elaborates that 'this key sentence [...] about the self shifts the burden of clarification from the term "self" to that of "identification," or rather "process of identification."'[28] Thus, the ecological self emerges when we come to identify the environment with ourselves – that is when we begin to understand that the self is constituted from many parts, some of which are beyond the confines of our physical body – to the extent that we realise that conservation of the natural world is simultaneously an act of self-preservation. A similar conclusion is drawn in Freya Matthews' work on *The Ecological Self*,[29] which she characterises as being holistically 'nested' in wider ecological systems. She explains that:

> Because the self stands in relations of ecological interdependence (direct or indirect) with the elements of that wider self, those elements (or its relations to them) are logically involved in its identity [...] Individuality in this framework is thus [...] a relative matter – it is a function of involvement in a wider system, the identity of which is implicated in the identities of each of its participant subsystems. The individual is thus in a very real sense a microcosm of the wider self in which it occurs.[30]

An ecological perspective on consciousness would see consciousness – just like any other element of an ecosystem – as being connected to all other elements of the system through various modes of interaction and relationship. Indeed, the science of ecology specifically highlights the complex connections between phenomena in the natural world, from interactions between species within an ecosystem, to interactions between ecosystems in the wider global system. The ecological perspective is an interconnected one (see Chapters One and Ten). In essence, then, the recognition of the ecological self is a realisation that there is no solid, impermeable boundary between the self and the ecosystem; the self is deeply embedded within, and part of, the wider ecological system, and is connected to all other aspects of it, though we are not always consciously aware of this.[31] Indeed, we could even take this further, drawing on Myers' conception of the 'polypsychic' self, and suggest that the self is a sort of ecosystem in itself.

In attempting to delineate precisely what is meant by the term 'ecopsychology,' Theodore Roszak argued that the 'core of the mind is the ecological unconscious.' This, he explains, consists of 'the living record of cosmic evolution, tracing back to distant initial conditions in the history of time' – an unconscious that connects us to all other life on Earth.[32] Could there be a connection between this conceptualisation of the ecological unconscious and Myers' notion of the subliminal mind and the multiplex self? In a manner similar to that highlighted by Freud, Roszak suggests that it is the repression of the ecological unconscious that has led to both the rise of widespread psychological distress in contemporary Western societies, and to our culture's destructive attitude towards the natural world.

Parapsychology

But the ecological self is not *just* a cultural or conceptual category, or a way of 'thinking,' and may in fact represent an *actual* extension of self and consciousness out into the wider natural environment. If we take the parapsychological data seriously – which suggests the existence of psi phenomena such as telepathy, pre-cognition, psychokinesis and so on – then the image of the self that emerges is quite different from the bounded, egoic notion of the individual that dominates scientific materialist psychology and culture (which perhaps helps to explain some of the antagonism towards parapsychology from mainstream science). In an essay titled 'Toward more subtle awareness,' which explores possible future directions for psi research, the transpersonal psychologist William Braud (1942–2012) suggested that psi research points towards the possibility that our 'identities may extend beyond their customarily assumed limits.' He goes on to explain that:

> [...] psi events suggest that these limited identities may be quirks of an unnecessarily limited and habituated attention, self-perception, and self-conception. Such an individual self concept may be, to a large extent, culturally conditioned, because—even without considering psi events—we can find, in other cultures, greater identifications with others (with one's extended family, one's community, one's ancestors; with aspects of the

natural world). Even within a Western, Eurocentric culture, we experience expansions of self-identity, beyond their usual bounds, in certain non-ordinary conditions of consciousness. Psi experiences suggest even further, and more profound, extensions of identity.[33]

Such extensions of identity, as Naess suggested with his concept of the ecological self, may go as far as identification with the natural world as a component of the self. William Braud suggests that the 'psi phenomena that we observe appear to require and to reveal [...] interconnectedness,' and that this 'connectedness seems more subtle, more extensive, and more profound than are the more familiar, conventional forms' of consciousness.[34] Arguing along similar lines, the ecospsychologist Joanna Macy has suggested that:

> Once we tune into our interconnectedness, responsibility toward self and other become indistinguishable, because each thought and act affects the doer as much as the one done to. Just as an amputee continues to feel twinges in the severed limb, so in a sense do we experience, in anguish for homeless people or hunted whales, pain that belongs to a separated part of our body—a larger body than we thought we had, unbounded by our skin.[35]

Frederic Myers would have referred to these feelings as *telepathic*. Indeed the term was coined by Myers from the Greek *tele* and *pathos*, literally 'feeling at a distance.' Other forms of extraordinary experience are also associated with the emergence of a sense of greater connectedness to the natural world. The work of the parapsychology and psychedelics researcher David Luke and colleagues, for instance, suggests that the altered states of consciousness associated with psychedelic states, induced through the ingestion of various psychoactive substances, are both conducive to psi experiences[36] and to an increased sense of connection to nature.[37] Lifetime experience with psychedelics has also been found to be associated with an enhanced sense of nature connectedness.[38] Meeting these two strands in the middle is an apparent renewed connection to nature associated with out-of-body experiences (OBE), near-death experiences (NDE), and alien abduction experiences[39] (see Chapter Four). Is it a coincidence that psi and other extraordinary experiences are associated with both expanded notions of the self and an enhanced sense of nature connectedness?

Greening the Paranormal

Taking Myers' lead, one approach to re-awakening a sense of 'environmental reciprocity' could be to re-engage with the extraordinary, mystical and paranormal. Just as Myers thought that these extraordinary states could give an insight into the nature of consciousness, so too might they give and insight into nature itself and our relationship with it. Indeed, there are a number of ecological threads that run through and connect the divergent strands of the paranormal, many of which are explored in the edited book *Greening the Paranormal.*[40] For the sake of brevity, and the limited purposes of this section, I will highlight some of the key themes explored in the book and explain how they might relate to the preceding discussions.

In my introductory chapter to the book I attempted to put forward the suggestion that the worldview implied by the paranormal – taken as a whole – suggests a cosmology of interconnection, and a cosmos populated by numerous different forms of mind and intelligence – gods, spirits, fairies, cryptozoological entities and other supernatural beings – of which human consciousness is just one variety (see Chapters Five and Six). There are echoes here of James' assertion that Myers' gothic psychology also incorporates the 'nonhuman' world. There are also resonances in this idea with what we might term an 'animistic' worldview (see Chapter Five).

In addition to the denizens of the paranormal ecosystem, psi phenomena, such as psychokinesis (PK) and telepathy – if real – also appear to embed consciousness and the self into wider networks of physical and non-physical communication with other elements of the cosmos. The Global Consciousness Project, for example, which collects data from random number generators in laboratories widely distributed around the world, seems to suggest that when human consciousness is collectively focussed it exerts an influence on the physical world. For instance, during times of global catastrophe (such as in the wake of natural disasters), or during periods of intense unity and solidarity (such as with the recent global climate strikes or the global coronavirus pandemic), the random number generators stop being random, and move towards patterning and coherence.[41] Drawing on such ideas, and the wider evidence and implications of parapsychology, the ecopsychologists Margaret Kerr and David Key have suggested 'that the human psyche is woven into nature in the same way that psi is interwoven into a larger emotional and physical context.'[42]

To briefly summarise, if the world truly is radically more alive than we have tended to give it credit for in the post-modern, post-industrial Western world – and if we are embedded into this system at subliminal levels – then we are right to call the Earth a 'haunted planet' – a term coined by the Fortean writer John Keel in his 1971 book of the same name.[43] Waking up to this expanded view of reality and our place within it – to the gothic complexity that arises from the interaction of the many different forms of consciousness and intelligence that surround us and populate the cosmos, and with which we are constantly engaging in relationships (whether we are aware of it or not) – may be understood through the lens of 're-enchantment.'[44] In recent years there has been a growing sense of dissatisfaction with the dominant materialist paradigms of Western science and academia, which leave very little room for the mythic, mystical and imaginal in scholarship. Re-enchantment offers an alternative perspective. In their recent edited book *Re-Enchanting the Academy*, Angela Voss and Simon Wilson write that:

> To feel enchanted is to step through a hidden portal into another way of seeing, into a new reality, where the reasonable, the certain, the measurable, and the predictable give way to the awesome, the wonderful, the delightful, the paradoxical, and the uncertain – and perhaps even the longing of the soul for some other kind of life beyond the exigencies of the everyday.[45]

Myers' gothic psychology, and his willingness to explore beyond the confines of the dominant models of self and consciousness may point us in the direction of a new way of conceiving of humanity and our relationship with the world around us – and may go some way towards enabling a re-enchantment of the natural world. In the epilogue to his posthumously published *Human Personality and its Survival of Bodily Death* Myers gives a hint of what this wider perspective entails, and where it might lead us in the future:

> [...] I mean no unreal opposition or forced divorcement of sacred and secular, of flesh and spirit [...] as our link with other spirits strengthens, as the life of the organism pours more fully through the individual cell, we shall feel love more ardent, wider wisdom, higher joy; perceiving that this organic unity of Soul, which forms the inward aspect of the telepathic law, is in itself the Order of the Cosmos, the Summation of Things.[46]

At this time of social, psychological and ecological crisis these ideas could represent both interesting and practical angles for further research and exploration as we continue forward into the twenty-first century.

Future Directions for Research

First, the ecological context for psi experiments could be taken into consideration in order to double down on the relationship between psi and nature connectedness. In previous publications I have suggested the importance of researching psi phenomena in their social and cultural context, but perhaps this context should also be expanded out to include the ecological context as well. For example, are there particular landscapes, sites, locations, or ecosystems that are more or less conducive to psi phenomena and experiences? The work of pioneering researchers in this area, such as Paul Devereux,[47] deserves further exploration, especially at a time when the re-establishment of a sense of connection to nature is needed more than ever before (see Chapter Eight). Secondly, further research should go into understanding the relationship between dividual forms of consciousness, such as the ecological self and plural systems, and psi research. Are practices that develop the ecological self, such as gardening, hiking, and other outdoor activities also psi conducive? How might this research be used to promote pro-environmental behaviours?

Summary

A full exploration of the ecological dimensions of psi and the paranormal, and their relation to the ecological self exceeds the limitations of this short book, but hopefully the relevance of this research is clear. Cultivation of the ecological self, as conceived by the deep ecologists, has been suggested as one way to bring about a transformation in human environmental behaviour. The evidence from parapsychology, however, seems to suggest that this expanded sense of self is more than just a belief system or cultural category, but is actually an expression of consciousness extending out into the world, reaching to make connections – this is what William Braud referred to as 'the long body.' Anthropological investigations of the 'non-Western' dividual self, deep ecological perspectives on the ecological self and parapsychological research all appear to coalesce in an image of consciousness as dynamic, multiple, interactive and inter-connective.

CHAPTER EIGHT:
Sacred Geography

This chapter is concerned with the land, landscapes, and the question of what makes something sacred – are there 'sacred places' in the land that have a power and influence of their own, or is sacred space purely a human construct?

What is Sacred Geography?

Anthony Thorley, one of the main proponents of sacred geography as taught in the Sophia Centre, has defined the field as being concerned with 'the study of qualities of the sacred and related cultural activities found in certain places and expressed in a spatial context.'[1] This notion is echoed by Brian Molyneaux and Piers Vitebsky, who characterise the study of sacred geography as an 'intelligent open-minded inquiry' into 'the sacred meanings given to the landscape by various cultures now foreign to us in time or space.'[2] Paul Devereux, a pioneer of sensory archaeology, has suggested that sacred geography can be conceived as the study of 'where the physical world and the "otherworlds" of spirit or mind meet.'[3] To this end Devereux employs the concept of 'mindscapes' to refer to the way in which human beings understand and map (both cognitively and cartographically) their surrounding environments. The ancient Greeks recognised this layering of human meaning and significance on top of the physical features of the land with their concepts of *topos* and *chora*. Devereux and colleagues explain that:

> Topos signifies a simple location, the physical, observable features of a locale. Chora, however, refers to the more subtle aspects of place, those that can trigger memory, imagination, and mythic presence.[4]

Devereux explains that the way in which a 'culture maps its world says much about its way of thinking about its environment,' and in particular 'about how its soul and the soul of the world [...] interact.'[5] Sacred geography is therefore concerned with understanding the subtle aspects of place, the ways in which human beings and the land on which they live interact with one another, and how this interaction is interpreted and enacted in cosmology, culture and behaviour.

The Sacred: Social Construction and Hierophany

There are, broadly speaking, two dominant approaches to understanding the nature of the sacred in the academic study of spirituality and religion. The sociological perspective suggests that the sacred is something that is socially constructed. In other words, that it is essentially human-made – manifested and maintained by human activity alone. Émile Durkheim, the father of this approach, for example, suggested that the sacred is created through a conceptual separation of the profane (the everyday world of mundane matter), and those things held to be somehow special by human social groups. Once this distinction is made, the special or sacred character of objects or places is reinforced through collective ritual and taboos, which alter human behaviour around the object or place.[6] Taken in its extreme form, then, the Durkheimian position is that there is nothing that is inherently sacred in itself, rather objects, places and people are *made sacred* by human beings and the things that they do around them. This is essentially the dominant perspective in most of the social sciences, and might be understood as a form of social and cultural constructivism.

On the other hand, for those who hold or experience a place to be sacred its sanctity is often understood as something that *actually exists* in the world, so that it is not so much created by human beings as experienced by them in particular places, and pre-exists any kind of social construction or elaboration. This view is clearly expressed in the writings of the controversial historian of religion Mircea Eliade (1907–1986), who argued in favour of understanding the sacred through the lens of *hierophany* – as a 'manifestation of the sacred.' He explains that:

> When the sacred manifests itself in any hierophany, there is not only a break in the homogeneity of space; there is also revelation of an absolute reality, opposed to the nonreality of the vast surrounding expanse. The manifestation of the sacred ontologically founds the world.[7]

The idea is that there is something external to human beings in the very fabric of the world, and perhaps dwelling or pooling in particular locations, that human beings can encounter and experience directly, and which manifests through interaction. In his *Patterns in Comparative Religion* Eliade also discusses the concept of Kratophany, literally defined as 'an emanation of power.'[8] Notions of power, place and the sacred are often intimately connected.

Sacred geography research is therefore especially concerned with the different ways in which a sense of the sacred is manifested in particular places through a combination of human (psychological, social and cultural) and non-human (other, extra-human) factors.

Haunted Places and the Numinous

The German theologian Rudolf Otto's perspective provides a sort of compromise between the two strong positions of the social construction of the sacred and ontological hierophany. He argued that there is a distinct kind of feeling-response that human beings experience when we encounter what he called the 'wholly other,' which – like Eliade's notion of hierophany – may erupt through the mundane fabric of the everyday world. He called this feeling response the *numinous*, and suggested that it might arise when we move into particular places where the 'wholly other' seeps through. These locations might be understood as 'thin places,' to use the terminology of Celtic Spirituality, which are places where there is thought to be a 'thinness of the boundary between this world and the spiritual world.'[9] The experience of the numinous may then go on to serve as the basis for further social and cultural elaboration (social construction). Otto explains that:

> [the] implicit meaning [of a place] may be rendered explicit. It is already the beginning of this explicative process [...] when a [person] says: '*It* is not quite right here'; '*It* is uncanny' [...] 'This place is haunted' [...] Here we have the obscure basis of meaning and idea rising into greater clarity and beginning to make itself explicit as the notion [...] of a transcendent Something, a real operative entity of a numinous kind, which later [...] assumes concrete form as a '*numen loci*,' a daemon, an 'El,' a Baal, or the like.[10]

In other words the hierophantic experience comes first – experienced through the body's innate numinous feeling-response – followed by stories, rituals, taboos and further cultural elaboration.[11] As Otto suggests, the idea that particular places are haunted by ancestors, spirits or other entities may be rooted in numinous experiences had by people in particular locations, transmitted in the form of what folklorists call *memorates* – stories that are believed to be true – that are later incorporated into cultural and religious traditions.[12] Indeed, parapsychologist Neil Dagnall and colleagues have suggested that hauntings are one of the 'oldest problems in environmental psychology,' raising important questions about the different ways that people experience, relate to and interpret their surroundings.[13] The Islamic philosopher Seyyed Hossein Nasr suggests that the sacred might in fact arise out of 'the spiritual interrelationship of human beings and the natural environment,'[14] an understanding that sees the sacred emerging through participation in the world, and which would seem to resonate with Otto's idea of phenomenologically haunted places and numinous experiences resulting in the designation of certain locations as sacred.

Landscape, Movement and Story

The meeting point between the physical landscape and human consciousness is in our embodied experience – the phenomenological experience of place as filtered through the subjectivity of our physical bodies, sense organs and cognitive conceptual categories. Landscapes play a centrally important role in the world's many spiritual and religious traditions, which have informed the ways in which geographical features and particular places have been experienced and interpreted by countless generations of humans. As the landscape archaeologist Barbara Bender explains:

> Landscapes and time are not objective, not 'a given,' not neutral. (Nor, for that matter, is 'nature' or any of the other categories that we might care to consider) [...] it is we, through our embodied understanding, our being-in-the world, who create the categories and the interpretations.[15]

Consider, for example, the importance of landscapes in the major world religions: the Holy Land for Jews, Christians and Muslims, or the Himalayas for Tibetan Buddhists, and the monuments and sacred locations that become sites of worship, devotion and pilgrimage for many thousands of believers around the world each year.[16] These give a good sense of the connection between the sacred and the geographic. Indeed, pilgrimage is a central point of connection between spirituality, the land and embodied experience, as pilgrims bodily move through significant landscapes and sacred sites to reflect on their faith. The scholar of religion Justine Digance suggests that pilgrimage in the twenty-first century calls for a flexible definition. She proposes the broad definition of 'undertaking a journey that is redolent with meaning,'[17] and explains that:

> Traditional religious pilgrimage is far from diminishing in popularity, with age-old centres such as Rome, Jerusalem and Lourdes still attracting the faithful, with newer sites such as Medjugorje and Sri Sathya Sai Baba's palatial Ashram at Puttaparthi in India, proving to be popular pilgrimage sites today. A veritable cornucopia of secular pilgrimages [also] abounds, far too numerous to cover in detail.[18]

As the archaeologist Christopher Tilley has suggested, a landscape is really 'a series of named locales, a set of relational places linked by paths, movements and narratives.' He suggests that the 'natural' topography of the land is 'perspectively linked to the existential Being of the body in societal space.'[19] In other words, landscapes are created through human perception, participation, movement and the telling of stories, as much as they are the product of geological and biological processes – they are, in essence, a co-creation.

This process contributes to a layering of meaning within landscapes. Adopting an Aristotelian perspective, sacred geographer Bernadette Brady suggests that as 'an area becomes rich with cultural layers [...] it will grow in its potential to influence human activity,' in particular rich cultural landscapes may promote 'such activity as wanting to maintain place names,' as well as establishing 'measures to protect storied locations.'[20] Tourism researchers Rachael Ironside and Stewart Massie have suggested that a folklore-centric gaze that shifts the focus of tourists towards a relational approach to landscape can be especially beneficial for both local communities and the non-human environment by helping to establish an emotional connection to place, and so encouraging pro-environmental behaviour.[21] Folklore and traditional stories of place may, therefore, play an important role in mediating relationships to the land, and may have practical applications for helping to establish a respectful relationship with natural environments, especially in the context of tourism and sustainability, though not without complications.[22]

The Dreaming

The Aboriginal Australian concept of 'the dreamtime' also goes a long way towards demonstrating the close relationship between story, spirituality and the landscape amongst indigenous communities. Many different indigenous Australian terms are translated into English as 'dreamtime' or 'dreaming,' making it a tricky concept to use accurately from an etic perspective. There are even varieties of meanings *within* aboriginal social groups, not to mention between them. The Warlpiri term Jukurrpa (dreaming), for example, has five meanings, as the anthropologists David Price-Williams and Rosslyn Gaines explain:

> The first referred to the Ancestral period, which although dictating a mythical past, also has a real temporal dimension in the present. The second meaning is designation of the whole category of Ancestral Beings. Third [...] [it] is used to refer to specific myths or Dreaming stories. The fourth meaning concerns the specific actions of an Ancestral Being [...] [The] fifth meaning is about '[night] dreams' that individuals have during their sleep which are later associated with a specific Dreaming.[23]

In spite of the variety of meanings of the dreaming, there are some defining characteristics across tribal groups that are worth mentioning in this context. Indeed, Alan Rumsey suggests that the apparent differences in defining the dreaming between groups are in fact representative of 'variants of a single "mode of orientation," to place,' in which 'enduring, physical features of the lived landscape [are the] prime locus of objectification.'[24] The dreaming may refer to ancestral creation myths – the stories of how the world and the features of the landscape came to be – while also simultaneously referring to an 'a-temporal metaphysical reality' that overlays and interpenetrates the everyday reality experienced with our physical senses.[25] In moving through the landscape along song-lines, through sacred sites and mythic locations, and telling and re-telling dreaming stories, it is possible to participate directly in the act of creation itself. Lynn Hume explains that the dreaming implies that:

> Everything is interconnected in a vast web of sacredness. Ancestor tracks and sites, and the Dreaming stories associated with them, make up the sacred geography of Australia. The entire continent is criss-crossed by

tracks that the Ancestors made on their travels [...] Those responsible must take care of the country by periodically following songlines pertaining to these myths, thus maintaining their connections to the land and keeping the land.[26]

For indigenous Australians the physical features of the natural landscape offer a direct connection to the creation event and are revered and protected as sacred sites,[27] many of which are currently under threat from government coal mining operations, despite their cultural, ecological, and spiritual significance.[28] Indigenous Australia's sacred landscapes and dreaming stories are also echoed and reflected in the indigenous and folk traditions of other parts of the world, which similarly portray the image of a living mythical landscape with which we can participate.[29]

Tending Sacred Landscapes and Gardens

It is possible to distinguish between religious and spiritual traditions that see the landscape as *naturally* expressive of the sacred (such as amongst the Indigenous Australian groups discussed above), and those who actively *shape* the landscape in order to express spiritual and philosophical teachings. Andrew Cunningham explains, for example, that the word *paradise* was adopted into Greek from Persian and literally refers to 'an enclosed park.' The term was, and still is, used in reference to the Garden of Eden, the first garden and the only garden not created by human hands. Cunningham continues that 'this equation is very important. Paradise is a garden: a garden is paradise. We can make a paradise on earth by making a garden.'[30] Gardens are, of course, an example of what might be referred to as 'domesticated landscapes.' They are carefully shaped by gardeners, often over generations. As Cunnigham explains, the 'gardener's work preserves their identity as gardens, and keeps them from slipping back into non-gardens.'[31] Ideas connecting gardens to cosmogonic stories and notions of divine order are not unique to the Judeo-Christian traditions, and are found widely distributed across different cultural contexts. In his book on *Religion and Geography*, for instance, the geographer Chris C. Park suggests that human transformation of the landscape 'is promoted in religions that see in the process of shaping the world a meaning [for] human existence.' He gives the example of the Dogon people of the Upper Volta Republic in West

Africa, who 'deliberately seek to reproduce in the landscape what they understand to be the original cosmic pattern.'[32]

A similar idea is expressed in the notion of 'philosophical gardens,' defined as gardens whose designs purposefully embody the teachings of a particular religious, spiritual or philosophical tradition. Japanese Buddhist Zen gardens are a classic example. Zen gardens usually employ gravel, stones and moss to create what the garden historian Sean McGovern describes as 'a way for complex philosophical perceptions and religious ideals to become tangible in topographical text form.'[33] Zen gardens, he writes, can be understood as three-dimensional *koans* – as puzzles or riddles, often without a solution, that are used to stimulate thought and ultimately contribute towards enlightenment. Sacred landscapes and gardens may also serve important ecological functions. As an illustration Swamy, Kumar and Sundarpandian report on sacred groves in Tamil Nadu, India, where:

> [...] people believe that any damage to the sacred grove, harm to the fauna residing in it or felling of any tree from it may invite the wrath of the local deity, causing diseases and failure of agricultural crops. Even taking a dry twig is forbidden, and any violation of the taboo, people say, will incur the wrath of the snake gods. Therefore, many people will not even take dead wood out of the sacred groves.[34]

By defining particular areas as sacred, or simply as gardens, human behaviour in those places in moderated, providing opportunities for biodiversity and psychodiversity to flourish. See Chapter Six for more on the role of gardens as meeting places between the human and non-human worlds.

Window Areas and Zones of Strangeness

There are certain locations around the world that have a reputation for supernatural occurrences. Particular regions or areas may become associated with certain traditions because of historical and legendary events that apparently took place there,[35] or with ghosts, witches, fairies, or UFOs because of experiences repeatedly reported in those areas over time.[36] The Skinwalker Ranch in Utah is one such example, where there are reports of all manner of highly unusual phenomena, including orbs of light, apparent portal-like manifestations, and even sightings of human-animal hybrid monsters, all in the vicinity of '480 acres of cottonwood trees, Russian olives and very lush pasture bordered by a creek.'[37] Cannock Chase in the UK, 'a 26-square mile area of woodland and heath,' is also widely regarded as a paranormal hot-spot, with reports of UFOs, mysterious big black cats and even large, hairy Bigfoot-type entities appearing in local newspapers.[38] There are numerous other regions like this around the world. The term 'window area' was coined by the Fortean writer and researcher John Keel to describe these places. He writes:

> We have a theory. It is not very scientific but it is based upon the known facts. These creatures and strange events tend to recur in the same areas year after year, even century after century. This, in itself, indicates that the creatures somehow live in those areas which we call 'windows.'[39]

For Keel, these 'strange creatures from time and space,' inhabit different frequencies of what he called 'the superspectrum' (see discussion in Chapter Four). The psychical researcher Peter McCue has similarly referred to these areas as 'Zones of Strangeness,' which has a nice ring to it. He points out, however, that when 'places are described as hot spots, the tacit assumption is that the geographical concentration of incidents is more than a statistical fluke.'[40] Only a concerted research effort to document the occurrence of such events in particular locations over time – in order to determine whether there is a causal relationship between a specific place and paranormal experiences reported there – would be able to settle this statistical issue.

Psychophysiological Influences from the Land

One approach to determining whether there is a causal relationship between the features of certain locations and extraordinary experiences is to investigate the possibility of subtle influences from the land itself. The neuroscientist and parapsychological researcher Michael Persinger (1945–2018) and colleagues, for instance, investigated the possible effects on human perception of subtle electromagnetic stimulation of the temporal lobes. They found that exposure to particular electromagnetic frequencies *can* (though not always)[41] result in the participant experiencing visions, a sense of presence, and other 'anomalous' phenomena and sensations.[42] Further research and theorising on the role of infrasound, radiation, and other subtle influences on human consciousness has also been carried out. The parapsychologist Serena Roney-Dougal, for example, has suggested the possibility that interaction with subtle magnetic fields at sacred sites, such as at stone circles and other prehistoric monuments, can stimulate the endogenous production of the highly psychactive compound DMT in the brain, giving rise to all manner of psychedelic and paranormal experiences in these locations.[43] The earth mysteries researcher and writer Paul Devereux has even suggested that these subtle environmental influences might give rise to other paranormal encounters, including with UFOs, and what he terms 'earth lights.' He explains:

> What are earth lights? Well they certainly have electrical and magnetic attributes, and some form of plasma is assumed. Modern witnesses who come close to earth lights typically report hallucinatory episodes – suggesting magnetic fields that are known to be able to affect parts of the brain.[44]

According to Devereux, earth lights are most likely to be experienced in the atmospheres of areas of high tectonic activity, such as along fault lines, 'as a result of electromagnetic events or "discharges" emanating from seismic activity.'[45] The Hessdalen lights in Norway are a prime example of the Earth-light phenomenon.[46]

As part of an innovative investigation into the influence of the environment on human consciousness, Devereux, along with Stanley Krippner, Robert Tartz and Adam Fish, conducted a study of dream content from dreams recorded at three outdoor sacred sites in Wales and Cornwall, which were compared to dreams recorded in the home. Their results confirmed their hypothesis that 'the content of dream reports from purported outdoor sacred sites would differ significantly from the content of dream reports collected by participants in their homes.' The results of the study suggested modest statistically significant differences between the content of dreams in the home and at outdoor sacred sites. In particular they noted 'more aggressive content in site dreams and more friendly content in home dreams.' A range of explanations are offered, including 'expectancy, suggestions, the effect of unfamiliar surroundings, the fact that the selected field sites possessed above average background levels of radiation or magnetism, and possible anomalous properties of the sacred sites' themselves.[47]

Do these perspectives lend any credence to the possibility of a natural sacredness that dwells in the land, just waiting for human interaction, or are the extraordinary experiences that apparently result from interaction with electromagnetism, and other subtle factors, simply hallucinatory by-products with no wider relevance?

Summary

Émile Durkheim suggested that the sacred is essentially socially constructed – created by the things that human beings do to make distinctions between different perceived orders of reality. Through ritual and taboos we create and sustain the sacred, which would suggest that sacred landscapes and places are a human construct. Eliade's perspective, on the other hand suggests that the sacred is something 'out there' in the world, waiting to be experienced in the form of hierophanies, in which case the land itself is inherently sacred. Otto's perspective bridges both of these positions, acknowledging that sacred places may be developed as a combination of the two – the numinous experience emerges when we interact with certain places inspiring the social creation of stories, rituals, taboos and other embellishments to maintain it. Researchers such as Michael Persinger and Paul Devereux have suggested that the numinous feeling-responses associated with some places might be caused by the influence of subtle emanations from the earth, initiating altered states of consciousness in anyone who happens to enter into their radius. But, is this a reductive way of thinking about hierophany and the power of place? Is explaining 'sacred' experiences and locations in terms of the influences of subtle magnetism, radiation or infrasound another way of 'explaining it away'? Or, is it possible that altered states of consciousness might be a necessary pre-condition for accessing 'numen loci'? Perhaps a complexity perspective, with multiple contributing factors, is better than any single reductive explanation. Above all else, sacred geography offers a glimpse of a re-enchanted way of looking at and living in the world. As Paul Devereux explains the view that the world is somehow 'alive, enchanted, sentient and capable of communicating with us' is the 'essence of all sacred geographies, regardless of specific cultural beliefs and differences.'[48] Anthony Thorley, whose definition of sacred geography was considered at the start of this chapter, adds that 'Sacred Geography is part of the important post-enlightenment academic rediscovery of an animistic worldview relevant to Western Culture.'[49]

CHAPTER NINE:
Traditional Ecological Knowledge

The notion that there are both 'traditional' and 'scientific' forms of ecological knowledge has already been touched upon in preceding chapters. Chapter One, for instance, provided an overview of some of the key concepts to have emerged from *scientific* ecology, including ideas such as 'systems,' 'succession' and 'trophic cascades.' These concepts and principles are usually couched in the context of a materialist metaphysics, and they are understood as referring to physical biological dynamics and processes.[1] This chapter will turn to consider *traditional* forms of ecological knowledge and the principles and perspectives that underlie their many different formulations.

What is Traditional Ecological Knowledge?

Traditional Ecological Knowledge (TEK) is a term that has been gaining increasing attention since the 1980s. The social ecologist Fikret Berkes, a pioneer of the cross-cultural study of ecological frameworks, explains that systems of traditional ecological knowledge represent the cumulation of 'experience acquired over thousands of years of direct human contact with the environment,'[2] which includes 'an intimate and detailed knowledge of plants, animals, and natural phenomena,' and the 'development and use of appropriate technologies for hunting, fishing, trapping, agriculture, and forestry.' The anthropologist Margaret Bruchac provides a useful survey of different forms of traditional knowledge and knowledge transmission, which include:

> [...] oral narratives that recount human histories; cosmological observations and modes of reckoning time; symbolic and decorative modes of communication; techniques for planting and harvesting; hunting and gathering skills; specialised understandings of local ecosystems; and the manufacture of specialised tools and technologies (e.g., flint-knapping, hide tanning, pottery-making, and concocting medicinal remedies).[3]

Tradtional ecological knowledge is, therefore, primarily scientific and technological in its outlook and practical application, and in these ways does not differ too much from scientific ecological knowledge. Indeed, Potowatomi biologist Robin Wall Kimmerer has argued that traditional ecological knowledge and scientific ecological knowledge have many points of overlap and might in fact represent complimentary ways of knowing about the world, explaining that the synergy of perspectives can be useful in a variety of different ways:

> Traditional ecological knowledge can be a source of new biological insights and potential models for conservation biology and sustainable development [...] Examination of traditional ecological knowledge explicitly brings multicultural perspectives into the core of the science curriculum, where they have generally been absent [...] Recognition of traditional ecological knowledge increases opportunities for productive partnerships between Western scientists and indigenous people [...] Traditional ecological knowledge integrates scientific and cultural concerns in a holistic manner.[4]

On the other hand, it is argued that systems of traditional ecological knowledge represent a form of 'holistic knowledge, or "world view" which parallels the scientific discipline of ecology,' but which never fully meet.[5] Furthermore, traditional knowledge often exists within a wider 'spiritual' framework that does not necessarily synergise with Western science (see the next section). In many ways traditional ecological knowledge systems resemble what deep ecologist Arne Naess called 'ecosophies,' or ecological philosophies of place.[6] There are, therefore, many different traditional ecological knowledges adapted to the unique features and characteristics of particular regions or landscapes. Although there is often an emphasis on Indigenous American perspectives in many books concerned with TEK, Robin Wall Kimmerer reminds us that systems of traditional ecological knowledge exist all over the world, 'independent of ethnicity.' Traditional ecological knowledge systems are 'born of long intimacy and attentiveness to a homeland and can arise wherever people are materially and spiritually integrated with their landscape.'[7]

TEK and Spirituality

Broadly speaking, biology and ecology are positivistic sciences, in the sense that they rely on empirical research methods and quantitative data that align them with the other so-called 'hard science' disciplines in the academy. There is little room in 'mainstream' ecological science for what might be termed the 'spiritual' (see Chapter Two). Biology and ecology generally (though not exclusively) adopt a materialist metaphysics.[8] Systems of traditional ecological knowledge, by contrast, are fully embedded in relational modes of understanding the world that see establishing good relationships between persons – human, non-human and other-than-human – as cosmologically foundational (see Chapter Five). As already noted, indigenous worldviews tend to collapse the binary distinctions that many Western knowledge systems are built on. In many indigenous contexts, spirituality is not something separate from the other domains of life, but is fundamentally wedded together with them. The indigenous research methodologist Linda Tuhiwai Smith explains that:

> The arguments of different indigenous peoples based on spiritual relationships to the universe, to the landscape, to stones, rocks, insects, and other things, seen and unseen, have been difficult arguments for Western systems of knowledge to deal with or accept. These arguments give a partial indication of the different world views and alternative ways of coming to know, and of being, which still endure within the indigenous world. It is one of the few parts of ourselves which the West cannot decipher, cannot understand and cannot control [...] yet.[9]

TEK and the Ecological Crisis

One of the main drivers of increased scholarly attention to traditional ecological knowledge systems has been their proposed utility as frameworks for assisting local communities to establish resilience in the face of impending climate emergencies. The United Nations Permanent Forum on Indigenous Issues, for example, suggests that traditional ecological knowledge 'has the potential to play a crucial role in sustainable development and for addressing the most pressing global problems, such as climate change, land management, land conservation, and to strengthen scientific, technological and medical research.'[10] Robin Kimmerer uses the analogy of 'braiding' to explain and understand how different knowledge systems can sustain and enhance one another. One way in which traditional forms of knowledge can be become part of the global project to mitigate the ecological crisis is through what Kimmerer calls 'reciprocal restoration ecology':

This approach arises from a creative symbiosis between traditional ecological knowledge (TEK) and restoration science, which honors and uses the distinctive contributions of both intellectual traditions. Reciprocal restoration recognizes that it is not just the land that is broken, but our relationship to it [...] Reciprocal restoration is the mutually reinforcing restoration of land and culture such that repair of ecosystem services contributes to cultural revitalization, and renewal of culture promotes restoration of ecological integrity.[11]

This perspective sees local cultures as intimately connected to their surrounding environments. One approach to ecological restoration, then, is to support and encourage the revitalisation of local communities, traditions, languages and knowledge, and in particular their sense of relationship and connection to their surrounding ecology. The possibilities of relational ontologies for framing environmental conservation efforts have also become an important subject for scholarly discussion. The anthropologists Andrew Paul, Robin Roth and Saw Sha Bwe Moo, for example, argue that 'in order to transform conservation biology through Indigenous perspectives, it is essential to pay attention to the relational world in which many Indigenous Peoples live.' They explain that:

Doing so helps support a conservation practice attentive to the inter-dependence of all life in ways that uphold Indigenous Peoples' rights of self-determination, cultural identity, and social relations with their ancestral lands. We argue that attending to these relations is essential to building community-based conservation collaborations.[12]

However, efforts to implement approaches and perspectives from traditional ecological knowledge into the movement toward global sustainability are far from unproblematic. The indigenous Australian scholar Tyson Yunkaporta illustrates this point with an illuminating 'yarn' (a free-flowing conversation on a particular theme) in his book *Sand Talk,* which considers some of these issues, including the appropriation of indigenous practices and the apparent incompatibility of the 'spiritual' components of traditional knowledge systems with the 'scientific' perspectives of Western ecological restoration efforts. He writes:

I have been to many conferences and talks about Indigenous Knowledge and sustainability, and have read numerous papers on the topic. Most carry the same simplistic message: First Peoples have been here for x-thousand years, they know how to live in balance with this place and we should learn from them to find solutions to sustainability issues today [...] They then offer some isolated examples of sustainable practices pre-colonisation, and that's it. The audience is left wondering, 'Yes, but how? What insight does this offer today, for the problems we are experiencing now?[13]

Yunkaporta's proposition for a more fruitful direction forward is to suggest that rather than taking specific practices that have developed in a particular socio-cultural-ecological context, and then transplanting it onto other locations to which it is not necessarily suited (tantamount to appropriation), we should instead look for and learn from the broader themes and patterns that emerge in indigenous traditions cross-culturally. Yunkaporta explains: 'I want to use an Indigenous pattern-thinking process to critique contemporary systems, and to impart an impression of the pattern of creation itself.'[14] Adopting a similar approach to overarching patterns in his introduction to the book *Traditional Ecological Knowledge*, the anthropologist Daniel Shilling highlights five cross-cultural elements of traditional ecological knowledge systems. He explains that:

Reciprocity and respect define the bond between all members of the land family [...] Reverence toward nature plays a critical role in religious ceremonies, hunting rituals, arts and craft, agricultural techniques, and other day-to-day activities [...] One's relationship to the land is shaped by something other than economic profit [...] To speak of an individual owning land is anathema, not unlike owning another person, akin to slavery [...] Each generation has responsibility to leave a healthy world to future generations.[15]

Furthermore, Shilling points out that these principles 'are not Romantic myths, New Age manifestos, or fables of a pre-historic Noble Savage, as detractors claim.'[16] Indeed, they represent very real ethical frameworks and profoundly practical modes of living in the world that resonate with the life ways of many indigenous societies around the globe. In a similar effort to distill principles, rather than specific practices, Robin Wall Kimmerer has suggested three core features of traditional ecological knowledge systems – *animacy, reciprocity* and *ceremony* – which may, in Theodore Roszak's terms possess a 'proven ecological utility.'[17]

Animacy

As previously noted, systems of traditional ecological knowledge are often embedded in wider holistic worldviews from which they cannot be separated. For many indigenous societies this worldview entails an understanding that the word is fundamentally alive in a sense that is not recognised by mainstream materialist science (see Chapter Five). As an illustration of this key difference between traditional and scientific knowledge systems Kimmerer gives the example of the Anishinaabe word *puhpowee,* which is defined as 'the force which causes mushrooms to push up from the earth over night.'[18] She adds that 'Western science has no such term, no words to hold this mystery [...] You'd think that biologists, of all people, would have words for life.' For Kimmerer, the makers of this word 'understood a world of being, full of unseen energies that animate everything.'[19] Anishinaabe natural science is, therefore, an animistic natural science.[20]

From the perspective of traditional ecological knowledge, then, it would come as little surprise to find – as Monica Gagliano and colleagues have done – that plants might possess consciousness and intelligence. In fact it might even be expected. At the very least plant consciousness could be accommodated into a broader framework of understanding that the category of personhood extends beyond the human. It is interesting to note, however, that while Western scientific ecology and conservation efforts are keen to draw on systems of traditional ecological knowledge for certain kinds of information – such as species classifications, population dynamics, habitat knowledge, animal behaviour patterns, and so on – the animate and personal understanding of the world is often dismissed in favour of the standard mechanistic and materialistic perspective, which denies that rocks can be persons, for example. Tyson Yunkaporta acknowledges, however, that for some in the Western world accepting the reality of plant consciousness, let alone other forms of other-than-human persons such as spirits, might be a step too far. In which case, there are other ways of bridging this gap, such as through an understanding of the role and significance of metaphor in influencing human behaviour. He explains that:

You don't need to believe in ghosts to balance spirit and live the right way in this world. You can use any metaphor you like [...] Whatever stories your cultural experience offers you, you can still perceive spirit through metaphor and bring it into balance.[21]

It is the metaphors that we use to understand the world around us, rather than whether we necessarily 'believe' them to be 'true' that impact our behaviour. What if, for example, the world was approached *as if* it were alive? How might our behaviour towards it be modified?

Reciprocity and Ceremony

The next of Kimmerer's characteristic features of traditional ecological knowledge systems is the notion of *reciprocity,* which serves as a guiding principle in human interactions with the living world in many indigenous societies. In a cosmos inhabited not just by human beings, but by all manner of other-than-human persons (upon whom humans depend for their survival), it is vital to be able to establish and maintain good relationships with them.[22] Falling out of favour could be catastrophic. From an animist perspective *reciprocity* – giving and receiving in an act of mutual exchange – is essential for making sure this does not happen. This is the starting point for what Kimmerer calls 'cultures of gratitude,' which characterise many indigenous worldviews. She explains that:

> In such cultures, people have a responsibility not only to be grateful for the gifts provided by Mother Earth, they are also responsible for playing a positive and active role in the well-being of the land. They are called not to be passive consumers, but to sustain the land that sustains them.[23]

This can be achieved in many ways, such as by tending and maintaining the land and by establishing ethical frameworks for the consumption of resources. Another way in which reciprocity is expressed and maintained is through *ceremony.* Kimmerer suggests that ceremony provides the means by which human beings strive to live reciprocally in the world. Culturally meaningful ritual interaction with the living environment enables the establishment of good relationships, and provides a framework for engaging with both humans and non-humans in a respectful manner:

Ceremonies are a form of reciprocity that renews bonds between land and people and focuses intention, attention, and action on behalf of the natural world, which is inclusive of the spiritual world.[24]

The performing of ceremonies as an act of reciprocity draws human attention towards the land for acknowledgment of its agency. Renée E. Mazinegiizhigoo-kwe Bédard, a scholar from the Dokis First Nation in Canada, provides a detailed account of the traditional origin myth associated with the ceremonial giving of offerings of tobacco (asemaa) in Anishinaabe tradition. According to traditional folklore the teaching to give offerings was first taught to humans by the Spirit Being Giizhigookwe, who:

> [...] instructed her children in the protocols and ceremony of offering asemaa, in prayer to Gizhew-Manidoo (Great Spirit, Great Mystery, the Creator), in gratitude for the bountiful gifts of the land, before entering the forest's sacred spaces, to ask permission to hunt or harvest food, and to plant or pick medicines. In these ways she showed Anishinaabeg how to perform mino-babanametwaawag (leaving a good presence) on the land to maintain the natural balance and harmony of the Earth. The belief encoded in babanametwaawag is that if something is taken, something is to be given, such as asemaa. A gift for a gift is the exchange and ceremony of mutuality.[25]

Taken together, the principles of animacy, reciprocity and ceremony provide an ethical, practical and personal framework for an ecological orientation that is rooted in indigenous perspectives, but which does not draw from any one particular tradition or practice.

Re-Indigenising

Rather than appropriating the indigenous practices of other societies, or artificially transferring cultural traditions from one bio-region to another, communities should instead be looking to reconnect with their own indigenous heritages, folklore and traditions. The human ecology researchers Iain Mackinon, Lewis Williams and Arianna Waller suggest that:

> This looking within both for what we have been and for what we have become is done in prospect of an imminent transformation, in order to

realize what we might yet become here on Earth. It is founded on the view that our diverse, necessary and good group identities here on Earth now also constitute membership of a common Indigenous humanity that is itself deeply enmeshed with, dependent upon and part of the natural fabric of a living Earth.[26]

There are many different ways that it might be possible to develop this sense of connection to the land. Getting to know the places in which we live, the sacred geographies of our own communities, the other-than-human persons who inhabit the spaces around us, and re-connecting with traditional folklore and narratives of place, may all contribute toward a re-indigenisation of local communities.

Indigenous cultures foster an *active* relationship with ecology, and understand that participation and interaction – through everyday activities as well as ritual and ceremony – are key to establishing good relationships with the non-human world. TEK, then, encourages our participation in the world,[27] while SEK encourages a sense of academic detachment from it. From this perspective Western science's difficulty in coming to terms with the possibility of plant (and other forms of) consciousness might arise from deeper cultural frameworks that deny animacy in the world. By fostering a closer relationship with ecology – framed in the language of animism – indigenous cultures encourage a personal relationship with the world, and so they experience it. It is also interesting to note, however, that participation itself – even without a pre-existing animist framework – seems to give rise to a sense of personal relationship with the natural world. The work of Botelho *et al.* (as discussed in Chapter Four) would seem to support this suggestion. In their study of the introduction of agro-forestry in rural Brazil, they observed what they described as 'a metaphysical reconfiguration of the self and the ecosystem' amongst the farmers, who developed a personal relationship with the land they worked with. It was through hands on participation with the local environment that these farmers came to develop a renewed sense of connection to the living world, and a rediscovery of traditional approaches to land management. Their sense of identification with the natural world was expanded.

Indigenous Research and Extraordinary Experience

Another potential contribution of traditional knowledge systems might be in the field of religious, spiritual and extraordinary experience research. The inclusion of indigenous research perspectives, and greater representation for indigenous research on extraordinary experience could provide useful frameworks for conceptualising these issues in their social and ecological contexts.[28] Religious experience researchers have tended to adopt a range of quantitative and qualitative research methodologies since the discipline's inception in the nineteenth century, which has contributed to a diverse and interdisciplinary field of research.[29] Increasingly, however, historians of science are demonstrating that the research paradigms of the human and social sciences continue to perpetuate – often in subtle ways – out-dated colonialist models for understanding the world, as well as building research programs on ontological assumptions that are not necessarily shared by non-Western (and especially indigenous) societies.[30]

There is a tendency – even in work on religious and extraordinary experience – for social-scientific research methods to adopt positivist perspectives, methods and approaches that by their nature are at odds with the subject matter of religious experience research. Similarly, scientific research on religious experience has tended to be reductive in nature, attempting to find the location of a 'God Spot' in the brain,[31] for example, or to create neat taxonomies of religious and spiritual experiences.[32] These tendencies are a part of the cultural baggage that scientific religious experience research continues to carry, even when its own research findings often seem to point toward different ontological possibilities. Extrovertive experiences, for instance – which are very well documented in the literature, as we have seen (see Chapter Four) – often seem to collapse any kind of distinction between the observer and the observed, or the subject and the object. This is, of course, a challenge to the notion of scientific objectivity itself, and leads to a sense of cognitive dissonance in the field of religious experience research between what the data suggests and what the dominant scientific paradigms will actually allow.

The growing field of indigenous research methods (which begin from very different ontological starting points to western scientific research), however, may offer new and exciting avenues for research on religious and other forms of extraordinary experience going forward – directions that do not rely on the assumptions that have shaped mainstream

Western approaches to religious experience research, or indeed to nature in general. The indigenous research methodologist Linda Tuhiwai Smith, for example, summarises the key differences between indigenous and dominant Western scientific epistemologies:

> The indigenous research agenda is broad in its scope and ambitious in its intent. There are some things which make this agenda very different from the research agenda of large scientific organisations or of various national science research programmes. There are other elements, however, which are similar to any research programme which connects research to the 'good' of society. The elements that are different can be found in key words such as healing, decolonization, spiritual, recovery. These terms seem at odds with the research terminology of Western science, much too politically interested rather than neutral and objective.[33]

Perhaps, unlike the positivist approach that has underlined most 'scientific' and 'social-scientific' research on extraordinary experience in the past – and which denies the spiritual *a priori* - an approach that draws from indigenous methodologies might place the spiritual reality that these experiences seem to indicate on a level playing field with the social, cultural, psychological and other factors that are at play (and which Western science is much more willing to engage with). Arguing along related lines in his chapter in *Greening the Paranormal*, Ioway historian Lance Foster re-tells the story of Plenty Coups (1848–1932), chief of the Crow Nation, and his encounter with a water spirit while crossing the Missouri River. After a terrifying ordeal Plenty Coups and his band escape the Water-person, but rather than return to the site to investigate further, or to hunt for the mysterious creature to bring it home as a trophy, an offering is left and the location noted as an inhabited place best avoided. The story presents a radically different approach to extraordinary experiences to that generally employed in the Western scientific study of extraordinary experience. Foster elaborates that:

> The indigenous way to encounter the invisible ecosystem was summed up by Plenty Coups: When you encounter strange things in this life, you just acknowledge their right to be here, the same as anything else; you leave them alone, and go on your way. But what I see is that it seems to be near impossible for the non-indigenous to leave things alone.[34]

135

As is clear by now, many indigenous societies understand that the world is fundamentally alive in a sense that is not recognised by mainstream materialist science. These are very different foundations to those upon which the Western social scientific study of religious experience are built. Indigenous research begins from an holistic perspective rather than attempting to dissect, break apart of reduce the complexity of experience in the world. Furthermore, indigenous perspectives have a very different attitude towards 'anomalous' phenomena and experiences. As Renée E. Mazinegiizhigo-kwe Bédard notes in the context of Anishinaabe worldview:

> The weird in Anishinaabeg contexts holds distinctive meanings that lie outside of Eurocentric expressions of the numinous and anomalous. We recognise the beings that dwell in the weirdness, weird time, and weird territories, as our relatives in the cosmic order of Creation and not outside the realm of possibility. We do not marginalise weirdness or weird beings. We welcome them and hold complex protocols, duties, and responsibilities to guard their sovereign rights. We acknowledge the presence of weirdness and of Spirit when we lay our semaa (sacred tobacco) down on the land.[35]

What, then, might the study of religious, spiritual and extraordinary experience look like if it started from the principle of an animate natural world, or from an ontology of relationship, or holism, or complexity, or from a perspective that rejects the division of self and other, or internal and external? These are big questions and exciting opportunities for future exploration.

Summary

There are many different varieties of Traditional Ecological Knowledge, with each system intimately tied to the unique socio-cultural-ecological niche in which it has emerged. These systems have been challenged, damaged, lost or destroyed through colonialism, but many systems of TEK still survive and thrive today. There are key themes that emerge from a cross-cultural perspective on TEK – with particular emphasis on principles of animacy, reciprocity and ceremony. Western science is just beginning to reveal what are conceived as the building blocks of consciousness and intelligence in non-human beings – the ability to sense the environment, to learn, remember, communicate and adapt to change amongst plants, for example – but interaction and participation bring these disparate components together into a complex whole that can be experienced and dialogued with. Culture and the imagination, then, both provide frameworks for interaction with the world, and consequently affect our relationship with it. What is clear is that if we do want to understand non-human consciousness we will have to participate with it in order to establish a relationship with it. Traditional ecological knowledge – with its emphasis on human embeddedness in ecosystems – in combination with scientific ecological knowledge, may offer fruitful avenues for investigating the sentience of plants and other elements of the living world through an holistic and non-reductive lens, as well as providing ethical frameworks for living in a complex world of many minds.

CHAPTER TEN:
Organic Ontologies

In philosophy, the word ontology is used to refer to the 'study of being', in other words to the study of *what exists*. *Ontologies*, then, are *models of what exists*. Ontologies may take many different forms, and human beings can approach the world from many different ontological perspectives.[1] This chapter suggests that organic ontologies – that is models of the world that build on and emphasise organic principles and processes, such as those that are observed in biological and ecological systems – might represent more useful frameworks for making sense of the world than standard reductionist and mechanistic models, and especially for making sense of phenomena such as mystical and paranormal experiences.

Is the world a watch or a vegetable?

In 1802 the Reverend William Paley's (1743–1805) famous 'Watchmaker' argument for the existence of a divine creator was first published, though earlier iterations of the idea had circulated for many years. Paley argued that the world resembles the intricate design of a pocket-watch mechanism in the way that it has apparently been 'put together' by a conscious designer.[2] He argued that if one were to find a pocket-watch on the ground and examine it, one would come to the conclusion that it had been designed, and so it is with the world. This is taken as evidence for the existence of the God of classical theism, and hence for a form of intelligent design creationism.[3] But does the world really resemble a watch mechanism? The Enlightenment philosopher David Hume (1711–1776) had earlier presented an argument against this line of reasoning in his *Dialogues Concerning Natural Religion*, published in 1779. Hume wrote that:

> The world plainly resembles more an animal or a vegetable than it does a watch or a knitting-loom. Its cause, therefore, it is more probable, resembles the cause of the former. The cause of the former is generation or vegetation. The cause, therefore, of the world, we may infer to be something similar or analogous to generation or vegetation.[4]

It is not often that I find myself in agreement with Hume, but in this instance I think that I do. Hume's critique of the design argument and the notion that the world has been 'put together' like a machine is to suggest that, when we really look at it, the world much more closely resembles a living organism than it does an artificial mechanism. From this Hume reasons that the cause of its existence, that is the origin of the universe, is much more likely to resemble similar, if not identical, processes to those observed in the sphere of biology – processes of organic growth and gradual development, rather than anything artificially put together by human hands. If we follow Hume's line of thinking here then it makes sense to suggest that biological, or organismic, models of the world might be a closer match to reality than mechanistic and reductionistic frameworks.

Organicism and Mechanism

Broadly speaking the distinction between organicism and mechanism concerns whether an holistic or reductionistic perspective on the world is adopted. The biologists Scott F. Gilbert and Sahotra Sarkar note that reductionism is the basis of physics and chemistry, and suggest that it has a two-fold function: firstly to serve as an *epistemology* – a way of finding out about the world by breaking it down into its constituent parts. This is an epistemological framework that also comes with an assumption that all scientific knowledge will eventually be *reduced* to the 'terms of physics.' Secondly, reductionism also serves as an *ontology* – an understanding that the world is best explained in terms of its constituent parts (particles and sub-atomic particles, for example), and that reality is structured from the 'bottom-up.'[5] It is this understanding of the world that justifies the millions spent on projects like the Large Hadron Collider, where physicists smash particles together to try to access the fundamental building blocks of the physical universe.[6] By contrast, the organicist view sees the holistic, top-down perspective as essential for understanding the world around us. The biologist Rupert Sheldrake is an example of an organicist thinker, and provides a useful definition of organicist philosophy. He explains how:

This philosophy denies that everything in the universe can be explained from the bottom up, as it were, in terms of the properties of subatomic particles, or atoms, or even molecules. Rather, it recognises the existence of hierarchically organised systems which, at each level of complexity, possess properties that cannot be fully understood in terms of the properties exhibited by their parts in isolation from each other; at each level the whole is more than the sum of its parts.[7]

The historian of science Garland E. Allen suggests that the eventual dominance of the mechanistic approach in biology was part of a drive in the 1850s to 'professionalize those aspects of biology that had previously been considered largely descriptive, speculative and not amenable to experimental analysis,'[8] a tendency that also likely helps to explain the prevalence of reductionist models throughout the social sciences and humanities, which have been similarly striving for recognition as objective sciences.[9] At any rate, an essential difference between the organicist and mechanistic views of ecology is in the extent to which each approach attributes directionality and understands the role of complexity in natural phenomena. For the organicist, individual organisms work together (consciously or not) in the direction of increasing complexity and greater interdependence, while for the mechanist there is no such collaboration – a perspective that suggests an essentially Newtonian picture of the world – or rather 'Newtonianist' as the historian of science Jonathan Louth points out[10] – that emphasises competition between individual organisms – the classic 'survival of the fittest' scenario.[11] See the discussion of the holism-reductionism debate in Chapter One for more on this.

Now, having outlined what is meant by the term 'organicism,' and how it differs from the mechanistic view, which still seems to dominate the physical and social sciences in many respects,[12] I want to shift attention to consider some key figures in the history of psychical research who have drawn on organicist models, metaphors and theories to understand the nature and dynamics of the paranormal.

Greening Theories of Mysticism and the Paranormal: An 'Ecological Outlook'

As has been noted in previous chapters, there is an apparent 'green' or ecological dimension to many paranormal and extraordinary experiences, not just in terms of the content and effects of extraordinary experiences (which often carry an ecological message, and occasionally result in a dramatic shift in ecological awareness for experiencers), but also in the sense that there appear to be deeper underlying ontological connections that run through both ecology and the dynamics of the paranormal.[13] Nature mystical experiences are a particularly good example, where engagement with the natural environment gives rise to extrovertive mystical experiences, and a shift in perspective for experiencers that reveals the deep interconnectedness of ecosystems (see Chapter Four). The idea suggested here is that models and concepts from biology and ecology might provide novel frameworks for understanding extraordinary experiences and phenomena and their place in the natural world. This is a sentiment that is echoed in the work of Sir Alister Hardy, the eminent biologist, marine ecologist and founder of the Religious Experience Research Centre, who was engaged in a lifelong quest to understand the relationship between religious experience and the wider contexts of biology and ecology. In his first Gifford Lecture (1963–64), Hardy wrote:

> I will confess that perhaps my main interest in ecology is the conviction that this science of inter-relationships of animals and their environment will eventually have a reaction for the benefit of [humankind] I believe that one of the great contributions of biology this century will be the working out of ecological principles that can be applied to human affairs: the establishment of an ecological outlook.[14]

The suggestion here, then, in the context of the wider themes of this book, is that we might be able to apply this 'ecological outlook' to our understanding of a wide range of 'human affairs,' including addressing the ecological crisis, understanding religious and paranormal experience, and illuminating other processes by which human beings make sense of their relationship to the world. An organic framework may provide better insights than the imposition of a reductionist or mechanistic ontological model ever could. As the parapsychologist John L. Randall (1933–2011) summarised in his 1975 book *Parapsychology and the Nature of Life*, 'the mechanist theory of life' can be critiqued on the following grounds':

> 1) that, despite strong claims to the contrary, it fails to provide a satisfactory explanation of the origin and evolution of living systems: its apparent success in this area arises partly from the ignoring of important facts which run contrary to the theory:

2) That it completely ignores the existence of such aspects of reality as consciousness, free-will and purpose, of which we have direct introspective awareness. It attempts to dismiss such phenomena as illusory, and to stigmatise their study as 'unscientific';

3) That it ignores, or attempts to dismiss as fraudulent, all the findings of parapsychology.'[15]

The philosopher Thomas Nagel might agree with Randall's assessment, referring to 'antireductionism' as an antidote to the excessive reductionism that characterises materialist science. He explains that there 'are some things that the physical sciences alone cannot fully account for. Other forms of understanding may be needed, or perhaps there is more to reality than even the most fully developed physics can describe.'[16] The next sections will consider whether organicist ontological perspectives yield any insights into the mysteries of the paranormal.

Organicism in Psychical Research

Spiritualists, psychical researchers and parapsychologists have all employed technological metaphors to understand paranormal phenomena and extraordinary experiences.[17] The metaphor of the 'spiritual telegraph' is a good example. According to the scholar of communications Jeremy Stolow, the concept was used by Spiritualists 'in order to elaborate a grand theory of supernatural presence, grounded in the power of electromagnetism.'[18] Similarly, the brain has been characterised as a 'receiver' of consciousness, using the analogy of radio broadcast and reception, which has been especially popular amongst researchers of psychics and mediums.[19] See, for example, Upton Sinclair's (1878–1968) book about his own experiments with telepathy and thought-transference, which he titled *Mental Radio*.[20] They have all borrowed models from physics, the queen of the 'hard sciences,' including concepts of forces, fields, waves and rays, for example.[21]

On the other hand, there are researchers who have taken their inspiration from organismic and biological models. Historical examples include Franz Anton Mesmer's (1784–1814) notion of 'animal magnetism' as a natural force that flows through and connects all lifeforms, and which may be manipulated for all manner of therapeutic purposes. Mesmer's notion of animal magnetism, sometimes also known as the 'mesmeric fluid,' was understood to be a semi-physical substance that imbues otherwise inanimate matter with life-force or vitality. The historian of parapsychology Carlos Alvarado (1955–2021) explains that Mesmer saw the fluid 'as emanating from the heavenly bodies and present in nature in general' as a sort of universal connecting principle.[22] Mesmer's idea was an early manifestation of what would later come to be known as Vitalism. This is the perspective that 'living organisms defy description in purely physico-chemical terms, because organisms possess some non-material, non-measurable forces or directive agents that account for their complexity.'[23] As Thomas Nagel summarises: 'if organisms with mental life are not miraculous anomalies but an integral part of nature – then biology cannot be a purely physical science.'[24]

The pioneering developmental biologist and psychical researcher Hans Driesch (1867–1941), for instance, saw resonances between biological and parapsychological processes and offered his own vitalist interpretation of certain paranormal phenomena. In his book *Psychical Research*, Driesch makes the case for what he terms 'a kind of super-vitalism' underlying all manner of normal and paranormal manifestations.[25] In a discussion of ostensible 'paraphysical materialisations' – such as those that were alleged to have been produced by the physical mediums of the early twentieth century[26] – Driesch suggests that they can simply be thought of as extensions of otherwise normal physiological processes:

> In fact, normal organisatory and constructive assimilation, as it appears, for instance, in regeneration, would have to be amplified only in regard to its effects ('small' and 'big' are always relative notions). Materialisation would at the same time be a supernormal embryology.[27]

The kind of materialisations Driesch is referring to here were documented by numerous scientific observers at the tail-end of the nineteenth century and the early decades of the twentieth. As an example, during séances with a prominent medium of the 1920s, Eva Carriere (1886–c.1922), the Nobel prize winning physiologist Charles Richet (1850–1935) claimed to have observed and documented a mysterious substance that on numerous occasions was seen to emanate from the medium's mouth, breasts, navel, fingertips, vagina and scalp. This substance was described as coalescing into crude limbs, referred to as 'pseudo-pods' (a term introduced by Richet into psychical research from cellular biology), and human-like heads which would move independently and were highly sensitive to both light and touch. Richet described in detail 'the formation of divers objects, which in most cases seem to emerge from a human body and take on the semblance of material realities, clothing, veils, and living bodies.'[28] These materialisations were also observed by other researchers at the time, including Baron Albert von Schrenck-Notzing (1862–1929), who saw them dissolve back into the medium's body and took numerous extraordinary photographic plates of the bizarre phenomenon.[29]

The term 'ectoplasm' (from the Greek: *ektos* meaning 'outside' and *plasma* meaning 'something formed or moulded'), was eventually coined by Richet to refer to these extraordinary phenomena, which were being observed in spiritualist séances right across Europe at the time.[30] Ectoplasm has since entered popular culture through the blockbuster *Ghostbusters* movies, in which it is usually portrayed as a sort of translucent green slime, though in the reports of psychical researchers ectoplasm was most frequently described as a white, wet and gauzy substance that was tepid to the touch. It is interesting to note in the context of this chapter that this influential term was also borrowed explicitly from the lexicon of cellular biology, deriving from the concept of protoplasm – the living part of cells. The historian of science Robert M. Brain has suggested that for experimental physiologists such as Richet, ectoplasmic materialisations 'became a special instance of protoplasm investigation, and therefore of Life in its most fundamental operations, yet within supernormal settings.'[31]

Another key figure in *fin-de-siècle* science whose work effectively blurred the distinction between natural and supernatural processes was Alfred Russel Wallace (1823–1913), co-formulator of the theory of natural selection with Charles Darwin. In addition to his status as a naturalist Wallace was also a prominent proponent of Spiritualism. Martin Fichman, emeritus professor of history at York University, has suggested that it was Wallace's conversion to Spiritualism in the 1860s that was the impetus for his 'enunciation of an explicit evolutionary teleology,' as distinct from Darwin's more mechanistic (and much less teleological) understanding of the process of natural selection.[32] For Wallace the evolutionary process was simultaneously physical *and* spiritual. A similar sentiment is felt in the later work of Sir Alister Hardy, who speaks of a 'Divine Flame' directing, and flowing throughout, the evolutionary process, echoing the vitalist understanding of life and blurring the line between the biological and the spiritual.[33]

Supernature: Growth, Habit and Process

The botanist Lyall Watson (1939–2008) referred to this trend as the 'natural history of the supernatural.' Watson argued in favour of what he called 'supernature,' explaining that there is 'one life' on Earth that 'embraces every animal and plant on the planet. Time has divided it up into several million parts, but each is an integral part of the whole.'[34] Biochemist and cellular biologist Rupert Sheldrake's book *The New Science of Life*, once denounced as a heretical book suitable for burning, is another influential example of this trend.[35] Though the book is not specifically parapsychological in nature, primarily dealing with broader themes in biology and physiology related to morphogenesis (the processes that give living organisms their shapes and structures), Sheldrake's theories have nevertheless been used to explain parapsychological phenomena, especially his notion of 'morphogenetic fields.'[36] In the preface to the 2009 edition of his book, originally published in 1981, Sheldrake explains the main thrust of his argument in the following terms:

> This book is about the hypothesis of formative causation, which proposes that nature is habitual [...] This hypothesis is radically different from the conventional assumption that nature is governed by eternal laws. But I believe that the idea of the habits of nature will have to be considered sooner or later, whether we like it or not, because modern cosmology has undermined the traditional assumptions on which science was based.[37]

Like the earlier organicists and vitalists discussed above, Sheldrake rejects the reductionist and mechanistic understanding of the cosmos, epitomised here with the example of 'fixed laws of nature.' Drawing on evidence from anomalies that challenge our established models – such as apparent fluctuations in measurements of the speed of light since the 1920s[38] – Sheldrake instead proposes that what science has defined as unchanging laws might in fact be something more like 'habits' of nature, subject to gradual dynamic change:

145

The idea that 'laws of nature' are fixed while the universe evolves is an assumption left over from pre-evolutionary cosmology. The laws may themselves evolve or, rather, be more like habits [...] the 'fundamental constants' may be variable, and their values may not have been fixed at the instant of the Big Bang. They still seem to be varying today.[39]

If, as Hume suggests, the world really does resemble more 'an animal or vegetable' than a mechanism, then might we not also expect natural laws to be dynamic rather than static, and to evolve, change and adapt over time like living organisms do? This form of organismic thinking takes us from the level of cell (Driesch), organism (Richet), and species (Wallace) right through to the the cosmic scale. From this perspective the cosmos – from the micro to the macro – becomes a seething mass of life constantly moving, changing and evolving. Just as Driesch thought that ectoplasmic materialisations might represent a super-extension of the otherwise normal processes of embryology, might we not also be able to super-extend other organic principles (at the very least metaphorically) to make sense of the dynamics of the paranormal?

Panpsychism, Idealism and New Materialism

Panpsychism argues that matter and consciousness are not separate or distinct substances, but have in fact co-evolved with one another, so that they are fundamentally interconnected. Mind, from this perspective, is thought to be distributed throughout the natural world as a property of matter in general.[40] Going a little further, philosopher of mind Peter Sjöstedt-Hughes explains that panpsychism refers to:

> [...] the doctrine that minds exist fundamentally throughout all of actuality – from humans, hawks, honeybees and trees, down to bacteria, mycelia, molecules, and the subatomic below these. All of matter includes minds.[41]

Panpsychism therefore encourages a re-evaluation of the nature of matter itself, and the physical things in the world around us, which may possess a subjective dimension that has been forgotten in the dominant ontology of Western science, but which continues to bubble away beneath the surface.[42] As transpersonal psychologist Les Lancaster summarises:

> Panpsychists [...] hold that mind is a property of the whole physical world, and is not limited only to brains [...] If mind is a property of the natural world, then [...] consciousness, is to be explained in terms of properties of the natural world as a whole, and not simply as a product of the brain.[43]

Panpsychism may provide a philosophical framework for interpreting and understanding a wide range of human interactions with the living world. The historian of astrology Garry Phillipson, for example, has suggested that it might provide a basis for understanding astrological influences, providing a grounding for the practice of astrology in the natural world. He explains that *if* 'panpsychism is a valid account, *then* consequences follow for our relationship to the cosmos which *might* extend so far as to support an account of astrology as divination.'[44] If matter possesses consciousness, then stars, planets and other celestial bodies may also possess minds, and may have agency and influence in the world in ways that mainstream materialist science does not recongise.[45] With some work and elaboration, panpsychism might also help to understand the nature of the wide variety of non-human forms of consciousness and intelligence discussed in Chapter Five, from organic organisms to more subtle forms of consciousness encountered in extraordinary experiences.

Idealism presents another holistic ontological possibility. Unlike panpsychism, which sees matter and consciousness as co-extensive, idealism holds that consciousness itself is the primary reality, with matter representing an expression of mind, within mind. The philosopher Bernardo Kastrup, for example, has suggested an idealist ontology, which he argues is 'more parsimonious and empirically rigorous [...] than mainstream physicalism, bottom-up panpsychism, and cosmopsychism.'[46] Kastrup summarises his idealist model in the following terms:

> There is only cosmic consciousness. We, as well as other living organisms, are but dissociated alters of cosmic consciousness, surrounded by its thoughts. The inanimate world we see around us is the revealed appearance of these thoughts. The living organisms we share the world with are the revealed appearances of other dissociated alters.[47]

Kastrup employs the analogy of whirlpools in water to describe the relationship between individuals and the wider cosmic consciousness. Each whirlpool represents a dissociated alter – an individual person or organism – and although the whirlpool is individuated it remains unseparated from the wider flow of the water. Matter, from this idealist perspective, is *within* consciousness and so is, in effect, an illusion.

A growing number of scholars in the humanities, however, are beginning to re-think matter itself. The scholar of communications Christopher Gamble and colleagues explain that the so-called 'new materialism' movement is a reaction to the 'perceived *neglect* or *diminishment* of matter in the dominant Euro-Western tradition as a passive substance intrinsically devoid of meaning.'[48] The new materialists argue that matter is in fact active and alive in the world, rather than dead and inert. The feminist theorist Karen Barad, for example, asks 'Why are language and culture granted their own agency and historicity while matter is figured as passive and immutable, or at best inherits a potential for change derivatively from language and culture?'[49]

Combined, these perspectives begin to come close to something resembling the 'philosophy of organism' developed by the philosopher Alfred North Whitehead (1861–1947), as part of his broader 'process philosophy.' Whitehead emphasised the fluid processual nature of reality, in contrast to the atomistic view of reality that dominates much of the materialist metaphysics underlying contemporary (popular) science. Whitehead calls for a radical shift in perspective, suggesting that 'the actual world is a process,' and that 'the process is the becoming of actual entities.'[50] Peter Sjöstedt-Hughes provides a useful summary of Whitehead's philosophy of organism as a framework that:

> [...] seeks to overcome the problems in the traditional metaphysical options of dualism, materialism, and idealism [...] The philosophy of organism seeks to resolve these issues by fusing the concepts of mind and matter, thereby creating an 'organic realism' as Whitehead also named his philosophy.[51]

The philosophy of organism, then, has the potential to reveal new insights into a range of phenomena that are not adequately explained by mainstream reductionist perspectives. Furthermore, it may provide a philosophical basis for ecological activism and a recognition of the world as both alive and active in a way that resonates with animistic worldviews and perspectives..

Fortean Organicism

As already noted, organicism has also become common in the theoretical repertoires of paranormal researchers and Fortean writers. Charles Fort, a collector of anomalies at the turn of the nineteenth into the twentieth century, who gives his name to the field of Fortean studies, developed several novel models to accomodate his extraordinary 'damned facts.' In order to make sense of the anomalies he had amassed – including everything from fish falling from the sky through to proto-UFO encounters[52] – Fort's thinking took him in some very novel directions. Indeed, he frequently rejected his own theories about the anomalous – preferring to *keep thinking*, rather than settle on any particular model – but scattered amongst his many mind-bending ideas are some truly binary-collapsing concepts that pre-empted later developments in science and philosophy. For example, Fort had an intuition that whatever the ultimate nature of these anomalies might be, they would not be understood using the 'cognitive grids of the pairs mental/material, real/unreal, subjective/objective.'[53] Fort's notion of 'the action of mind-matter upon matter-mind,' for instance, points in the direction of panpsychism. As already noted, the Fortean writer John Keel also came to the conclusion that 'the Earth is really a living organism, and that it in turn is a part of an even larger organism.'[54] For Keel, life extends outwards beyond the physical into more subtle dimensions. He referred to this idea as the 'superspectrum,' which he defined as:

> [...] a hypothetical spectrum of energies that are known to exist but that cannot be accurately measured with present-day instruments. It is a shadowy world of energies that produce well-observed effects, particularly on biological organisms (namely humans). This superspectrum is the source of all paranormal manifestations from extrasensory perception (ESP) to flying saucers; little green men; and tall, hairy monsters. It is hard to pin down scientifically because it is extradimensional – meaning that it exists outside our own space-time continuum yet influences everything within our reality.[55]

The resonances here with what Lance Foster has called the 'invisible ecoystem,'[56] what the writer Anthony Peake has labelled 'The Hidden Universe,'[57] and what Julia Wright refers to as 'subtle ecologies'[58] are striking. More recently still, Fortean writer Joshua Cutchin has employed the concept of the ecosystem to help make sense of the kaleidoscopic mysteries of the paranormal, which together encompass what he calls the 'Ecology of Souls.'[59] According to his model, all manner of paranormal occurrences – from near-death experiences to fairy encounters – have something intrinsically to do with the natural cycles of life and death through which all living organisms must pass. He explains how:

> Paranormal entities – faeries, aliens, even many cryptids – might best be understood as an ecology of souls, viewed through the lenses of death and human soul tradition [...] topics as disparate as altered states of consciousness, shamanism, ancient monuments, and ley lines enter the conversation, creating what is hopefully a fresh, wholistic perspective on these mysterious beings and [humankind's] relationship to them.[60]

The image of complexity and interconnection implied by what Alister Hardy called the 'ecological outlook' continues to give inspiration for Fortean thinkers, and to provide new frameworks for making sense of the myriad ways in which the paranormal manifests and expresses itself in the lives of human beings. It reminds us that we are not the centre of the universe, and that there is much more going on in the cosmos than we are usually aware of.

Participatory Ecologies

Much like the double-slit experiment in quantum physics, which seems to suggest that the act of measurement determines the outcome of the experiment,[61] the concept of the ecosystem reminds us that we are also participants in the system. From the ecological perspective we cannot remove ourselves from the system we are observing, whether we are observing a forest ecosystem, conducting a laboratory experiment or participating in a séance in a garden shed. Ecosystems are participatory – the world is participatory. In his recent book *Ecologies of Participation*, Zayin Cabot explains his preference for the idea of 'ecologies' over the notion of 'ontologies' precisely for the reason that ecology implies our own participation in the system:

> I use the term ecologies to allow us to interact. Ontology by itself breeds conflict, implying that 'I' am closer than 'you.' Ontologies, while

provocative, remain useful paradoxes, but have little place in our lives. Ecologies are more useful and liveable, if we are going to come together, and thus I argue for participation, allowing for some sort of process whereby words actually do create the worlds in which we live.[62]

Ecologies invite our participation in a way that the notion of ontologies might not, presenting the opportunity for us to enter into different ways of looking at the living environment that surrounds us, and allowing for the possibility of real communication and conversation between worlds.

Summary

There are many possible ontological models. Scientific ontologies have often tended towards mechanistic and reductionistic perspectives on the world, but there are also frameworks that emphasise complexity, holism and the organic, such as the models that arise from the observation of ecological systems. As already noted in the context of succession, ecosystems tend generally towards greater complexity, biodiversity and interconnection. If complexity of this sort is a principle of the natural world, then, perhaps we as social scientists and investigators should also embrace the complexity of the world, rather than perpetually trying to reduce it down to simple explanations. This chapter has suggested that ontological models that draw from organicist perspectives might provide useful frameworks for making sense of human encounters with the mystical, paranormal and other-than-human. The vitalist parapsychologist Hans Driesch suggested that paranormal phenomena might best be understood as 'super-extensions' of ordinary biological processes, Charles Richet drew on his knowledge of cellular biology to make sense of mediumistic materialisations, and Alfred Russel Wallace conceived of a stream of cosmic evolution that is both biological and spiritual in nature. While the philosophical positions of panpsychism and idealism are often presented to be at odds with one another, they both present holistic models of the cosmos in which consciousness plays a fundamental role, while the New Materialists remind us not to forget about matter itself, which may be far more active, alive and significant than it is often given credit for. Much of this work resonates with philosophical perspectives that emphasise process, dynamism and complexity over reduction and simplicity, as well as with the animistic cosmological perspectives discussed in previous chapters. Finally, Zayin Cabot's notion of 'participatory ecologies' allows for the possibility that we can move between different ontological perspectives in our approach to the world. A dynamic participatory approach for a living cosmos.

CHAPTER ELEVEN:
Education and Nature Connection

The aim of this final chapter is to explore different ways that the ideas discussed in the preceding chapters might be put into some kind of practical action in the world. After all, the environmental problems that are facing the planet are very much of *this world* – physical, biological and material. Any spiritual or conceptual response must also be coupled with a practical, material dimension. In particular education is suggested as an essential component of a wider cultural shift toward ecocentrism and the establishment of a sense of connection to the natural world.

Nature Connectedness

Many commentators have suggested that the current ecological crisis has its roots in the perceived disconnection between human beings and our natural environments.[1] This sense of disconnection has emerged, especially in the Western world, over the last two hundred years or so, and is closely tied to the rise of the techno-scientific worldview,[2] though as, we have seen, others have suggested earlier origins (see Chapter Three). The restoration of a sense of connection to the natural world has, therefore, been proposed as one important way of bringing about a broad-scale change in social attitudes and behaviours towards the environment.[3] In an influential paper in the *Journal of Environmental Psychology,* Stephan Mayer and Cynthia Frantz outlined their 'connectedness to nature scale' – a psychometric tool for measuring the extent to which people feel they are 'emotionally connected to the natural world.' In the paper they define connection to nature as an 'individual's' experiential sense of oneness with the natural world,'[4] reminiscent of Naess' notion of the 'ecological self' as a deep seated identification with the ecological environment.[5] Furthermore, they found that individuals with a higher sense of emotional connection to nature were more likely to engage in pro-environmental behaviours. In a review of the research literature on what has come to be known as 'connectedness to nature theory' (CNT), the sustainable development researchers Brian Restall and Elisabeth Conrad explain that:

[...] a relationship with the natural world directly affects people's physical, mental, and overall wellbeing due to benefits gained by increased exposure to nature and positive experiences in the natural world [...] Direct experiences with natural settings seem to have very profound emotional effects on people [...] and a stronger commitment to nature could lead to higher human interest in environmental protection.[6]

Similarly, a recent study of 4,960 adults in the UK found that visiting green spaces more than once a week 'was positively associated with general health and household pro-environmental behaviours.'[7] Nature experiences in childhood also seem to be particularly powerful influences. In a recent study on the effects of nature experiences on pro-environmental behaviour in adults, Claudio Rosa and colleagues found evidence to suggest that childhood experiences 'have a lasting effect until adulthood, encouraging nature experiences later in life, which, in turn, promote pro-environmentalism.'[8] Studies such as these suggest that one important way of making a practical contribution to mitigating the climate crisis is by helping in the facilitation of a sense of connection to nature – to develop the 'ecological self.' Rosa *et al.* suggest that the school-setting in particular is an ideal venue for enabling young people develop a sense of connection to the natural world. Education and access to green spaces are therefore key, and combining the two could have enormous benefits. Furthermore, it is my suggestion that Religious Education lessons in particular – because of their cross-cultural concern for exploring different worldviews – might be a useful venue for discussing and developing this sense of connection to nature in the school setting. This could be made especially effective through the combination of teaching and learning with philosophising in outdoor settings – from simply walking and talking outside to working in outdoor classrooms, or in school or community gardens.[9]

Education as a Response to Climate Change

No doubt many teachers have been inundated with questions and comments from their students about the climate crisis in recent years, owing in large part to the impact of Greta Thunberg, her Fridays for Future youth movement and her powerful speeches.[10] Indeed, awareness of the issues facing our planet has never been higher. In 2019 the UK government officially declared a

'Climate Emergency,' partly in response to the Extinction Rebellion protests that were taking place in London at the time.[11] The government's declaration signalled an official recognition of the climate crisis.[12] A 2019 Ipsos Mori survey suggested that '85% of Britons are now concerned about climate change.'[13] It is, therefore, a topic ripe for discussion in the classroom. Recent research suggests that conversations around 'social justice concerns,' such as those that might be explored through discussions about environmental ethics in the classroom, can be just as influential in motivating pro-environmental behaviour as, for example, childhood experiences in nature.[14] But is there a way of tying teaching and learning into meaningful, hands-on action to promote biodiversity and build resilience against climate change? One approach might be through the incorporation of permaculture principles into the education curriculum.

Permaculture

Permaculture is a process for designing sustainable and regenerative garden systems that takes its inspirations from the principles of ecology. It was developed in the 1970s by the Australian ecologist Bill Mollison (1928– 2016) and his student David Holmgren.[15] The term itself derives from the conjunction of the words 'permanent' and 'culture' (or 'agriculture'), so *Perma*-culture could be understood as a design system for creating ecologically rooted 'permanent cultures' that are 'regenerative,' rather than just 'sustainable.'[16] One of the most popular formulations of Permaculture makes use of twelve key design principles, and three ethical precepts, drawing primarily from the work of David Holmgren, and in particular from his book *Permaculture: Principles and Pathways Beyond Sustainability*.[17] The twelve principles are:

1. Observe and Interact.
2. Catch and Store Energy.
3. Obtain a Yield.
4. Apply Self-Regulation and Accept Feedback.
5. Use and Value Renewable Resources and Services.
6. Produce No Waste.
7. Design from Patterns to Details.

8. Integrate Rather than Segregate.

9. Use Small and Slow Solutions.

10. Use and Value Diversity.

11. Use Edges and Value the Marginal.

12. Creatively Usxe and Respond to Change.[18]

These twelve principles are themselves couched within the wider tripartite Permaculture ethic of:

1. Earth care.

2. People care.

3. Fair share.

Holmgren's twelve principles are often used to provide the structure for the Permaculture Design Course (PDC), an intensive, usually residential, course in the principles of ecology, systems thinking, regenerative agriculture, ecological design and so on. The content of the PDC was formally codified in 1984.[19] For many people, the permaculture design course represents a pivotal moment in thier lives, and frequently leads to transformations of lifestyle. Participants in PDCs are awarded with a certificate in Permaculture Design on completion of the course (I completed my own PDC in 2017 at Chester Cathedral). A further intensive teacher training diploma course, which comprises the compilation of a detailed portfolio of successful Permaculture design projects, must be undertaken if an individual wants to progress further to become a teacher themselves. In the UK, PDCs are usually accredited by the Permaculture Association, the official body governing Permaculture practitioners.[20]

Permaculture and Spirituality

It is important to point out that Permaculture is not a spiritual movement, though it does possess certain 'religion-like qualities.'[21] It is certainly not intended as a means to induce extraordinary or spiritual experiences in practitioners (though in effect, it often does, see Chapter Four). At its core it is a scientific (broadly materialist), practical and hands-on approach to building sustainable gardens and regenerating ecological systems. Indeed, many Permaculture practitioners would likely reject any association with 'woo-woo' subjects, for fear of detracting from Permaculture's eminently practical, science-based, significance.[22] Bill Mollison was insistent to point out, for instance, that:

> [...] permaculture is not biodynamics, nor does it deal in fairies, devas, elves, after-life, apparitions or phenomena not verifiable by every person from their own experience, or making their own experiments. We permaculture teachers seek to empower any person by practical model-making and applied work, or data based on verifiable investigations.[23]

Nevertheless, Permaculture is, for many of those who engage with it, something much more than 'just' a regenerative ecological design tool – it represents an holistic worldview based on the principles of ecology and systems thinking that highlights the fundamental interconnectedness of all life on Earth.[24] Moreover, for many the permaculture design course experience itself is often understood as a 'religious experience' leading to a sense of 'empowerment' for the individual.[25] This clearly suggests an association with spirituality for some practitioners of Permaculture. David Holmgren's attitude to spirituality is much less antagonistic than Mollison's. He writes of the attractiveness of Permaculture to both the scientifically and spiritually inclined:

> Permaculture attracts many people raised in a culture of scientific rationalism because its wholism does not depend on a spiritual dimension. For others, permaculture reinforces their spiritual beliefs, even if these are simply a basic animism that recognises the earth as alive and, in some unknowable way, conscious. For most people on the planet, the spiritual and rational still coexist in some fashion. Can we really imagine a sustainable world without spiritual life in some form?[26]

Permaculture is not without its critics, however. In a remarkable document created by indigenous leaders and organisations, Western Permaculture and regenerative agriculture perspectives are criticised for their appropriation of indigenous practices, and especially for not going far enough in challenging the dominant worldviews that have contributed to the ecological crisis. The document explains that while Permaculture and regenerative agriculture 'borrow practices from Indigenous cultures, critically, they leave out our world views and continue the pattern of erasing our history and contributions to the modern world.' In this respect Permaculture may be unwittingly reproducing colonial attitudes.[27] While this may be the case, there is nevertheless the potential for permaculture to become much more critically aware of its own attitudes and approaches. Indeed, there are other regenerative horticulture practices that do not begin with the same assumptions. The Japanese horticulturalist and philosopher Masanobu Fukuoka's (1913–2008) 'natural farming' approach, for example, begins from very a different ontological position but with the core principles of 'no cultivation' (digging or ploughing, for example), 'no chemical fertilizer or prepared compost,' 'no weeding by tillage or herbicides' and 'no dependence on chemicals.'[28] The aim is to promote biodiversity alongside productivity, while building soil, all of which is couched in a wider holistic philosophical framework. Fukuoka explains:

> Scientists think they can understand nature. That is the stand they take. Because they are convinced they can understand nature, they are committed to investigating nature and putting it to use. But I think an understanding of nature lies beyond the reach of human intelligence [...] Why is it impossible to know nature? That which is conceived to be nature is only the *idea* of nature arising in each person's mind. The ones who see true nature are infants. They see without thinking straight and clear [...] An object seen in isolation from the whole is not the real thing.[29]

It is, therefore, possible to conceive of regenerative farming and gardening practices from a range of different spiritual and philosophical orientations, echoing the cultural ecologies discussed in Chapter One, and Julia Wright's notion of differing 'subtle agroecologies.'[30]

Learning Gardens and Bio-Psychodiversity

Like Zen gardens, permaculture gardens can also be conceived as philosophical gardens (see Chapter Eight). They encapsulate the principles of ecological design and the philosophy and ethics of permaculture and so represent a living illustration, while also providing very real environmental and social benefits. These are the perfect outdoor teaching spaces, where the principles of natural systems can be observed *in situ*. Outdoor learning, especially over an extended period of time, has been shown to 'evoke immediate shifts towards a stronger nature connectedness among students' in primary and secondary school settings.[31] The sustainability education researchers Dilafruz Williams and Jonathan Brown even go so far as to suggest that what they call 'learning gardens' can serve as an antidote to the compartmentalisation, individualism and competitiveness of mainstream education reforms, and provide an alternative to the mechanistic models that underpin them, by promoting a more holistic way of looking at the world. They explain that:

> School grounds and schoolyards are prime milieu that serve as the basis for ecological alternatives that contrast dominant mechanistic metaphors. Not only can learning gardens enhance mastery over literacy, numeracy, as well as life skills, but for us, soil and learning gardens also serve as animate options for reorienting the metaphoric imagination guiding modern education.[32]

Not only does an educational garden in the school setting provide opportunities for enhancing students' 'experiential sense of oneness with the natural world,'[33] thus promoting pro-environmental behaviour, but the garden itself can also become a hub for biodiversity, and so also, as discussed in Chapter Five, for *psychodiversity*. In the learning garden individual spiritual development, philosophical reflection and ecological enhancement can go hand in hand.

One School One Planet

Between 2016–19 I had the great fortune of being involved in the *One School One Planet* project with Steve Jones, a permaculture teacher with 25 years of experience in community gardening initiatives.[34] The project, funded by Powys County Council and the European Union Rural Development Fund, sought to investigate ways of incorporating permaculture principles and perspectives into the mainstream education curriculum. We did this by working with our local High School, exploring different approaches to teaching the principles of ecosystem functioning and regenerative agriculture – from 'traditional' classroom based sessions, with whiteboards and worksheets, to practical outdoor sessions working on a community garden project to promote biodiversity. Students from the High School, primarily from the Welsh Baccalaureate course, were actively involved in the construction of the garden, which served as an outdoor classroom for exploring the principles of permaculture, ecology and regenerative agriculture. Our efforts are documented in two short books[35] and in an interdisciplinary permaculture textbook called *Small and Slow Solutions*.[36] The project was from the outset an inter-disciplinary exploration, and the textbook we have created is intended to be accessible to teachers from across the school curriculum, for different ages and subject areas.

An important lesson that was learned over the course of the *One School One Planet* project is that collaboration in-school – between subjects and departments, for example – as well as between school and community groups is essential. The *One School One Planet* project was predominantly a community project with most of the outdoor activities away from the school campus, but much of the practical work was carried out in collaboration with Welsh Baccalaureate and Land-Based studies students from the school in order to meet their course requirements. Indeed, this kind of symbiotic relationship and stacking of functions is just the kind of ecological principle that permaculture gardens exemplify. Perhaps, then, there is room for collaboration between teachers and their classes and community gardening projects – where outdoor experiential learning and practical efforts to protect and enhance biodiversity can be used to underpin deeper philosophical reflection.

Spirituality and Practical Engagement

Religious Education is uniquely placed amongst the subjects taught in secondary schools to provide a place for the exploration and critical examination of different worldviews, and ways of understanding the roles and impacts of human beings in the world.[37] It could also provide a useful framework for exploring the different attitudes to the natural world that emerge from different religious, spiritual and philosophical traditions.[38] For example, as discussed in Chapter Three, in the build up to the United Nations Paris Climate Summit (COP21) in 2015 statements were issued by representatives of the major world religions calling on members of their respective faith communities to take positive action on climate change.[39] The climate declarations of the major world religions could be used to encourage discussion and debate in the classroom. In addition to classroom based discussion, outdoor learning, especially in the context of interconnected permaculture gardens, might also serve to facilitate reflection on, and understanding of complex concepts relating to different worldviews and cosmological models. The Norwegian religious education researcher Geir Skeie, for example, suggests that outdoor engagement with the world in the context of religious education can be particularly effective. He explains that:

> [...] religious education may offer a rich space for teaching and learning from and about space. [...] The material artefacts and religious places that are available in the local community offer possibilities for experiential learning, as do the encounter with people of different faiths and beliefs. Moving within, but also beyond established traditions and organised religion, there is even a possibility and challenge to engage in a personal relationship with the world.[40]

It may, therefore, be possible to foster a closer relationship with our ecology from a young age through outdoor learning, school gardening, or other forms of hands-on engagement with the living world.[41] This, in turn, may be used to explore deeper issues of philosophy, metaphysics and spirituality, including holistic, interconnected models of a living world. Furthermore, interacting with the living systems of gardens and wider landscapes may also serve the important function of enhancing understanding of the underlying metaphysical perspectives of the world religions, while also practically contributing to boosting biodiversity and to students' sense of wellbeing.

Summary

At the very least, the themes discussed in this chapter could be used to stimulate discussion in the classroom. Or, even better, as suggested by Rosa *et al.*, contact with nature 'could also be promoted during class time by taking students outside during lessons or by motivating them to engage in outdoor adventure experiences.'[42] It is unlikely that many schools will have the necessary resources, time or money to create on-campus permaculture or philosophical gardens, but there are other ways to bring nature and ecological principles into our teaching. Nature is, after all, all around us – we simply have to step outside to see natural processes in action. Indeed, going outside for a walk may be one of the simplest methods of connecting learning with the natural world. 'Philosophy walks' around the school campus – much as Aristotle is reputed to have done with his students – could quite easily connect teaching and learning with the elements, with long-lasting impacts on people's worldviews and behaviour.

CONCLUDING REMARKS

The vision that emerges from the tangle of strands discussed in this book is one that sees minds, and expressions of minds, as fundamental. A mind-based cosmology emerges. Taken together, panpsychism, animism, relational ontology and perspectivism, as well as insights from paranormal research, would seem to point in the direction of a complex cosmology – a cosmos of many minds interacting. Just as ecological systems tend toward maximum biodiversity, so might consciousness tend toward maximum psychodiversity. But there are other factors at work as well, which prevent these processes from occurring and flourishing – such as the many devastating impacts of anthropogenic climate change. One of the broader themes explored in this book is the role that a re-engagement with non-human intelligence – in the form of plants, animals, fairies, spirits and so on – might have in renewing our sense of connection to the natural world and in practically helping to promote biodiversity. Perhaps by re-enchanting our view of the natural world, re-connecting with the varieties of non-human intelligence that surround us, and leaving wild and green spaces for fairies at the bottom of the garden, we can contribute to halting the dramatic loss of biodiversity (and psychodiversity) that is currently blighting our planet. Cultivating and nurturing human and non-human minds, then – allowing the full expression of the visible and invisible – should be the responsibility of each and every one of us, and will become a central feature of a cosmology for the future. Education will play a key role in disseminating access to different models of engaging with the world, and subjects such as Religious Education in schools can provide an important platform for this, especially when combined with practical engagement with ecosystems and the enhancement of biodiversity through practices such as permaculture, 'natural farming,' or agroforestry. Animistic, spiritual, relational, perspectivist, panpsychist and paranormal understandings of the world all provide frameworks for conceptualising a personal relationship with the non-human world that surrounds and sustains us in new (and old) ways that can help us to escape from the anthropocene. If pro-environmental behaviours can be made meaningful to peoples' lives because of their spiritual resonances, then all the better. The possibilities offered by relational ontologies and other forms of traditional ecological knowledge for framing environmental conservation efforts have also become an important subject for scholarly discussion. These worldviews suggest that the living world is much more than just biomass – it is a super natural world teeming with all manner of different forms of life and mind, in which we all participate on a daily basis, and with which we must establish mutually beneficial relationships. It is up to us to work out how we are going to negotiate these relationships with the other-than-human world, but what is clear is that a new (or perhaps very old) inclusive approach to human and non-human minds in nature is needed to take us into the future.

NOTES

Notes to the Foreword by Nicholas Campion

1. Nicholas Campion, ed., *The Harmony Debates: Exploring a Practical Philosophy for a Sustainable Future* (Lampeter: Sophia Centre Press, 2020).

2. See Paul Griffiths and Stefan Linquist, 'The Distinction Between Innate and Acquired Characteristics', *The Stanford Encyclopaedia of Philosophy* (Spring 2022 Edition), Edward N. Zalta, ed., https://plato.stanford.edu/archives/spr2022/entries/innate-acquired/.

3. For spiders, see Fiona R. Cross and Robert R. Jackson, 'The execution of planned detours by spider-eating predators', *Journal of the Experimental Analysis of Behaviour* 105, no. 1 (18 January 2016): pp. 194–210; for ants, see Antoine Wystrach, 'We've Been Looking at Ant Intelligence the Wrong Way', *The Conversation*, 30 August 2013, https://theconversation.com/weve-been-looking-at-ant-intelligence-the-wrong-way-17619 [accessed 20 March 2023]; for lions, see Jason G. Goldman, 'Lions are the Brainiest of the Big Cats', *Scientific American* (1 December 2016), https://www.scientificamerican.com/article/lions-are-the-brainiest-of-the-big-cats/ [accessed 20 March 2023]; for starlings, see Royal Society for the Protection of Birds, 'Starling Murmurations' https://www.rspb.org.uk/birds-and-wildlife/wildlife-guides/bird-a-z/starling/starling-murmurations/. [accessed 20 March 2023].

4. 'Bees learn and "teach" others', *Nature* 538, 293 (2016), https://doi.org/10.1038/538293b.

5. Daniel Chamowitx, *What a Plant Knows: A Field Guide to the Senses* (London: Scientific American / Farrar, Straus & Giroux, 2017 [2012]); Eduardo Kohn, *How Forests Think: Toward an Anthropology Beyond the Human* (Berkeley: University of California Press, 2013); Stefano Mancuso, *The Revolutionary Genius of Plants: A New Understanding of Plant Intelligence and Behavior* (New York: Atria Books, 2018).

6. Arne Naess, 'The Shallow and the Deep, Long-Range Ecology Movement', *Inquiry* 16, no. 1–4 (1973): pp. 95–100 (p. 95).

7. Philippe Descola, *Beyond Nature and Culture* (Chicago: University of Chicago Press, 2005), p.307.

8. Andrew Benjamin, *Towards a Relational Ontology: Philosophy's Other Possibility* (Albany, NY: SUNY Press, 2015), p. 2.

9. Kenneth J. Gergen, *Relational Being: Beyond Self and Community* (Oxford: Oxford University Press, 2009).

10. Luci Attala, *How Water Makes Us Human: Engagements with the Materiality of Water* (Cardiff: University of Wales Press, 2019).

11. Øyvind Grøn and Arne Naess, *Einstein's Theory: A Rigorous Introduction for the Mathematically Untrained* (New York: Springer, 2011), p. 3.

12. Gilles Deleuze and Félix Guattari, *A Thousand Plateaus* (London: Bloomsbury 1999 [1988]), p. 6.

13. Plato, *Timaeus*, trans. R.G. Bury (Cambridge, MA: Harvard University Press, 1931), 30 C-D.

14. Timothy Morton, *Being Ecological* (London: Pelican, 2018), p. 1.

15. Morton, *Being Ecological*, p. 2.
16. Paul Heelas, Linda Woodhead, Benjamin Seel, Karin Tusting and Bron Szerszynski, *The Spiritual Revolution: Why Religion Is Giving Way to Spirituality* (Oxford: Blackwell, 2005), p. 5.

Notes from the Introduction

1. Jack Hunter, 'The MA in Ecology and Spirituality: Background and Interview with Dr. Andy Letcher', *Journal for the Study of Religious Experience* 7, no. 2 (2021): pp.140–45.
2. Steve Jones and Jack Hunter, *One School One Planet Vol. 1: Climate. Education. Innovation* (Llanrhaeadr-ym-Mochnant: Psychoid Books, 2018); Steve Jones and Jack Hunter, *One School One Planet Vol. 2: Permaculture, Education and Cultural Change* (Llanrhaeadr-ym-Mochnant: Psychoid Books, 2019).
3. Jack Hunter, 'Preliminary Report on Extraordinary Experience in Permaculture: Collapsing the Natural/Supernatural Divide', *Journal of Exceptional Experiences and Psychology* 6, no. 1 (2018): pp.12–22.
4. Jack Hunter, *Manifesting Spirits: An Anthropological Study of Mediumship and the Paranormal* (London: Aeon Books, 2020).
5. Jack Hunter, *Greening the Paranormal: Exploring the Ecology of Extraordinary Experience* (Hove: August Night, 2019).
6. Diana Espirito Santo and Jack Hunter, *Mattering the Invisible: Technologies, Bodies and the Realm of the Spectral* (Oxford: Berghahn, 2021); Jack Hunter and Rachael Ironside, *Folklore, People and Place: International Perspectives on Tourism and Tradition in Storied Places* (Abingdon: Routledge, 2023).
7. See for example Theodore Roszak, *The Voice of the Earth: An Exploration of Ecopsychology* (New York: Bantam, 1993); Warwick Fox, *Toward a Transpersonal Ecology: Developing New Foundations for Environmentalism* (Foxhole: Resurgence Books, 1995); Paul Devereux, *Re-visioning the Earth: A guide to opening the healing channels between mind and nature* (New York: Atria Books, 1996); Stephan Harding, *Animate Earth: Science, Intuition and Gaia* (Cambridge: Green Books, 2009); Bron Taylor, *Dark Green Religion: Nature Spirituality and the Planetary Future* (Chicago: University of Chicago Press, 2010); Lesley J. Sponsel, *Spiritual Ecology: A Quiet Revolution* (Westport: Praeger, 2012); Llewellyn Vaughan-Lee, *Spiritual Ecology: The Cry of the Earth* (Point Reyes: The Golden Sufi Center, 2019).

Notes from Chapter One

1. Eugene Odum, *Ecology* (New York: Holt, Rinehart and Winston, 1975): pp. 1–4.
2. Frank N. Egerton, 'A History of the Ecological Sciences: Early Greek Origins', *Bulletin of the Ecological Society of America* 82, no. 1 (2001): pp. 93–97; Anna Pavord, *The Naming of Names: The Search for Order in the World of Plants* (London: Bloomsbury, 2005), p. 21.
3. Bruce Winterhalder, 'The behavioural ecology of hunter gatherers', in *Hunter-Gatherers: An Interdisciplinary Perspective,* ed. Catherine Panter-Brick, Robert H. Layton and Peter A. Rowley-Conwy, (Cambridge: Cambridge University Press, 2001), pp. 12–13.

4. Fikret Berkes, 'Traditional Ecological Knowledge in Perspective', in *Traditional Ecological Knowledge: Concepts and Cases,* ed. Julian T. Inglis, (Ottawa: International Program on Traditional Ecological Knowledge, 1993), pp. 1–10.

5. Robert C. Stauffer, 'Haeckel, Darwin, and Ecology', *The Quarterly Review of Biology* 32, no. 2 (1957): pp. 138–44.

6. Richard Weikart, 'Progress through Racial Extermination: Social Darwinism, Eugenics, and Pacifism in Germany, 1860–1918', *German Studies Review* 26, no. 2 (2003): p. 275.

7. Frank N. Egerton, 'History of Ecological Sciences, Part 47: Ernst Haeckel's Ecology', *Bulletin of the Ecological Society of America* 94, no. 3 (2013): pp. 222–24.

8. Odum, *Ecology,* p. 1.

9. Daniel Simberloff, 'A Succession of Paradigms in Ecology: Essentialism to Materialism and Probabilism', *Synthese* 43, no. 1 (1980): pp. 3–39.

10. Taylor, *Dark Green Religion.*

11. Charles O. Frake, 'Cultural Ecology and Ethnography', *American Anthropologist* 64, no. 1 (1962): p. 53.

12. Roy A. Rappaport, *Ecology, Meaning, and Religion* (Berkeley: North Atlantic Books, 1979), p. 97.

13. Bron Taylor, *Avatar and Nature Spirituality* (Waterloo: Wilfrid Laurier University Press, 2013); Dell deChant, 'Religion and Ecology in Popular Culture', in *Religion and Popular Culture,* ed. Terry Ray Clark and Dan W. Clanton, Jr., (Abingdon: Routledge, 2012).

14. Suzanne W. Simard *et al.,* 'Mycorrhizal networks: Mechanisms, ecology and modelling', *Fungal Biology Reviews* 26 (2012): pp. 39–60.

15. O.T. Oss and O.N. Oeric, *Psilocybin Magic Mushroom Grower's Guide* (Grand Junction: Quick American Archives, 2006); Paul Stamets, *Mycelium Running: How Mushrooms Can Help Save the World* (Berkeley: Ten Speed Press, 2005); Peter Wohlleben, *The Hidden Life of Trees: What they Feel, How they Communicate — Discoveries from a Secret World* (London: William Collins, 2016); Merlin Sheldrake, *Entangled Life: How Fungi Make Our Worlds, Change Our Minds, and Shape Our Futures* (London: Vintage, 2020); Aliya Whiteley, *The Secret Life of Fungi: Discoveries from a Hidden World* (London: Elliott and Thompson Ltd., 2020).

16. Aubrey Byron, 'The People Who Study Fungus Know Why It's Suddenly Taking Over Horror: The Last of Us isn't the only recent story to rely on fungal fright', https://slate.com/culture/2023/02/last–of–us–hbo–mushroom–fungus–horror.html [accessed 25 February 2023].

17. Eugene Odum, 'The Strategy of Ecosystem Development', *Science,* 164 (1969): p. 262.

18. Gordon Dickinson and Kevin Murphy, *Ecosystems* (Abingdon: Routledge, 2007), p. 11.

19. Fritjof Capra and Pier Luigi Luisi, *The Systems View of Life: A Unifying Vision* (Cambridge: Cambridge University Press, 2014).

20. Dickinson and Murphy, *Ecosystems,* p. 11–13.

21. Lucie M. Bland, *et al.,* 'Developing a standardized definiton of ecosystem collapse for risk assessent', *Frontiers in Ecology and the Environment* 16, no. 1 (2018): pp. 29–36.

22. Dickinson and Murphy, *Ecosystems,* p. 4.

23. Dickinson and Murphy, *Ecosystems,* p. 2.

24. Frederic E. Clements, *Plant Succession and Indicators* (New York: H.W. Wilson, 1928).

25. Odum, 'The Strategy of Ecosystems Development', p. 262.

26. Lawrence R. Walker, David A. Wardle, Richard D. Bardgett and Bruce D. Clarkson, 'The use of chronosequences in studies of ecological succession and soil development', *Journal of Ecology* 98 (2010): pp. 725–36.

27. Lynn Margulis and Bermudes, 'Symbiosis as a Mechanism of Evolution: Status of Cell Symbiosis Theory', *Symbiosis* 1 (1985): 101–24; Michael W. Gray, 'Lynn Margulis and the endosymbiont hypothesis: 50 years later', *Molecular Biology of the Cell* 28, no. 10 (2017).

28. Dickinson and Murphy, *Ecosystems*, p. 24.

29. Robert T. Paine, 'Food Web Complexity and Species Diversity', *The American Naturalist* 100, no. 910 (1966): pp. 65–75.

30. Michael L. Pace *et al.*, 'Trophic cascades revealed in diverse ecosystems', *Trends in Ecology and Evolution* 14, no. 12 (1999): p. 483.

31. George Monbiot, *Feral: Rewilding the Land, Sea and Human Life* (London: Penguin, 2014), pp. 84–85.

32. Pace *et al.*, 'Trophic cascades revealed in diverse ecosystems', p. 483.

33. See Nicholas Campion, 'Introduction', in Nicholas Campion (ed.), *The Harmony Debates: Exploring a practical philosophy for a sustainable future* (Lampeter: Sophia Centre Press, 2020), pp. 17–29; Jack Hunter, 'Harmony and Ecology', in Campion (ed.), *The Harmony Debates*, pp. 209–20; Stephan Harding, 'Nature's Fragile Seminars', in Campion (ed.), *The Harmony Debates*, pp. 221–36; Angie Polkey, 'The Permaculture Path to Harmony: a study of personal emergence', in Campion (ed.), *The Harmony Debates*, pp. 411–16; John Sauven, 'Harmony and the Climate Crisis', Campion (ed.) *The Harmony Debates*, pp, 439–43; Rupert Sheldrake, 'Harmony, Science and Spirituality', in Campion (ed.), *The Harmony Debates:*, pp. 237–45.

34. Mario Bunge, 'Survey of the Interpretations of Quantum Mechanics', *American Journal of Physics* 24, no. 4 (1956): pp. 272–86; Christopher A. Fuchs and Asher Peres, 'Quantum Theory Needs No "Interpretation,"' *Physics Today* 53, no. 3 (2000): pp. 70–71.

35. Simberloff, 'A Succession of Paradigms in Ecology'.

36. Thomas Kuhn, *The Structure of Scientific Revolutions* (Chicago: University of Chicago Press, 1962), p. 10.

37. Donato Bergandi, 'Multifaceted Ecology Between Organicism, Emergentism and Reductionism', in *Ecology Revisited: Reflecting on Concepts, Advancing Science,* ed. A. Schwarz and K. Jax, (Dordrecht: Springer, 2011), pp. 31–43.

38. John B. Foster and Brett Clark, 'The Sociology of Ecology: Ecological Organicism Versus Ecosystem Ecology in the Social Construction of Ecological Science, 1926–1935', *Organization and Environment* 21, no. 3 (2008): p. 326.

39. Charles Mann, 'Lynn Margulis: Science's unruly Earth Mother', *Science* 252, no. 5004 (1991): pp. 378–81.

40. Michel Loreau *et al.*, 'A New Look at the Relationship Between Diversity and Stability', in *Biodiversity and Ecosystem Functioning,* ed. Michel Loreau, Shahid Naeem and Pablo Inchausti (Oxford: Oxford University Press, 2002), p. 79.

41. Loreau *et al.*, 'A New Look at the Relationship Between Diversity and Stability', p. 80.

42. Shigeo Yachi and Michel Loreau, 'Biodiversity and ecosystem productivity in a fluctuating environment: The insurance hypothesis', *PNAS* 96, no. 4 (1999): p. 483.

43. Loreau *et al.*, 'A New Look at the Relationship Between Diversity and Stability'.

44. James Lovelock, *Gaia: A New Look at Life on Earth* (Oxford: Oxford University Press, 2000).

45. James Lovelock and Lynn Margulis, 'Atmospheric homeostasis by and for the biosphere: the gaia hypothesis', *Tellus* 26, nos. 1–2 (1974): pp. 2–10.

46. Luciano Onori and Guido Visconti, 'The GAIA theory: from Lovelock to Margulis. From homeostatic to a cognitive autopoietic worldview', *Rend. Fis. Acc. Lincei* 23 (2012): p. 376.

47. James Lovelock, 'Atmospheric Fluorine Compounds as Indicators of Air Movements', *Nature* 230 (1971): p. 379.

48. James Lovelock, 'A Physical Basis for Life Detection Experiments', *Nature* 207 (1965): pp. 568–70.

49. Richard Dawkins, *The Extended Phenotype: The Gene as the Unit of Selection* (Oxford: Oxford University Press, 1982), p. 237.

50. James Kirchner, 'The Gaia Hypotheses: Are They Testable? Are They Useful?' *Philosophical Foundations of Gaia* (1991): pp. 38–46.

51. Kirchner, 'The Gaia Hypotheses', p. 39.

52. Richard J. Huggett, 'Ecosphere, biosphere, or Gaia? What to call the global ecosystem', *Global Ecology and Biogeography* 8 (1999): p. 425.

53. Huggett, 'Ecosphere, biosphere, or Gaia?', p. 430.

54. Kirchner, 'The Gaia Hypotheses', p. 46.

55. Taylor, *Dark Green Religion*, p. 16.

56. Harding, *Animate Earth*.

57. Timothy M. Lenton and Bruno Latour, 'Gaia 2.0 – Could humans add some level of self-aware-ness to Earth's self-regulation?' *Science* 361, no. 6407 (2018): p. 1066.

Notes to Chapter Two

1. Margaret Chatterjee, *The Concept of Spirituality* (New Delhi: Allied Publishers Private Limited, 1989), p. vi.

2. René Descartes, *Discourse on Method and The Meditations* (London: Penguin, 1968), pp. 164–65.

3. Jan G. Platvoet, 'Does God have a Body? On the Materiality of Akan Spirituality', in *New Paths in the Study of Religions: Festschrift in Honour of Michael Pye on his 65th Birthday.* ed. C. Kleine, M. Schrimpf and K. Triplett (Munich: Biblion Verlag, 2004), pp. 175–76.

4. Platvoet, 'Does God have a Body?', p. 186.

5. Martin Mills, 'Anthropology and Religious Studies', in *The SAGE Handbook of Social Anthropology*, ed., R. Fardon, *et al.* (London: Sage, 2012), pp. 183–96.

6. Émile Durkheim, *The Elementary Forms of the Religious Life* (Oxford: Oxford University Press, 2008).

7. Edward Burnett Tylor, *Anthropology: An Introduction to the Study of Man and Civilization* (London: C. A. Watts, 1930).

8. William James, *The Varieties of Religious Experience* (New York: Barnes and Noble, 2004); Max Weber, *The Sociology of Religion* (London: Methuen, 1965); Sigmund

Freud, *Totem and Taboo* (Abingdon: Routledge, 2007).

9. Bronislaw Malinwoski, *Coral Gardens and their Magic: A Study of the Methods of Tilling Soil and Agricultural Rites in the Trobriand Islands* (Woking: Unwin Brothers, 1935).

10. Fiona Bowie, *The Anthropology of Religion* (Oxford: Blackwell, 2006), p. 151.

11. Arnold van Gennep, *The Rites of Passage* (Chicago: University of Chicago Press, 1961).

12. Victor Turner, 'Liminality and Communitas', in *Readings in the Anthropology of Religion*, ed. Michael Lambek, (Oxford: Blackwell, 2004), pp. 358–74.

13. Margit Warburg, 'Graduation in Denmark: Secular Ritual and Civil Religion', *Journal of Ritual Studies* 23, no. 2 (2009): pp. 31–42.

14. Edward E. Evans-Pritchard, *Witchcraft, Oracles and Magic Among the Azande* (Oxford: Oxford University Press, 1975), p. 30.

15. Auguste Comte, 'The Positive Philosophy', in *Sociological Perspectives*, ed. Kenneth Thompson and Jeremy Tunstall, (London: Penguin, 1976), pp. 18–32.

16. Durkheim, *The Elementary Forms of Religious Life*.

17. Kenneth Surin, 'Marxism and religion', *Critical Research on Religion* 1, no. 1 (2013): pp 9–14.

18. Marion Bowman, 'More of the Same? Christianity, Vernacular Religion and Alternative Spirituality in Glastonbury', in *Beyond New Age: Exploring Alternative Spirituality*, ed. Steven Sutcliffe and Marion Bowman, (Edinburgh: Edinburgh University Press, 2000), p. 85.

19. Navtej K. Purewal and Virinder S. Kalwa, 'Women's 'popular' practices as critique: Vernacular religion in Indian and Pakistani Punjab', *Women's Studies International Forum* 33 (2010): p. 383.

20. Jeff Astley, *Ordinary Theology: Looking, Listening and Learning in Theology* (Aldershot: Ashgate, 2002).

21. Madeline Castro *et al.*, 'The paranormal is (still) normal: The sociological implications of a survey of paranormal experiences in Great Britain', *Sociological Research Online* 19, no 3 (2014).

22. Paul Heelas and Linda Woodhead, *The Spiritual Revolution: Why Religion is Giving Way to Spirituality* (Oxford: Blackwell, 2005), p. 1.

23. Heelas and Woodhead, *The Spiritual Revolution,* p. 6.

24. Graham Harvey, 'If 'Spiritual But Not Religious' People Are Not Religious What Difference Do They Make?' *Journal for the Study of Spirituality* 6, no. 2 (2016): pp. 128–41.

25. Jeff Astley and Ann Christie, *Taking Ordinary Theology Seriously* (Cambridge: Grove Books, 2007).

26. Edith Turner, *Experiencing Ritual: A New Interpretation of African Healing* (Philadelphia: University of Pennsylvania Press, 1998), p. 149.

27. Edith Turner, 'The reality of spirits: A tabooed or permitted field of study?' *Anthropology of Consciousness* 4, no. 1 (1993): pp. 9–12.

28. Castro *et al.*, 'The paranormal is (still) normal'; Neil Dagnall *et al.*, 'Paranormal Experience, Belief in the Paranormal and Anomalous Beliefs', *Paranthropology: Journal of Anthropological Approaches to the Paranormal* 7, no. 1 (2015): pp. 4–14; David J. Hufford, *The Terror That Comes in the Night: An Experience-Centered Study of Supernatural Assault Traditions* (Philadelphia: University of Pennsylvania Press, 1982).

29. Bowman, 'More of the same?', pp. 86–93.

30. Adam Possamai and Murray Lee, 'Hyper-real religions: Fear, anxiety and late-modern religious innovation', *Journal of Sociology* 47, no. 3 (2011): pp. 227–42.

31. Taylor, *Avatar and Nature Spirituality*.

32. Gordon Lynch, *Understanding Theology and Popular Culture* (Oxford: Blackwell, 2005).

33. Greg McCann, 'Bioregions and Spirit Places: Taking Up Jim Dodge's Long-Lost Suggestion', *The Trumpeter* 27, no. 3 (2017): pp. 10–26.

34. John Grim, 'Indigenous Traditions: Religion and Ecology', in *The Oxford Handbook of Religion and Ecology,* ed. R.S. Gottlieb, (Oxford: Oxford University Press, 2006).

35. Grim, 'Indigenous Traditions'.

36. Suzanne Owen, 'The World Religions paradigm: time for a change', *Arts and Humanities in Higher Education* 10, no. 3 (2011): pp. 253–68.

37. Denise Cush, 'Paganism in the Classroom', *British Journal of Religious Education* 19, no. 2 (1998): pp. 83–94; James D. Holt, 'The Church of Jesus Christ of Latter-Day Saints in the RE classroom', *Resource* 24, no. 3 (2002): pp. 6–8; James D. Holt, 'Jehovah's Witnesses and the RE Classroom', *Resource* 26, no. 2 (2004): pp. 16–19.

38. Jacomijn C. Van de Kooij, Doret J. de Ruyter and Siebren Miedema, 'The Merits of Using "Worldview" in Religious Education', *Religious Education* 112, no. 2 (2016): pp. 172–84.

39. James, *Varieties of Religious Experience*, p. 39.

40. Stanley Krippner, 'Personal Mythology: An Introduction to the Concept', *The Humanistic Psychologist* 18, no. 2 (1990): p. 139.

41. Nicholas Campion, *Astrology and Cosmology in the World's Religions* (New York: New York University Press, 2012), p. 10.

42. Hunter, *Manifesting Spirits*.

43. David Hay and Rebecca Nye, *The Spirit of the Child* (London: Jessica Kingsley Publishing, 2006), p. 22.

44. Doug Oman, 'Defining religion and spirituality', in *Handbook of the psychology of religion and spirituality,* ed. R. F. Paloutzian & C. L. Park, (Guildford: The Guildford Press, 2013), p. 24.

Notes to Chapter Three

1. 'Our Living Planet Report', WWF, https://wwf.panda.org/knowledge_hub/all_publications/living_planet_report_2018/ [accessed 23 January 2023].

2. Aelys M. Humphreys *et al.*, 'Global dataset shows geography and life form predict modern plant extinction and rediscovery', *Nature Ecology and Evolution* 3 (2019): pp. 1043–47.

3. Bruno Latour, *Facing Gaia: Eight Lectures on the New Climatic Regime* (Cambridge: Polity Press, 2017), p. 9.

4. Antoinette Mannion, *Global Environmental Change* (Harlow: Longman Scientific and Technical, 1994).

5. Timothy Morton, *The Ecological Thought* (Cambridge, MA: Harvard University Press, 2010), p. 130; Timothy Morton, *Hyperobjects: Philosophy and Ecology after the End of the World* (Minneapolis: University of Minnesota Press, 2013).

6. J. R. Petit, *et al.*, 'Climate and atmospheric history of the past 420,000 years from the

Vostok ice core, Antarctica', *Nature* 399 (1999): 429–36.

7. Markku Rummukainen, 'Changes in climate and weather extremes in the 21st century', *Wiley Interdisciplinary Reviews: Climate Change* 3, no. 2 (2012): pp. 115–29.

8. Tanja Bosak *et al.*, 'Morphological record of oxygenic photosynthesis in conical stromatolites', *PNAS* 106, no. 27 (2009): pp. 10939–43.

9. 'Emissions Gap Report 2022', UNEP, https://www.unep.org/re- sources/emissions-gap-report-2022 [accessed 28 December 2022].

10. Svante Arrhenius, 'On the influence of carbonic acid in the air upon the temperature of the ground', *The London, Edinburgh and Dublin Philosophical Magazine and Journal of Science* 41, no. 241 (1896): pp. 365–87.

11. Susan Solomon *et al.*, 'Irreversible climate damage due to carbon dioxide emissions', *PNSA* 106, no. 6 (2008): pp. 1704–9.

12. Jones and Hunter, *One School One Planet Vol. 2*.

13. David Pimentel *et al.*, 'Environmental and Economic Costs of Soil Erosion and Conservation Benefits', *Science* 267 (1995): pp. 1117–23.

14. W. Hoffman, J. Beyea and J.H. Cook, 'Ecology of agricultural monocultures: Some consequences for biodiversity in biomass energy farms', *Second biomass conference of the Americas: Energy, environment, agriculture, and industry. Proceedings* (1995).

15. Ken Norris, 'Agriculture and biodiversity conservation: opportunity knocks', *Conservation Letters* 1 (2008): p. 2.

16. Bradley J. Cardinale *et al.*, 'Biodiversity loss and its impact on humanity', *Nature* 486, 7401 (2012): pp. 59–67.

17. Cardinale *et al.*, 'Biodiversity loss', pp. 2–5.

18. Cardinale *et al.*, 'Biodiversity loss', pp. 2–5.

19. Paul Jepson and Cain Blythe, *Rewilding: The Radical New Science of Ecological Recovery* (London: Icon Books, 2020).

20. Andrew Glikson, 'Fire and human evolution: The deep-time blueprints of the Anthropocene', *Anthropocene* 3 (2013): pp. 89–92.

21. Simon L. Lewis and Mark A. Maslin, 'Defining the Anthropocene', *Nature* 519 (2015): p. 177.

22. Lewis and Maslin, 'Defining the Anthropocene', p. 177.

23. Lynn White Jr., 'The Historical Roots of Our Ecologic Crisis', *Science* 155, no. 3767 (1967): p. 1205.

24. White Jr., 'The Historical Roots of Our Ecologic Crisis'.

25. White Jr., 'The Historical Roots of Our Ecologic Crisis'.

26. White Jr., 'The Historical Roots of Our Ecologic Crisis', p, 1205.

27. Jason W. Moore, 'The Capitalocene, Part I: on the nature and origins of our ecological crisis', *Journal of Peasant Studies* 44, no 3 (2017): pp. 594–630.

28. Donna Harraway, 'Anthropocene, Capitalocene, Plantationocene, Chthulucene: Making Kin', *Environmental Humanities* 6 (2015): p. 160.

29. Harraway, 'Anthropocene, Capitalocene, Plantationocene, Chthulucene', p. 160.

30. Harraway, 'Anthropocene, Capitalocene, Plantationocene, Chthulucene', p. 160.

31. Rachel Carson, *The Silent Spring* (Boston: Houghton and Mifflin, 1962).

32. Frank Zelko, 'Scaling Greenpeace: From Local Activism to Global Governance', *Historical Social Research* 42 (2017): pp. 318–42.

33. Neil Gunningham, 'Averting Climate Catastrophe: Environmental activism, Extinction Rebellion and Coalitions of Influence', *King's Law Journal* 30, no. 2 (2019):

pp. 194–202.

34. Christopher Rootes, 'Environmental movements: From the local to the global', *Environmental Politics* 8, no. 1 (1999): pp. 1–12.

35. Greta Thunberg, *No One Is Too Small to Make a Difference* (London: Penguin, 2019).

36. 'What is the Paris Agreement?' UNFCCC, https://unfccc.int/process-and-meetings/the-paris-agreement [accessed 25 February 2023].

37. Johann Rockström *et al.*, 'A Roadmap for Rapid Decarbonization', *Science* 355, no. 6331 (2017): pp. 1269–71.

38. 'World is off track to meet Paris Agreement climate targets', UNEP, https://unepccc.org/world-is-off-track-to-meet-paris-agreement-climate-targets/ [accessed 27 February 2023].

39. White Jr., 'The Historical Roots of Our Ecologic Crisis', p. 1207.

40. Bron Taylor, Gretel Van Wieren and Bernard Daley Zaleha, 'Review: Lynn White Jr. and the greening of religion hypothesis', *Conservation Biology* 30, no. 5 (2016): pp. 1000–9.

41. Jonathan Chaplin, 'The global greening of religion', *Palgrave Communication* 2, 16047 (2016).

42. Pope Francis, *Laudato Si,* [accessed 25 February 2023], https://www.vatican.va/content/dam/francesco/pdf/encyclicals/documents/papa-francesco_20150524_enciclica-laudato-si-en.pdf

43. Morton, *The Ecological Thought,* p. 130.

44. Chaplin, 'The Global Greening of Religion, p. 2.

45. Chaplin, 'The Global Greening of Religion, p. 3.

46. 'Islamic Declaration on Global Climate Change', https://cambridgecentralmosque.org/wp-content/uploads/2020/03/writings-climate-declaration-mwb.pdf [accessed 13 March 2023].

47. Val Plumwood, 'Nature in the Active Voice', *Australian Humanities Review* 46 (2010): pp. 113–29.

48. Randolph Haluza-DeLay, 'Religion and climate change: varieties in viewpoints and practices', *Wiley Interdisciplinary Reviews: Climate Change* 5, no. 2 (2014): p. 263.

49. Arne Naess, 'The Shallow and the Deep, Long Range Ecology Movement. A Summary', *Inquiry* 16 (1973): pp. 95–100.

50. Edward O. Wilson, 'Biophilia and the Conservation Ethic', in *Evolutionary Perspectives on Environmental Problems*, ed. Dustin J. Penn and Iver Mysterud, (Abingdon: Routledge, 2007).

51. Arne Naess, 'Intrinsic value: Will the defenders of nature please rise', in *Wisdom in the Open Air*, ed. P. Reed and D. Rothenberg, (Minneapolis: University of Minnesota Press, 1993), pp. 70–82.

52. Arne Naess, 'Self-realization: An ecological approach to being in the world', in *Deep ecology for the twenty-first century,* ed. George Sessions, (Boston: Shambhala, 1995).

53. Arne Naess, *Ecology of Wisdom* (London: Penguin Books, 2008).

54. Whit Hibbard, 'Ecopsychology: A Review', *The Trumpeter* 9, no. 2 (2003): p. 27.

55. Roszak, *The Voice of the Earth.*

56. Roszak, *The Voice of the Earth,* p. 16.

57. Roszak, *The Voice of the Earth,* p. 16.

58. Ralph Metzner, *Green Psychology: Transforming Our Relationship to the Earth*

(Rochester: Park Street Press, 1999), p. 2.
59. Joanna Macy, 'Working Through Environmental Despair', in *Ecopsychology: Restoring the earth, healing the mind*, ed. T. Roszak *et al.*, (Sierra Club Books, 1995).
60. John Seed *et al.*, *Thinking Like a Mountain: Towards a Council of All Beings* (Gariola Island: New Catalyst Books, 2007), p. 15.
61. Alysha Jones and David Segal, 'Unsettling Ecopsychology: Addressing Settler Colonialism in Ecopsychology Practice', *Ecopsychology* 10, no. 3 (2018): pp. 127–36.
62. Laura Sewall and Thomas L. Fleischner, 'Why Ecopsychology Needs Natural History', *Ecopsychology* 11, no. 2 (2019): pp. 78–80.
63. Patrick Curry, *Ecological Ethics* (London: Polity, 2019), p. xi.
64. Curry, *Ecological Ethics*, p. xiii.

Notes to Chapter Four

1. Jeffrey J. Kripal, *The Flip: Epiphanies of Mind and the Future of Knowledge* (New York: Bellevue Literary Press, 2019).
2. Dewi Arwel Hughes, 'Mysticism: the perennial philosophy?', in *Mysticisms East and West,* ed. C. Partridge and T. Gabriel, (Cumbria: Paternoster, 2003), p. 306.
3. James, *Varieties of Religious Experience.*
4. Caroline Franks Davis, *The Evidential Force of Religious Experience* (Oxford: Oxford University Press, 1989).
5. Brian L. Lancaster, *Approaches to Consciousness: The Marriage of Science and Mysticism* (Basingstoke: Palgrave Macmillan, 2004), pp. 21–24.
6. Robert.C. Zaehner, *Mysticism Sacred and Profane* (Oxford: Oxford University Press, 1957).
7. 'Sir Alister Hardy (1896–1985) Inventor of the CPR', Continuous Plankton Recorder Survey, https://www.cprsurvey.org/about-us/sir-alister-hardy-and-the-continuous-plankton-recorder-cpr-survey/ [accessed 25 February 2023].
8. 'Religious Experience Research Centre', RERC, https://www.uwtsd.ac.uk/research/humanities-lampeter/religious-experience-research-centre-/ [accessed 25 February 2023].
9. Taylor, *Dark Green Religion*, p. 13.
10. David Hay, 'Zoology and Religion', https://metanexus.net/zoology-and-religion-work-alister-hardy/ [accessed 25 February 2023].
11. Taylor, *Dark Green Religion.*
12. Aldo Leopold, *A Sand County Almanac: And Sketches Here and There* (Oxford: Oxford University Press, 1949).
13. James, *Varieties of Religious Experience.*
14. Walter T. Stace, *Mysticism and Philosophy* (London: Macmillan, 1960), p. 15.
15. Alister Hardy, *The Spiritual Nature of Man* (Lampeter: Religious Experience Research Centre,1979), p. 81.
16. Paul Marshall, *Mystical Encounters with the Natural World: Experiences and Explanations* (Oxford: Oxford University Press, 2005), p. vii.
17. Roszak, *The Voice of the Earth.*
18. Jasmine L. Trigwell, Andrew J.P. Francis and Kathleen L. Bagot, 'Nature Connectedness and Eudaimonic Well-Being: Spirituality as a Potential Mediator', *Ecopsychology* 6, no.4 (2014): pp. 241–51.
19. Francis-Vincent Anthony, Chris A. M. Hermans and Carl Sterkens, 'A comparative

study of mystical experience among Christian, Muslim, and Hindu students in Tamil Nadu, India', *Journal for the Scientific Study of Religion* 49, no. 2 (2010): pp. 264–77.

20. RERC Reference: 10003, Male, no details.

21. RERC Reference: 002780, Male, 1941.

22. RERC Reference: 003039, Female, 1922.

23. Graham Harvey, *Animism: Respecting the Living World* (London: Hurst & Company, 2005), p. xi.

24. RERC Reference: 000035, Male, 1917.

25. RERC Reference: 002384, Female, 1960.

26. Clements, *Plant Succession*.

27. Jack Hunter, *Deep Weird: The Varieties of High Strangeness Experience* (Hove: August Night, 2023).

28. Rudolf Otto, *The Idea of the Holy* (Oxford: Oxford University Press, 1958), p. 13.

29. Simon Young, *The Fairy Census, 2014–2017*, http://www.fairyist.- com/wp-content/ uploads/2014/10/The-Fairy-Census-2014-2017-1.pdf [accessed 22 July 2019].

30. Fairy Census, §78, England (Lincolnshire). Male; 1980s.

31. Fairy Census, §190, Wales (Rhondda). Female; 2000s.

32. David Bryce Yaden, *et al.*, 'The Varieties of Self-Transcendent Experience', *Review of General Psychology* 21, no. 2 (2017): pp. 1–18.

33. Kripal, *The Flip*.

34. John E. Mack, *Abduction: Human Encounters with Aliens* (New York: Ballantine Books, 1995), pp. 434–35.

35. Kenneth Ring and Evelyn Elsaesser Valarino, *Lessons from the light: What we can learn from the Near-Death Experience* (Needham: Moment Point Press, 2006), p. 125.

36. Matthias Forstmann and Christina Sagioglou, 'Lifetime experience with (classic) psychedelics predicts pro-environmental behavior through an increase in nature relatedness', *Journal of Psychopharmacology* 31, no. 8 (2017): pp. 975–88.

37. Peter McCue, *Zones of Strangeness: An Examination of Paranormal and UFO Hot Spots* (Bloomington: AuthorHouse, 2012): p. 489.

38. Val Plumwood, 'Surviving a Crocodile Attack', https://www.utne.- com/arts/being-prey/ [accessed 31 December 2022].

39. Lance Foster, 'The Invisible Ecosystem', in *Greening the Paranormal: Exploring the Ecology of Extraordinary Experience*, ed. Jack Hunter, (Hove: August Night, 2019).

40. Timothy Grieve-Carlson, 'The Hidden Predator', in *Greening the Paranormal: Exploring the Ecology of Extraordinary Experience*, ed. Jack Hunter, (Hove: August Night, 2019).

41. Hunter, 'A Preliminary Report on Permaculture and Extraordinary Experience'.

42. Hunter, 'A Preliminary Report on Permaculture and Extraordinary Experience'.

43. Maria Izabel Vieira Botelho *et al.*, '"I made a pact with God, with nature and with myself": exploring deep ecology', *Agroecology and Sustainable Food Systems* 40, no. 2 (2016): p. 218.

44. Mark A. Schroll, *Ecology, Cosmos and Consciousness: Comic-Book Lore, Dreams and Inquiries into Various Other Transpersonal Ecosophical States* (Llanrhaeadr-ym-Mochnant: Psychoid Books, 2018), p 37.

Notes to Chapter Five

1. James Gallagher, 'More than half of your body is not human', BBC News, https://www.bbc.co.uk/news/health-43674270 [accessed 25 February 2023].

2. 'The Water in You: Water and the Human Body', USGS, https://www.usgs.gov/special-topics/water-science-school/science/water-you-water-and-human-body [accessed 28 February 2023].

3. R. A. Houghton, 'Biomass', in *Encyclopedia of Ecology,* ed. S.E. Jørgensen & B.D. Fath, (Elsevier, 2008).

4. R. B. Myneni, *et al.*, 'A large carbon sink in the woody biomass of northern forests', *Earth, Atmospheric and Planetary Sciences* 98, no. 26 (2001): pp. 14784–89.

5. 'Plant for the Planet: The Billion Tree Campaign', UNEP, https://www.unep.org/resources/publication/plant-planet-billion-tree-campaign [accessed 28 February 2023].

6. 'Forestry Facts and Figures 2021: A summary of statistics about woodland and forestry in the UK', Forestry Research, https://cdn.forestresearch.gov.uk/ 2021/09/frfs021_zgb9htp.pdf [accessed 28 February 2023].

7. Jeremy Narby, *Intelligence in Nature: An Inquiry into Knowledge* (New York: Tarcher-perigee, 2006), p. 43.

8. Janet Mann and Eric M. Patterson, 'Tool Use by Aquatic Animals', *Philosophical Transactions of the Royal Society – Biological Sciences* 368, no. 1630 (2013): pp. 1–11.

9. Peter Godfrey-Smith, *Other Minds: The Octopus and the Evolution of Intelligence Life* (London: William Collins, 2017).

10. Stefano Mancuso and Alessandra Viola, *Brilliant Green: The Surprising History and Science of Plant Intelligence* (London: Island Press, 2015), p. 146.

11. Mancuso and Viola, *Brilliant Green,* p. 5.

12. Monica Gagliano et al., 'Experience teaches plants to learn faster and forget slower in environments where it matters', *Oecologia* 175, no. 1 (2014): pp. 63–72.

13. Monica Gagliano et al., 'Tuned in: plant roots use sound to locate water', *Oecologia* 184, no. 1 (2017): pp. 151–60.

14. Monica Gagliano, 'Green symphonies: a call for studies on acoustic communication in plants', *Behavioural Ecology* 24, no. 4 (2013): pp. 789–96.

15. Brenner *et al.*, 'Plant neurobiology: an integrated view of plant signalling', *TRENDS in Plant Science* 11, no. 8 (2006): pp. 413–19.

16. Wohlleben, *The Hidden Life of Trees.*

17. Sharon Elizabeth Kingsland, 'Facts or Fairy Tales? Peter Wohlleben and the Hidden Life of Trees', *Bulletin of the Ecological Society of America* 99, no. 4 (2018).

18. Rupert Sheldrake, *The Science Delusion* (London: Coronet, 2012).

19. Andrew Adamatzky, 'Language of fungi derived from their electrical spiking activity', *Royal Society Open Science* 9 (2022).

20. Monica Gagliano, *Thus Spoke the Plant: A Remarkable Journey of Groundbreaking Scientific Discoveries and Personal Encounters with Plants* (Berkeley: North Atlantic Books, 2018).

21. Peter Tompkins and Christopher Bird, *The Secret Life of Plants* (New York: Harper, 2002), p. 4.

22. Cleve Backster, 'Evidence of Primary Perception in Plant Life', *International Journal of Parapsychology* 10, no. 4 (1968): pp. 329–48.

23. Backster, 'Evidence of Primary Perception in Plant Life', pp. 333–45.

24. Tompkins and Bird, *The Secret Life of Plants*.

25. Mancuso and Viola, *Brilliant Green*, p. 5.

26. Tylor, *Anthropology*, p. 88.

27. Charles Darwin, *On the Origins of Species* (London: Penguin, 1985).

28. George W. Stocking Jr., *Race, Culture, and Evolution: Essays in the History of Anthropology* (Chicago: University of Chicago Press, 1982).

29. Harry Olúdáre Garuba, 'On animism, modernity/colonialism and the African order of knowledge: Provisional reflections', in *Contested Ecologies: Dialogues in the South on Nature and Knowledge,* ed. L. Green, (Cape Town: HSRC Press, 2013), p. 45.

30. Harvey, *Animism*, p. xi.

31. Wesley J. Wildman, 'An Introduction to Relational Ontology', in *The Trinity and an Entangled World: Relationality in Physical Science and Theology*, ed. John Polkinghorn, (Michigan: Wm B. Eerdmans, 2010), p. 55.

32. Robin Wall Kimmerer, 'Restoration and Reciprocity: The Contributions of Traditional Ecological Knowledge', in *Human Dimensions of Ecological Restoration: Integrating Science, Nature and Culture,* ed. D. Egan, E.E. Hjerpe & J. Abrams, (Washington, DC: Island Press, 2011), p. 257.

33. Roszak, *The Voice of the Earth*, p. 84.

34. Kenneth M. Morrison, 'The cosmos as intersubjective: Native American other-than-human Persons', in *Indigenous Religions: A Companion,* ed. Graham Harvey, (New York: Cassell, 2000).

35. Eduardo Viveiros de Castro, 'Cosmological Deixis and Amerindian Perspectivism', in *A Reader in the Anthropology of Religion,* ed. Michael Lambek, (Oxford: Blackwell, 2006), pp. 307–8.

36. Morrison, 'The Cosmos as Intersubjective', p. 25.

37. Angela Voss and William Rowlandson, *Daimonic Imagination: Uncanny Intelligence* (Newcastle: Cambridge Scholars Press, 2013).

38. Hunter, *Greening the Paranormal*.

39. Cited in Jeffrey J. Kripal, *Authors of the Impossible: The Paranormal and the Sacred* (Chicago: University of Chicago Press, 2010), p. 67.

40. Charles Fort, *The Book of the Damned: The Collected Works of Charles Fort* (London: Tarcher Penguin, 2008).

41. John Keel, *The Eighth Tower: On Ultraterrestrials and the Superspectrum* (Charlottesville: Anomalist Books, 2013), p. 248.

42. Steven Mizrach, 'The Para-Anthropology of UFO Abductions: The Case for the Ultraterrestrial Hypothesis', in *Strange Dimensions: A Paranthropology Anthology,* ed. Jack Hunter, (Llanrhaeadr-ym-Mochnant: Psychoid Books, 2015), pp. 299–336.

43. Keel, *The Eighth Tower*, p. 17.

44. John Keel, *Our Haunted Planet* (London: Neville Spearman, 1971).

45. Julia Wright, *Subtle Agroecologies: Farming with the Hidden Half of Nature* (Abingdon: CRC Press, 2021), p. xxix.

46. Foster, 'The Invisible Landscape'.

47. Alfred Irving Hallowell, 'Ojibwa Ontology, Behavior and World View', in *Readings in Indigenous Religions* (London: Continuum, 2002), p. 25.

48. Hallowell, 'Ojibwa Ontology', p. 25.

49. Wirt Sikes, *British Goblins: Welsh Folklore, Fairy Mythology, Legends and Traditions* (Cockatrice Books, 2020 [1880]), p. 384.

50. Fabian Graham, 'Money God Cults in Taiwan: A Paranthropological Approach', *Paranthropology: Journal of Anthropological Approaches to the Study of the Paranormal* 3, no. 1 (2012): pp. 9–19.

51. Holly Walters, *Shaligram Pilgrimage in the Nepal Himalayas* (Amsterdam: Amsterdam University Press, 2020), p. 13.

52. Ping Xu, 'An Interdisciplinary Study: Rock Worship in Chinese Classical Gardens', *International Journal of Arts and Sciences* 7, no. 5 (2014): pp. 547–58.

53. Michael F. Brown and Margaret L. Van Bolt, 'Aguaruna Jivaro Gardening Magic in the Alto Rio Mayo, Peru', *Ethnology* 19, no. 2 (1980): p. 173.

54. Owen Davies and Ceri Houlbrook, *Building Magic: Ritual and Re-enchantment in Post-Medieval Structures* (Palgrave Macmillan, 2021), pp. 95–119.

55. Marju Kõivupuu, 'Tradition in landscape, landscape in tradition: discourse of natural sanctuaries in Estonia', *Time and Mind* 13, no. 3 (2020): pp. 267–81.

56. Thomas W. Hancock, 'Llanrhaiadr-yn-Mochnant: Its Parochial History and Antiquities', *Collections Historical and Archaeological Relating to Montgomeryshire* 6 (1873): pp. 319–20.

57. Jeffrey A. Weinstock, *The Monster Theory Reader* (Minneapolis: University of Minnesota Press, 2020).

58. Weinstock, *The Monster Theory Reader*, p. 26.

59. Anthony Lioi, 'Of Swamp Dragons: Mud, Megalopolis, and a Future for Ecocriticism', in *The Monster Theory Reader,* ed. Jeffrey A. Weinstock, (Minneapolis: University of Minnesota Press, 2020), pp. 453–54.

60. Mark A. Schroll and Claire Polansky, 'Character Analysis of Some Specific Heroes and a Continuing Exploration of Their Ability to Demonstrate Transpersonal Ecosophical Consciousness', in *Ecology, Cosmos and Consciousness,* ed. Mark A. Schroll, (Llanrhaeadr-ym-Mochnant: Psychoid Books, 2018), pp.122–23.

61. Simon Bacon, *Eco-Vampires: The Undead and the Environment* (Jefferson, NC: McFarland, 2020), p. 192.

62. Hunter, *Greening the Paranormal.*

63. Heather Swanson, Anna Tsing, Nils Bubandt and Elaine Gan, 'Introduction', in *Arts of Living on a Damaged Planet,* ed. A. Tsing, *et al.,* (Minneapolis: University of Minnesota Press, 2017): m2–m3.

64. Paul Robichaud, *Pan: The Great God's Modern Return* (London: Reaktion Books, 2021).

65. Kenneth Grahame, *The Wind in the Willows* (London: Methuen and Co., 1936), pp. 126–27.

66. Robichaud, *Pan.*

67. 'Our Living Planet Report', WWF, https://wwf.panda.org/knowl- edge_hub/all_ publications/living_planet_report_2018/ [accessed 23 January 2023].

68. Aelys M. Humphreys *et al.,* 'Global dataset shows geography and life form predict modern plant extinction and rediscovery', *Nature Ecology and Evolution* 3 (2019): pp. 1043–47.

69. Kevin Laland and William Hoppitt, 'Do Animals Have Culture?' *Evolutionary Anthropology* 12, no. 3 (2003): p 151.

70. Gareth Willmer, 'Bats have different song cultures and chatter about food, sleep, sex and other bats', https://ec.europa.eu/research-and-innovation/en/horizon-magazine/bats-have-different-song-cultures-and-chatter-about-food-sleep-sex-and-other-bats [accessed

25 February 2023].
71. Willmer, 'Bats have different song cultures'.

Notes to Chapter Six

1. David E. Cooper, *Senses of Mystery: Engaging with Nature and the Meaning of Life* (Abingdon: Routledge, 2018), p. 24.
2. Claude Lévi-Strauss, *Structural Anthropology, Volume I* (London: Penguin,1986).
3. Michel Conan, *Sacred Gardens and Landscapes: Ritual and Agency* (Cambridge, MA: Harvard University Press, 2007), p. 7.
4. Andrew Cunningham, 'The Culture of Gardens', in *Cultures of Natural History*, ed. N. Jardine *et al.*, (Cambridge: Cambridge University Press, 1996): 39.
5. Conan, *Sacred Gardens and Landscapes,* p. 7.
6. Jeremy Naydler, *Gardening as Sacred Art* (Edinburgh: Floris Books, 2011), pp. 14–20.
7. David Young and Michiko Young, *The Art of the Japanese Garden: History, Culture, Design* (Rutland: Tuttle, 2019), p.10.
8. Hunter, *Manifesting Spirits.*
9. Hunter, *Manifesting Spirits*, p. xx.
10. Alfred Gell, 'Technology and Magic', *Anthropology Today* 4, no. 2 (1988): p. 9.
11. Eric Keys, 'Kaqchikel Gardens: Women, Children, and Multiple Roles of Gardens among the Maya of Highland Guatemala', *Yearbook (Conference of Latin Americanist Geographers)* 25 (1999): p. 8.
12. Brown and Van Bolt, 'Aguaruna Jivaro Gardening Magic', pp. 102–72.
13. Brown and Van Bolt, 'Aguaruna Jivaro Gardening Magic', p. 173.
14. Joe Cooper, *The Case of the Cottingley Fairies* (London: Pocket Books, 1997).
15. Nicola Brown, '"There are fairies at the bottom of our garden": Fairies, fantasy and photography', *Textual Practice* 10 (1999): p. 57.
16. Daniel Harms, 'Of Fairies: An Excerpt from a Seventeenth-Century Magical Manuscript', *Folklore* 129, no. 2 (2018): pp. 192–98.
17. Twigs Way, *Garden Gnomes: A History* (Oxford: Shire Publications, 2009), p. 11.
18. Way, *Garden Gnomes,* p. 20.
19. Way, *Garden Gnomes,* pp. 23–24.
20. Ian C. Duggan, 'The cultural history of the garden gnome in New Zealand', *Studies in the History of Gardens and Designed Landscapes: An International Quarterly* 36, no. 1 (2016): pp. 78–88.
21. Way, *Garden Gnomes,* p. 35.
22. The Findhorn Foundation, *The Findhorn Garden: Pioneering a New Vision of Humanity and Nature in Cooperation* (Findhorn: Findhorn Press, 1975), pp. 58–59.
23. Rudolf Steiner, *Agriculture Course: The Birth of the Biodynamic Method* (Forest Row: Rudolf Steiner Press, 2004).
24. M. Turinek, S. Grobelnik-Mlakar, M. Bavec and F. Bavec, 'Biodynamic agriculture research progress and priorities', *Renewable Agriculture and Food Systems* 24, no. 2 (2009): pp. 146–54.
25. Alessandra Castellini, Christine Mauracher and Stefania Troiano, 'An overview of the biodynamic wine sector', *International Journal of Wine Research* 9 (2017): pp. 1–11.
26. Dennis Gaffin, *Running with the Fairies: Towards a Transpersonal Anthropology of Religion* (Newcastle: Cambridge Scholars Press, 2012), p. 70.

27. Young, *The Fairy Census*.

28. Simon Young, 'Children Who See Fairies', *Journal for the Study of Religious Experience* 4, no. 1 (2018): p. 91.

29. Claude Lecouteux, *Demons and Spirits of the Land: Ancestral Lore and Practice* (Rochester: Inner Traditions, 2015), pp. 55–56.

30. Ronald M. James, 'Knockers, Knackers, and Ghosts: Immigrant Folklore in the Western Mines,' *Western Folklore* 51, no. 2 (1992): pp. 153–77.

31. Way, *Garden Gnomes*, pp. 20–21.

32. Arthur Conan Doyle, *The Coming of the Fairies* (Gloucester: Dodo Press, 2022).

33. Robert Sheaffer, 'Do Fairies Exist?', *The Zetetic* (Fall/Winter, 1977): p. 46.

34. §209A) Canada (Quebec). Female (third person); 1980s; 51–60; in a garden; alone.

35. §337) US (New York State). Male; 1990s; 41–50.

36. Amy Whitehead, 'A method of "things": a relational theory of objects as persons in lived religious practice', *Journal of Contemporary Religion* 30, no. 2 (2020): 231–50.

37. Michael Robert Pearce, 'Accommodating the discarnate: Thai spirit houses and the phenomenology of place', *Material Religion* 7, no. 3 (2015): pp. 344–72.

38. Wright, *Subtle Agroecologies*.

39. Wright, *Subtle Agroecologies*, p. xxix.

40. Espirito Santo and Hunter, *Mattering the Invisible*.

41. Patrick MacManaway, 'Land Whispering: Practice Applications of Consciousness and Subtle Energy Awareness in Agriculture', in *Subtle Agroecologies: Farming with the Hidden Half of Nature* (Abingdon: CRC Press, 2021), p. 299.

42. Andy Letcher, 'The Scouring of the Shire: Fairies, Trolls and Pixies in Eco-Protest Culture,' *Folklore* 112 (2001): pp. 147–61.

43. Way, *Garden Gnomes*, p. 21.

44. Jack Hunter, 'Through a Crystal Darkly: Cultural, Experiential and Ontological Reflections on Faery', in *Fairy Films: Wee-Folk on the Big Screen*, ed. Joshua Cutchin, (Educated Dragon Publishing, 2023).

Notes to Chapter Seven

1. Brian Restall and Elisabeth Conrad, 'A literature review of connectedness to nature and its potential for environmental management', *Journal of Environmental Management* 159 (2015): pp. 1–15.

2. Charles D. Laughlin, 'Communing with the Gods: The Dreaming Brain in Cross-cultural Perspective', *Time and Mind: Journal of Archaeology, Consciousness and Culture* 4, no. 2 (2011): p. 159.

3. Olga Solomon, 'Sense and the Sense: Anthropology and the Study of Autism', *Annual Review of Anthropology* 39, no. 1 (2010): pp. 241–59.

4. Penny Spikins, 'Autism, the Integrations of 'Difference' and the Origins of Modern Human Behaviour', *Cambridge Archaeological Journal* 19, no. 2 (2009): pp. 179–201.

5. Catriona Pickard, Ben Pickard and Clive Bonsall, ,Autistic Spectrum Disorder in Prehistory', *Cambridge Archaeological Journal* 21, no. 3 (2011): pp. 357–64.

6. Yafit Kedar, Gil Kedar and Ran Barkai, 'Hypoxia in Paleolithic decorated caves: the use of artificial light in deep caves reduces oxygen concentration and produces altered states of consciousness', *Time and Mind* 14, no. 1 (2021): pp. 1–36.

7. 'Society for Psychical Research', SPR, https://www.spr.ac.uk [accessed 2 March 2023].

8. Donald West, 'Society for Psychical Research', https://psi-encyclopedia.spr.ac.uk/articles/society-psychical-research [accessed 25 February 2023].

9. Frederic W.H. Myers, *Human Personality and its Survival of Bodily Death* (Norwich: Pelegrin Trust, 1992), p. 13.

10. Myers, *Human Personality*, pp. 13–14.

11. Sonu Shamdasani, 'Introduction', in *From India to the Planet Mars: A Case of Multiple Personality with Imaginary Languages*, ed. Theodore Flournoy, (Princeton: Princeton University Press,1994), p. xv.

12. Frederic W.H. Myers, 'Multiplex Personality' (1886), https://www.bl.uk/collection-items/multiplex-personality-from-the-nineteenth-century [accessed 26 February 2023].

13. William James, 'Frederic Myers's service to psychology', *Proceedings of the Society for Psychical Research* 17 (1901): pp. 1–23.

14. C.G. Jung, *Psychology and the Occult* (Abingdon: Routledge, 2007).

15. Ann Taves, 'Religious Experience and the Divisible Self: William James (and Frederic Myers) as Theorist(s) of Religion', *Journal of the American Academy of Religion* 71, no. 2 (2003): pp. 306–11.

16. Myers, *Human Personality*, p. 19.

17. Clifford Geertz, 'From the native's point of view: On the nature of anthropological understanding', *Bulletin of the American Academy of Arts and Sciences* 28, no. 1 (1974): p. 31.

18. Charles Taylor, *A Secular Age* (Cambridge, MA: Harvard University Press, 2007), pp. 37–41.

19. Hazel R. Markus and Shinobu Kitayama, 'Culture and the self: Implications for cognition, emotion and motivation', *Psychological Bulletin* 98, no. 2 (1991): pp. 224–353.

20. Willy de Craemer, 'A Cross-Cultural Perspective on Personhood', *The Milbank Memorial Fund Quarterly: Health and Society* 61, no. 1 (1983): p. 26.

21. Hunter, *Manifesting Spirits*.

22. 'HVN: a positive approach to voices and visions', Hearing Voices Network, http://www.hearing-voices.org/about-us/hvn-values/ [accessed 26 February 2023].

23. Christopher Laursen, 'Plurality through imagination: The emergence of online tulpa communities in the making of new identities', in *Believing in bits: Digital media and the supernatural,* ed. Simone Natale and Diana W. Pasulka, (Oxford: Oxford University Press, 2019), p. 168.

24. Laursen, 'Plurality through imagination', pp. 172–73.

25. Hunter, *Manifesting Spirits*.

26. Bill Devall and George Sessions, 'Deep Ecology', in *Thinking Through the Environment: A Reader*, ed. M.J. Smith, (Abingdon: Routledge, 1999), pp. 200–7.

27. Freya Matthews, *The Ecological Self* (Abingdon: Routledge, 2006), p. 3.

28. Arne Naess, 'Self-realization', p. 227.

29. Matthews, *The Ecological Self*.

30. Matthews, *The Ecological Self*, p. 144.

31. Matthews, *The Ecological Self*, pp. 129–33.

32. Roszak, *The Voice of the Earth*.

33. William Braud, 'Toward more subtle awareness: Meanings, implications, and possible new directions for psi research', *Mindfield* 3, no. 1 (2000): p. 1.

34. Braud, 'Toward more subtle awareness', p. 3.

35. Macy, 'Working through environmental despair'.

36. David Luke and Marios Kittenis, 'A preliminary survey of paranormal experiences with psychoactive drugs', *Journal of Parapsychology* 69, no. 2 (2005): pp. 305–27.

37. Sam Gandy *et al.*, 'The potential synergistic effects between psychedelic administration and nature contact for the improvement of mental health', *Health Psychology Open* 7, no. 2 (2020): pp. 1–21.

38. Forstmann and Sagioglou, 'Lifetime experience with (classic) psychedelics'.

39. Ring and Valarino, *Lessons from the Light*, p. 125.

40. Hunter, *Greening the Paranormal*.

41. Roger Nelson and Peter Bancel, 'Effects of Mass Consciousness: Changes in Random Data during Global Events', *Explore: Journal of Science and Healing* 7, no. 6 (2011): pp. 373–83.

42. Margaret Kerr and David Key, 'The Ouroboros (Part 1): Towards an ontology of connectedness in ecopsychology research', *European Journal of Ecopsychology* 2 (2011): p. 52.

43. Keel, *Our Haunted Planet*.

44. For an interesting series of articles on 'super-nature' see Timothy Grieve Carlsons posts on the *Paracultures* blog: https://www.paracultures.com/post/supernature-1

45. Angela Voss and Simon Wilson, *Re-Enchanting the Academy* (Auckland: Rubedo Press, 2017), p. 13.

46. Myers, *Human Personality*, p. 289.

47. Devereux, *Re-Visioning the Earth*.

Notes to Chapter Eight

1. Anthony Thorley, 'Sacred Geography: a conceptual work in progress', *SPICA: Postgraduate Journal for Cosmology in Culture* 4, no. 2 (2016): p. 8.

2. Brian Leigh Molyneaux and Piers Vitebsky, *Sacred Earth, Sacred Stones* (San Diego: Laurel Glen, 2001), p. 7.

3. Paul Devereux, *Sacred Geography: Deciphering Hidden Codes in the Landscape* (London: Gaia, 2010), p. 6.

4. Paul Devereux, Stanley Krippner, Robert Tartz and Adam Fish, 'A Preliminary Study on English and Welsh Sacred Sites and Home Dream Reports', in *Transpersonal Ecosophy Vol. 1: Theory, Methods and Clinical Assessments*. ed. Mark A. Schroll, (Llanrhaeadr-ym-Mochnant: Psychoid Books, 2016), p. 412.

5. Devereux, *Sacred Geography*, p. 9.

6. Durkheim, *The Elementary Forms of the Religious Life*.

7. Mircea Eliade, *The Sacred and the Profane: The Nature of Religion* (New York: Harcourt, 1987), p. 21.

8. Mircea Eliade, *Patterns in Comparative Religion* (Lincoln: University of Nebraska Press, 1996).

9. Laura Béres, 'A Thin Place: Narratives of Space and Place, Celtic Spirituality and Meaning', *Journal of Religion and Spirituality in Social Work* 31, no. 4 (2012): pp. 394–413.

10. Otto, *The Idea of the Holy*, p. 126.

11. Hufford, *The Terror that Comes in the Night*.

12. Lauri Honko, 'Memorates and the Study of Folk Beliefs', *Journal of the Folklore Institute* 1, no. 1/2 (1964): pp. 5–19.

13. Neil Dagnall *et al.*, 'Things that go bump in the literature: An environmental appraisal of "haunted houses"', *Frontiers in Psychology*.

14. Norris Brock Johnson, 'Geomancy, sacred geometry, and the idea of a garden: Tenryu-ji temple, Kyoto, Japan', *The Journal of Garden History* 9, no. 1 (1989): p. 2.

15. Barbara Bender, 'Time and Landscape', *Current Anthropology* 43, Supplement (2002): S104.

16. Anthony Thorley and Celia M. Gunn, *Sacred Sites: An Overview* (London: The Gaia Foundation, 2008).

17. Justine Digance, 'Religious and secular pilgrimage: Journeys redolent with meaning', in *Tourism, Religion and Spiritual Journeys,* ed. D.J. Timothy and D.H. Olsen, (Abingdon: Routledge, 2006), p. 36.

18. Digance, 'Religious and secular pilgrimage', p. 37.

19. Christopher Tilley, *Phenomenology of Landscape* (Oxford: Berg, 1994), p. 34.

20. Bernadette Brady, 'Mountains Talk of Kings and Dragons, the Brecon Beacons', in *Space, Place and Religious Landscapes: Living Mountains,* ed. Darrelyn Gunzburg and Bernadette Brady, (London: Bloomsbury, 2022), p. 184.

21. Rachael Ironside and Stewart Massie, 'The Folklore-Centric Gaze: A Relational Approach to Landscape, Folklore and Tourism', *Time and Mind: Journal of Archaeology, Consciousness and Culture* 13, no. 3 (2020): pp. 227–44.

22. Hunter and Ironside, *Folklore, People and Place.*

23. David Price-Williams and Rosslyn Gaines, 'The Dreamtime and Dreams of Northern Australian Aboriginal Artists', *Ethos* 22, no. 3 (1994): p. 375.

24. Alan Rumsey, 'The Dreaming, Human Agency and Inscriptive Practice', *Oceania* 65 (1994): p. 126.

25. Lynn Hume, 'The dreaming in contemporary Aboriginal Australia', in *Indigenous Religions: A Companion,* ed. Graham Harvey, (London: Cassell, 2000), p. 125.

26. Hume, 'The dreaming in contemporary Aboriginal Australia', p. 127.

27. Thorley and Gunn, *Sacred Sites.*

28. Gareth Lewis and Ben Scambary, 'Sacred Bodies and Ore Bodies: Conflicting Commodification of Landscape by Indigenous Peoples and Miners in Australia's Northern Territory', in *The Right to Protect Sites: Indigenous Heritage Management in the Era of Native Title,* ed. P.F. McGrath, (Canberra: Australian Institute of Aboriginal and Torres Strait Islander Studies, 2016), pp. 221–52.

29. Hunter and Ironside, *Folklore, People and Place.*

30. Cunningham, 'The Culture of Gardens', p. 39.

31. Cunningham, 'The Culture of Gardens', p. 38.

32. Chris Park, *Sacred Worlds: An Introduction to Geography and Religion* (Abingdon: Routledge, 1994), p. 198.

33. Sean McGovern, 'The Ryôan-ji Zen garden: textual meanings in topographical form', *Visual Communication* 3, no. 3 (2004): pp. 344–59.

34. P. S. Swamy, M. Kumar and S. M. Sundarpandian, 'Spirituality and ecology of sacred groves in Tamil Nadu, India', *Unasylva* 54, no. 213 (2003): p. 55.

35. Ronald L. Baker, 'The Role of Folk Legends in Place-Name Research', *The Journal of American Folklore* 85, no. 338 (1972): pp. 367–73.

36. McCue, *Zones of Strangeness,* p. 91.

37. Colm A. Kelleher and G. Knapp, *Hunt for the Skinwalker: Science Confronts the Unexplained at a Remote Utah Ranch* (New York: Paraview Pocket Books, 2005), p. 10.

38. McCue, *Zones of Strangeness*, pp. 228–48.

39. John Keel, *Strange Creatures from Time and Space* (Greenwich: Fawcett, 1970), p. 15.

40. McCue, *Zones of Strangeness*, p. 91.

41. Greg Taylor, 'Michael Persinger Defends the "God Helmet", says Richard Dawkins Was Affected by Alcohol When He Tried It', The Daily Grail, https://www.dailygrail.com/2015/11/michael-persinger-defends-the-god-helmet-says-richard-dawkins-was-affected-by-alcohol-when-he-tried-it/ [accessed 3 March 2023].

42. Michael A. Persinger *et al.*, 'The Electromagnetic Induction of Mystical and Altered States within the Laboratory', *Journal of Consciousness Exploration and Research* 1, no. 7 (2010): pp. 808–30.

43. Serena Roney-Dougal, *Where Science and Magic Meet* (Glastonbury: Green Magic, 2002).

44. Paul Devereux, http ://www.pauldevereux.co.uk.

45. Paul Devereux, *Earth Lights: Towards an Understanding of the UFO Enigma* (Wellingborough: Turnstone Press, 1982), p. 195.

46. 'Project Hessdalen', http://www.hessdalen.org/index_e.shtml [accessed 14 March 2023].

47. Devereux, Krippner,Tartz and Fish, 'A Preliminary Study on English and Welsh Sacred Sites', pp. 381–417.

48. Devereux, *Sacred Geography*, p, 152.

49. Thorley, 'Sacred Geography', p. 8.

Notes to Chapter Nine

1. Simberloff, 'A Succession of Paradigms in Ecology', pp. 3–39.

2. Berkes, 'Traditional Ecological Knowledge in Perspective', p. 1.

3. Margaret M. Bruchac, 'Indigenous Knowledge and Traditional Knowledge', in *Encyclopedia of Global Archaeology*, ed. C. Smith, (New York: Springer Science and Business Media, 2014), p. 3814.

4. Robin Wall Kimmerer, 'Weaving Traditional Ecological Knowledge into Biological Education: A Call to Action', *BioScience* 52, no. 5 (2002): pp. 432–35.

5. James Bourque, Julian T. Inglis and Patrice LeBlanc, 'Preface', in *Traditional Ecological Knowledge: Concepts and Cases,* ed. J.T. Inglish (Ottawa: International Program on Traditional Ecological Knowledge, 1993), p. vii.

6. Naess, 'Self-realization'.

7. Robin Wall Kimmerer, 'Weaving Traditional Ecological Knowledge into Biological Education,' p. 433.

8. Simberloff, 'A Succession of Paradigms in Ecology'.

9. Linda Tuhiwai Smith, *Decolonizing Methodologies: Research and Indigenous Peoples* (London: Zed Books, 2012), p. 78.

10. 'Backgrounder – Traditional Ecological Knowledge', UN Permanent Forum on Indigenous Issues, https://www.un.org/development/desa/indigenouspeoples/wp-content/uploads/sites/19/2019/04/Traditional-Knowledge-backgrounder-FINAL.pdf [accessed 4 March 2023].

11. Robin Wall Kimmerer, 'Restoration and Reciprocity: The Contributions of Traditional Ecological Knowledge', in *Human Dimensions of Ecological Restoration: Integrating Science, Nature and Culture*, ed. D. Egan, E.E. Hjerpe & J. Abrams, (Washington, DC:

Island Press, 2011), p. 258.

12. Andrew Paul, Robin Roth and Saw Sha Bwe Moo, 'Relational ontology and more-than-human agency in Indigenous Karen conservation practice', *Pacific Conservation Biology* 27, no. 4 (2021): pp. 376–90.

13. Tyson Yunkaporta, *Sand Talk: How Indigenous Thinking Can Save the World* (Melbourne: The Text Publishing Company, 2019), pp. 18–19.

14. Yunkaporta, *Sand Talk*, pp. 19–20.

15. Daniel Shilling, 'The Soul of Sustainability', in *Traditional Ecological Knowledge: Learning from Indigenous Practices for Environmental Sustainability*, ed. M.K. Nelson & D. Schilling, (Cambridge: Cambridge University Press, 2018), p. 12.

16. Shilling, 'The Soul of Sustainability'.

17. Roszak, *The Voice of the Earth*, p. 84.

18. Robin Wall Kimmerer, *Braiding Sweetgrass: Indigenous Wisdom, Scientific Knowledge, and the Teachings of Plants* (Minneapolis: Milkweed, 2013), p. 49.

19. Kimmerer, *Braiding Sweetgrass*, p. 49.

20. Harding, *Animate Earth*.

21. Yunkaporta, *Sand Talk*, p. 109.

22. Harvey, *Animism*, p. xi.

23. Kimmerer, 'Restoration and Reciprocity: The Contributions of Traditional Ecological Knowledge', p. 257.

24. Robin Wall Kimmerer, '*Mishkos Kenomagwen*, the Lessons of Grass: Restoring Reciprocity with the Good Green Earth', in *Traditional Ecological Knowledge: Learning from Indigenous Practices for Environmental Sustainability*, ed. Melissa K. Nelson and Dan Shilling, (Cambridge: Cambridge University Press, 2018), p. 31.

25. Renée E. Mazinegiizhigoo-kwe Bédard, 'Sacred Anishinaabeg Folklore: Okikendawt Mnisiing, the Island of the Sacred Kettles', in *Folklore, People and Place: International Perspectives on Tourism and Tradition in Storied Places*, ed. Jack Hunter and Rachael Ironside, (Abingdon: Routledge, 2023).

26. Iain Mackinnon, Lewis Williams and Arianna Waller, 'The re-indigenization of humanity to Mother Earth: A learning platform to cultivate social-ecological resilience and challenge the Anthropocene', *Journal of Sustainability Education* 16 (2017).

27. Graham Harvey, 'Animism and ecology: Participating in the world community', *The Ecological Citizen* 3, no. 1 (2019): pp. 79–84.

28. Melissa Taitimu, 'Ngā whakawhitinga: standing at the crossroads: Māori ways of understanding extra-ordinary experiences and schizophrenia', (PhD Thesis, University of Auckland, 2008).

29. Bettina Schmidt, *The Study of Religious Experience: Approaches and Methodologies* (Sheffield: Equinox, 2016).

30. Tuhiwai Smith, *Decolonizing Methodologies*.

31. Isabel Clarke, 'Beyond the God Spot: Transcendence and the Brain', *The Way* 53, no. 1 (2014): pp. 49–55.

32. Yaden *et al.*, 'The Varieties of Self Transcendent Experience'.

33. Tuhiwai Smith, *Decolonizing Methodologies*, p. 122.

34. Foster, 'The Invisible Ecosystem', p. 96.

35. Renée E. Mazinegiizhigo-kwe Bédard, 'Jiisakiiwigaan: Shaking Tent Ceremony as Sacred Metamorphosis', in *Deep Weird: The Varieties of High Strangeness Experience*, ed. Jack Hunter, (Hove: August Night, 2023): p. 337.

Notes to Chapter Ten

1. Martin Holbraad and Morten Axel Pedersen, *The Ontological Turn: An Anthropological Exposition* (Cambridge: Cambridge University Press, 2017).

2. William Paley, *Natural Theology: Or, Evidences of the Existence and Attributes of the Deity, Collected from the Appearances of Nature* (Cambridge: Cambridge University Press, 2009).

3. Michael J. Behe, 'Intelligent Design', in *Science, Religion and Society: An Encyclopaedia of History, Culture and Controversy, Volume One,* ed. Arri Eisen and Gary Laderman, (New York: M.E. Sharpe, date missing), pp. 467–74.

4. David Hume, *Dialogues Concerning Natural Religion* (Oxford: Oxford University Press, 1993).

5. Scott F. Gilbert and Sahotra Sarkar, 'Embracing complexity: Organicism for the 21st century', *Developmental Dynamics* 219 (2000): pp. 1–2.

6. 'The Large Hadron Collider', CERN, https://www.home.cern/science/accelerators/large-hadron-collider [accessed 5 March 2023].

7. Rupert Sheldrake, *A New Science of Life* (London: Icon Books, 2009), p. 26.

8. Garland E. Allen, 'Mechanism, vitalism and organicism in late nineteenth and twentieth-century biology: The importance of historical context', *Studies in History and Philosophy of Science Part C Studies in History and Philosophy of Biological and Biomedical Sciences* 36, no. 2 (2005): pp. 262–63.

9. Eline N. van Basten, 'The history of quantification and objectivity in the social sciences', *Social Cosmos* 5, no. 1 (2014): pp. 8–14.

10. Jonathan Louth, 'From Newton to Newtonianism: Reductionism and the Development of the Social Sciences', *Emergence: Complexity and Organization* 13, no. 4 (2011): pp. 63–83.

11. Dawkins, *The Selfish Gene.*

12. Petri Yilkoski, 'Micro, Macro and Mechanism,' in *The Oxford Handbook of Philosophy of Social Science*, ed. Harold Kincaid, (Oxford: Oxford University Press, 2012), pp. 21–45.

13. Hunter, *Greening the Paranormal.*

14. Alister Hardy, *The Divine Flame: Natural History and Religion* (London: Collins, 1966), p. 24.

15. John L. Randall, *Parapsychology and the Nature of Life* (London: Souvenir Press, 1975), pp. 222–23.

16. Thomas Nagel, *Mind and Cosmos: Why the Materialist Neo-Darwinian Conception of Nature is Almost Certainly False* (Oxford: Oxford University Press, 2012), p. 14.

17. Espirito Santo and Hunter, *Mattering the Invisible.*

18. Jeremy Stolow, 'Techno-Religious Imaginaries: On the Spiritual Telegraph and the Circum-Atlantic World of the 19th Century', *Institute on Globalization and the Human Condition, McMaster University, Working Paper Series* (2006).

19. Anthony Enns, 'Psychic Radio: Sound Technologies, Ether Bodies and Spiritual Vibrations', *The Senses and Society* 3, no. 2 (2008): pp. 137–52.

20. Upton Sinclair, *Mental Radio* (Charlottesville: Hampton Roads Publishing, 2001).

21. Simone Natale, 'The Invisible Made Visible: X-rays as attraction and visual medium at the end of the nineteenth century', *Media History* 17, no. 4 (2011): pp. 345–58.

22. Carlos Alvarado, 'Human radiations: Concepts of force in mesmerism, spiritualism

and psychical research', *Journal of the Society for Psychical Research*, 70 (2006): p. 139.

23. Allen, 'Mechanism, vitalism and organicism', pp. 266–67.

24. Nagel, *Mind and Cosmos,* p. 15.

25. Hans Driesch, *Psychical Research* (London: Collins, 1933): p. 171.

26. Zofia Weaver, 'The Mystery of Ectoplasm: Where Biology and Imagination Meet', in *Deep Weird: The Varieties of High Strangeness Experience*, ed. Jack Hunter, (Hove: August Night, 2023).

27. Driesch, *Psychical Research*, p. 119.

28. Charles Richet, *Thirty Years of Psychical Research: A Treatise on Metapsychics* (London: Macmillan, 1923), p. 4.

29. Andreas Sommer, 'Tackling Taboos—From Psychopathia Sexualis to the Materialisation of Dreams: Albert von Schrenck-Notzing (1862–1929)', *Journal of Scientific Exploration* 23, no. 3 (2009): p. 304.

30. M. Brady Brower, *Unruly Spirits: The Science of Psychic Phenomena in Modern France* (Urbana: University of Illinois Press, 2010), p. 85.

31. Robert M. Brain, 'Materialising the Medium: Ectoplasm and the Quest for Supra-Normal Biology in Fin-de-Siècle Science and Art', in *Vibratory Modernism,* ed. A. Enns and S. Trower, (Basingstoke: Palgrave, 2013), p. 113.

32. Martin Fichman, 'Science in Theistic Contexts: A Case Study of Alfred Russel Wallace on Human Evolution', *Osiris* 16 (2001): p. 228.

33. Hardy, *The Divine Flame.*

34. Lyall Watson, *Supernature: A Natural History of the Supernatural* (London: Hodder and Stoughton, 1973), p. 3.

35. Alex Gomez-Martin, 'Facing biology's open questions: Rupert Sheldrake's "heretical" hypothesis turns 40', *Bioessays* 43, no. 6 (2021).

36. Mark A. Schroll, *Transpersonal Ecosophy Vol. 1: Theory, Methods and Clinical Assessments* (Llanrhaeadr-ym-Mochnant: Psychoid Books, 2016).

37. Sheldrake, *A New Science of Life*, p. 1.

38. Sheldrake, *The Science Delusion*, p. 108.

39. Sheldrake, *The Science Delusion*, p. 108.

40. Max Velmans, 'The Co-evolution of Matter and Consciousness', *Synthesis Philosophica* 22, no. 44 (2007): pp. 273–82.

41. Peter Sjöstedt-Hughes, *Modes of Sentience: Psychedelics, Metaphysics, Panpsychism* (Falmouth: Psychedelic Press, 2022), p. 1.

42. Espirito Santo and Hunter, *Mattering the Invisible.*

43. Lancaster, *Approaches to Consciousness,* p. 6.

44. Garry Phillipson, 'Panspychism and Astrology', in *Skylights: Essays in the History and Contemporary Culture of Astrology,* ed. Frances Clynes, (Lampeter: Sophia Centre Press, 2022), p. 180.

45. Rupert Sheldrake, 'Is the Sun Conscious?' *Journal of Consciousness Studies* 28, no. 3-4 (2021): pp. 8–28.

46. Bernardo Kastrup, 'The Universe in Consciousness', *Journal of Consciousness Studies* 25, no. 5–6 (2018): pp. 125–55.

47. Kastrup, 'The Universe in Consciousness', p. 153.

48. Christopher N. Gamble, Joshua S. Hanan and Thomas Nail, 'What is New Materialism?' *Angelaki: Journal of the Theoretical Humanities* 24, no. 6 (2019): p. 111.

49. Karen Barad, 'Posthumanist Performativity: Toward an Understanding of How

Matter Comes to Matter', *Journal of Women in Culture and Society* 28, no. 3 (2003): p. 801.

50. Alfred North Whitehead, *Process and Reality* (London: Free Press, 1978), p. 22.

51. Peter Sjöstedt-H., 'The Philosophy of Organism', *Philosophy Now* (June/July 2016): p. 14.

52. Fort, *The Book of the Damned.*

53. Jeffrey J. Kripal, *Comparing Religions: Coming to Terms* (Chichester: Wiley Blackwell, 2014), p. 259.

54. Keel, *The Eighth Tower*, p. 248.

55. Keel, *The Eighth Tower*, p. 71.

56. Lance Foster, 'The Invisible Ecosystem.'

57. Anthony Peake, *The Hidden Universe: An Investigation into Non-Human Intelligences* (London: Watkins, 2019).

58. Wright, *Subtle Agroecologies.*

59. Joshua Cutchin, *Ecology of Souls: A New Mythology of Death and the Paranormal, Vol. One* (Horse & Barrel Press, 2022).

60. Cutchin, *Ecology of Souls*, p, 13.

61. Dean Radin, *et al.*, 'Consciousness and the double-slit interference pattern: Six experiments', *Physics Essays* 25, no. 2 (2012): pp. 157–71.

62. Zayin Cabot, *Ecologies of Participation: Agents, Shamans, Mystics, and Diviners* (London: Rowman & Littlefield, 2018), p. 10.

Notes to Chapter Eleven

1. Matthew J. Zylstra, *et al.*, 'Connectedness as a Core Conservation Concern: An Interdisciplinary Review of Theory and a Call for Practice', *Springer Science Reviews* 2 (2014): pp. 119–43.

2. Roszak, *The Voice of the Earth.*

3. Michael Thomas Braito, Kerstin Bok, Courtney Flint, Andreas Muhar and Marianne Penker, 'Human–Nature Relationships and Linkages to Environmental Behaviour', *Environmental Values* 26, no. 3 (2017): pp, 365–89.

4. F. Stephan Mayer and Cynthia McPherson Frantz, 'The Connectedness to Nature Scale: A Measure of Individuals' Feeling in Community with Nature', *Journal of Environmental Psychology* 24, no. 4 (2004): p. 504.

5. Naess, 'Self-Realization'.

6. Restall and Conrad, 'A literature review of connectedness to nature', p. 1.

7. Leanne Martin *et al.*, 'Nature contact, nature connectedness and associations with health, wellbeing and pro-environmental behaviours', *Journal of Environmental Psychology* 68 (2020).

8. Claudio D. Rosa *et al.*, 'Nature Experiences and Adults' Self-Reported Pro-environmental Behaviors: The Role of Connectedness to Nature and Childhood Nature Experiences', *Frontiers in Psychology* 9, no. 1055 (2018): p. 8.

9. Justin Dillon, Mark Rickinson, Kelly Teamey, Marian Morris, Mee Young Choi, Dawn Sanders and Pauline Benefield, 'The value of outdoor learning: evidence from research in the UK and elsewhere', in *Towards a Convergence Between Science and Environmental Education,* ed. Justin Dillon, (Abingdon: Routledge, 2016).

10. Thunberg, *No One Is Too Small to Make a Difference.*

11. William E. Scheuerman, 'Political Disobedience and the Climate Emergency', *Philosophy and Social Criticism* 48, no. 6 (2022).

12. 'United Kingdom: Bipartisan UK Parliament declares a climate emergency', Climate Emergency Declaration, https://climateemergencydeclaration.org/united-kingdom-bipartisan-uk-parliament-declares-a-climate-emergency/ [accessed 6 March 2023].

13. 'Concern about climate change reaches record levels with half now 'very concerned'' Ipsos Mori, accessed https://www.ipsos.com/en-uk/concern-about-climate-change-reaches-record-levels-half-now-very-concerned [accessed 26 February 2023].

14. Rachel A. Howell and Simon Allen, 'Significant life experiences, motivations and values of climate change educators', *Environmental Education Research* 25, no. 6 (2019): pp. 813–31.

15. Bill Mollison and David Holmgren, *Permaculture One: A Perennial Agriculture for Human Settlements* (Tyalgum: Tagari Publications, 1990).

16. Christopher J. Rhodes, 'Permaculture: Regenerative – not merely sustainable', *Science Progress* 98, no. 4 (2014): pp. 403–12.

17. David Holmgren, *Permaculture: Principles & Pathways Beyond Sustainability* (Hepburn: Holmgren Design Services, 2006).

18. Holmgren, *Permaculture*.

19. Laura Centemeri, 'Commons and the new environmentalism of everyday life: Alternative value practices and multispecies commoning in the permaculture movement', *Rassegna Italiana di Sociologia* 59, no. 2 (2018): p. 8.

20. www.permaculture.org.uk

21. Chris Marsh, 'Permaculture (and) Religion', https://www.academia.edu/7131096/Permaculture_and_Religion [accessed 26 February 2023].

22. Marsh, 'Permaculture (and) Religion'.

23. Bill Mollison, *Travel in Dreams: 'One Fat Foot after Another': The Autobiography of Bill Mollison* (Stanley: Tagari Press, 1996): p. 623.

24. Marsh, 'Permaculture (and) Religion'.

25. Caroline Smith, 'The Getting of Hope: Personal Empowerment Through Permaculture', *Proceedings of the Sixth International Permaculture Conference September-October 1996, Perth, Western Australia* (1996).

26. Holmgren, *Permaculture*, p. 3.

27. 'Whitewashed Hope: A Message from 10+ Indigenous Leaders and Organisations: regenerative agriculture and permaculture offer narrow solutions to climate crisis', https://www.culturalsurvival.org/news/whitewashed-hope-message-10-indigenous-leaders-and-organizations [accessed 6 March 2023].

28. Masanobu Fukuoka, *The One-Straw Revolution* (New York: New York Review of Books, 2009), pp. 33–34.

29. Fukuoka, *The One-Straw Revolution*, pp. 25–26.

30. Wright, *Subtle Agroecologies*.

31. Tina Braun and Paul Dierkes, 'Connecting students to nature – how intensity of nature experience and student age influence the success of outdoor education programs', *Environmental Education Research* 23, no. 7 (2017): pp. 937–49.

32. Dilafruz R. Williams and Jonathan Brown, *Learning Gardens and Sustainability Education: Bringing Life to Schools and Schools to Life* (Abingdon: Routledge, 2012), p. 8.

33. Mayer and Frantz, 'The Connectedness to Nature Scale', p. 504.

34. http://www.sector39.co.uk

35. Jones and Hunter, *One School One Planet Vol. 1; One School One Planet Vol. 2.*

36. Steve Jones, Jack Hunter and Angharad Rees, A., *Small and Slow Solutions: Unleashing the Creativity of the Climate Change Generation* (Llanrhaeadr-ym-Mochnant: Sector39, 2019).

37. James D. Holt, *Religious Education in the Secondary School* (Abingdon: Routledge, 2014).

38. Stefan Altmeyer, 'Religious education for ecological sustainability: an initial reality check using the example of everyday decision-making', *Journal of Religious Education* 69 (2021): pp. 57–74.

39. Chaplin, 'The Global Greening of Religion'.

40. Geir Skeie, 'Transforming local places into learning spaces in religious education: Revisiting a collaborative research project', in *Location, Space and Place in Religious Education*, ed. Martin Rothgangel, Kerstin von Bromssen, Hans-Gunter Heimbrock and Geir Skeie, (Munster: Waxmann, 2017), p. 128.

41. Sandra Austin, 'The school garden in the primary school: meeting the challenges and reaping the benefits', *International Journal of Primary, Elementary and Early Years Education* 50, no. 6 (2016): pp. 707–21.

42. Rosa *et al.*, 'Nature Experiences and Adults' Self-Reported Pro-environmental Behaviors', p. 7.

.

.

REFERENCES

Adamatzky, Andrew. 'Language of fungi derived from their electrical spiking activity'. *Royal Society Open Science* 9 (2022).

Allen, Garland E. 'Mechanism, vitalism and organicism in late nineteenth and twentieth–century biology: The importance of historical context'. *Studies in History and Philosophy of Science Part C Studies in History and Philosophy of Biological and Biomedical Sciences* 36, no. 2 (2005): pp. 262–263.

Altmeyer, Stefan. 'Religious education for ecological sustainability: an initial reality check using the example of everyday decision-making'. *Journal of Religious Education* 69 (2021): pp. 57–74.

Alvarado, Carlos. 'Human radiations: Concepts of force in mesmerism, spiritualism and psychical research'. *Journal of the Society for Psychical Research* 70 (2006): pp. 138–62.

Anthony, Francis-Vincent, Chris A.M. Hermans and Carl Sterkens. 'A comparative study of mystical experience among Christian, Muslim, and Hindu students in Tamil Nadu, India', *Journal for the Scientific Study of Religion* 49, no. 2 (2010): pp. 264–77.

Arrhenius, Svante. 'On the influence of carbonic acid in the air upon the temperature of the ground'. *The London, Edinburgh and Dublin Philosophical Magazine and Journal of Science* 41, no. 241 (1896): pp. 365–87.

Astley, Jeff. *Ordinary Theology: Looking, Listening and Learning in Theology*. Aldershot: Ashgate, 2002.

———, and Ann Christie. *Taking Ordinary Theology Seriously*. Cambridge: Grove Books, 2007.

Attala, Luci. *How Water Makes Us Human: Engagements with the Materiality of Water*. Cardiff: University of Wales Press, 2019.

Austin, Sandra. 'The school garden in the primary school: meeting the challenges and reaping the benefits'. *International Journal of Primary, Elementary and Early Years Education* 50, no. 6 (2016): pp. 707–21.

Backster, Cleve. 'Evidence of Primary Perception in Plant Life'. *International Journal of Parapsychology* 10, no. 4 (1968): pp. 329–48.

Bacon, Simon. *Eco-Vampires: The Undead and the Environment*. Jefferson, NC: McFarland, 2020).

Barad, Karen. 'Posthumanist Performativity: Toward an Understanding of How Matter Comes to Matter'. *Journal of Women in Culture and Society* 28, no. 3 (2003): pp. 801–31.

Basten, Eline N. van. 'The history of quantification and objectivity in the social sciences'. *Social Cosmos* 5, no. 1 (2014): pp. 8–14.

Bédard, Renée E. Mazinegiizhigoo-kwe. 'Sacred Anishinaabeg Folklore: Okikendawt Mnisiing, the Island of the Sacred Kettles', in *Folklore, People and Place: International Perspectives on Tourism and Tradition in Storied Places*, ed. Jack Hunter and Rachael Ironside, (Abingdon: Routledge, 2023).

'Bees learn and "teach" others'. *Nature* 538, 293 (2016), https://doi.org/10.1038/538293b.

Behe, Michael J. 'Intelligent Design', in *Science, Religion and Society: An Encyclopaedia*

of History, Culture and Controversy, Volume One, ed. Arri Eisen and Gary Laderman, (New York: M. E. Sharpe), pp. 467–74.

Bender, Barbara. 'Time and Landscape'. *Current Anthropology* 43, Supplement, (2002):
s103–s112.

Benjamin, Andrew. *Towards a Relational Ontology: Philosophy's Other Possibility.*
Albany, NY: SUNY Press, 2015.

Béres, Laura. 'A Thin Place: Narratives of Space and Place, Celtic Spirituality and Meaning'. *Journal of Religion and Spirituality in Social Work* 31, no. 4 (2012): 394–413.

Bergandi, Donato. 'Multifaceted Ecology Between Organicism, Emergentism and Reductionism', in *Ecology Revisited: Reflecting on Concepts, Advancing Science*, ed.
A. Schwarz and K. Jax, (Dordrecht: Springer, 2011), pp. 31–43.

Berkes, Fikret. 'Traditional Ecological Knowledge in Perspective'. in *Traditional Ecological Knowledge: Concepts and Cases*, ed. Julian T. Inglis, (Ottawa: International
Program on Traditional Ecological Knowledge, 1993), pp. 1–10.

Bland, Lucie M., Jessica A. Rowland, Tracey J. Regan, David A. Keith, Nicholas J. Murray, Rebecca E. Lester, Matt Linn, Jon Paul Roriguez and Emily Nicholson. 'Developing a standardized definiton of ecosystem collapse for risk assessent'. *Frontiers in
Ecology and the Environment* 16, no. 1 (2018): pp. 29–36.

Bosak, Tanja, Biqing Liang, Min Sub Sim and Alexander P. Petroff. 'Morphological
record of oxygenic photosynthesis in conical stromatolites'. *PNAS* 106, no. 27
(2009): pp. 10939–43.

Botelho, Maria Izabel Vieira, I.M Cardosa, and K. Otsuki. '"I made a pact with God,
with nature and with myself": exploring deep ecology'. *Agroecology and Sustainable Food Systems* 40, no. 2 (2016): pp. 116–31.

Bourque, James, Julian T. Inglis and Patrice LeBlanc. 'Preface', in *Traditional Ecological
Knowledge: Concepts and Cases*, ed. J.T. Inglish, (Ottawa: International Program
on Traditional Ecological Knowledge, 1993), pp. vi–vii.

Bowie, Fiona. *The Anthropology of Religion*. Oxford: Blackwell, 2006.

Bowman, Marion. 'More of the Same? Christianity, Vernacular Religion and Alternative
Spirituality in Glastonbury', in *Beyond New Age: Exploring Alternative Spiritual-
ity*, ed. Steven Sutcliffe and Marion Bowman, (Edinburgh: Edinburgh University
Press, 2000), pp. 83–104.

Brady, Bernadette. 'Mountains Talk of Kings and Dragons, the Brecon Beacons', in
Space, Place and Religious Landscapes: Living Mountains, ed. Darrelyn Gunzburg
and Bernadette Brady, (London: Bloomsbury, 2022), pp. 173–90.

Brain, Robert M. 'Materialising the Medium: Ectoplasm and the Quest for Supra-Normal Biology in Fin-de-Siècle Science and Art', in *Vibratory Modernism*, ed. A. Enns
and S. Trower, (Basingstoke: Palgrave, 2013), pp. 112–41.

Braito. Michael Thomas, Kerstin Bok, Courtney Flint, Andreas Muhar and Marianne
Penker. 'Human–Nature Relationships and Linkages to Environmental Behaviour'.
Environmental Values 26, no. 3 (2017): pp. 365–89.

Braud, William. 'Toward more subtle awareness: Meanings, implications, and possible
new directions for psi research'. *Mindfield* 3, no. 1 (2000): pp. 1–8.

Braun, Tina and Paul Dierkes. 'Connecting students to nature – how intensity of nature
experience and student age influence the success of outdoor education programs'.
Environmental Education Research 23, no. 7 (2017): pp. 937–49.

Brenner, E.D., R. Stahlber, S. Mancuso, J. Vivanco, F. Baluska and E. Van Volkenburgh.
'Plant neurobiology: an integrated view of plant signalling'. *TRENDS in Plant Sci-*

ence 11, no. 8 (2006): pp. 413–19.

Brower, M. Brady. *Unruly Spirits: The Science of Psychic Phenomena in Modern France.* Urbana: University of Illinois Press, 2010.

Brown, Nicola. '"There are fairies at the bottom of our garden": Fairies, fantasy and photography'. *Textual Practice* 10, (1999): pp. 57–82.

Brown, Michael F. and Margaret L. Van Bolt. 'Aguaruna Jivaro Gardening Magic in the Alto Rio Mayo, Peru'. *Ethnology* 19, no. 2 (1980): pp. 169–90.

Bruchac, Margaret M. 'Indigenous Knowledge and Traditional Knowledge', in *Encyclopedia of Global Archaeology,* ed. C. Smith (New York: Springer Science and Business Media, 2014), pp. 3814–24.

Bunge, Mario. 'Survey of the Interpretations of Quantum Mechanics'. *American Journal of Physics* 24, no. 4, (1956): pp. 272–86.

Byron, Aubrey. 'The People Who Study Fungus Know Why It's Suddenly Taking Over Horror: The Last of Us isn't the only recent story to rely on fungal fright'. https://slate.com/culture/2023/02/last-of-us-hbo-mushroom-fungus-horror.html [accessed 27 February 2023].

Cabot, Zayin. *Ecologies of Participation: Agents, Shamans, Mystics, and Diviners.* London: Rowman & Littlefield, 2018.

Cadman, David. 'Principles of Harmony', in *The Harmony Debates: Exploring a practical philosophy for a sustainable future,* ed. Nicholas Campion, (Lampeter: Sophia Centre Press, 2020), pp. 43–45.

Campion, Nicholas. *Astrology and Cosmology in the World Religions.* New York: New York University Press, 2012.

———, ed. *The Harmony Debates: Exploring a practical philosophy for a sustainable future.* Lampeter: Sophia Centre Press, 2020.

Cardinale, Bradley J., E. Duffy, A. Gonzalez, D.U. Hooper, C. Perrings, P. Venail, A. Narwani, G.M. Mace, D. Tilman, D.A. Wardle, A.P. Kinzig, G.C. Daily, M. Loreau, J.B. Grace, A. Larigauderie, D. Srivastava, and S. Naeem. 'Biodiversity loss and its impact on humanity'. *Nature* 486, 7401 (2012): pp. 59–67.

Carson, Rachel. *The Silent Spring.* Boston: Houghton and Mifflin, 1962.

Castro, Madeline A., R. Burrows, and Robin Wooffitt. 'The paranormal is (still) normal: The sociological implications of a survey of paranormal experiences in Great Britain'. *Sociological Research Online* 19, no 3. (2014).

Centemeri, Laura. 'Commons and the new environmentalism of everyday life: Alternative value practices and multispecies commoning in the permaculture movement'. *Rassegna Italiana di Sociologia* 59, no. 2 (2018): p. 8.

'The Large Hadron Collider'. CERN. https://www.home.cern/science/accelerators/large-hadron-collider [accessed 5 March 2023].

Chamowitx, Daniel. *What a Plant Knows: A Field Guide to the Senses.* London: Scientific American / Farrar, Straus & Giroux, 2017 [2012].

Chaplin, Jonathan. 'The global greening of religion'. *Palgrave Communication* 2, 16047 (2016).

Chatterjee, Margaret. *The Concept of Spirituality.* New Delhi: Allied Publishers Private Limited, 1989.

Clarke, Isabel. 'Beyond the God Spot: Transcendence and the Brain'. *The Way* 53, no. 1 (2014): pp. 49–55.

Clements, Frederic E. *Plant Succession and Indicators.* New York: H.W. Wilson, 1928.

'United Kingdom: Bipartisan UK Parliament declares a climate emergency'. Climate

Emergency Declaration. https://climateemergencydeclaration.org/united-king-dom-bipartisan-uk-parliament-declares-a-climate-emergency/ [accessed 6 March 2023].

Comte, Auguste. 'The Positive Philosophy', in *Sociological Perspectives*, ed. Kenneth Thompson and Jeremy Tunstall, (London: Penguin, 1976), pp. 18–32.

Conan, Michel. *Sacred Gardens and Landscapes: Ritual and Agency*. Cambridge, MA: Harvard University Press, 2007.

Cooper, Joe. *The Case of the Cottingley Fairies*. London: Pocket Books, 1997.

Cross, Fiona R., and Robert R. Jackson. 'The execution of planned detours by spider-eating predators'. *Journal of the Experimental Analysis of Behaviour* 105, no. 1 (18 January 2016): pp. 194–210.

Cunningham, Andrew. 'The Culture of Gardens', in *Cultures of Natural History*, ed. N. Jardine, J. A. Secord and E.C. Spary. Cambridge: Cambridge University Press, 1996.

Curry, Patrick. *Ecological Ethics*. London: Polity, 2019.

Cush, Denise. 'Paganism in the Classroom'. *British Journal of Religious Education*, 19 no. 2 (1998): pp. 83–94.

Cutchin, Joshua. *Ecology of Souls: A New Mythology of Death and the Paranormal*, Vol. One. Horse & Barrel Press, 2022.

Dagnall, Neil, Ken Drinkwater, Andrew Parker, A. and Peter Clough. 'Paranormal Experience, Belief in the Paranormal and Anomalous Beliefs'. *Paranthropology: Journal of Anthropological Approaches to the Paranormal* 7, no. 1 (2015): pp. 4–14.

———, K.G. Drinkwater, C. O'Keeffe, A. Ventola, M.A. Jawer, B. Massullo, G.B. Caputo, and J. Houran. 'Things that go bump in the literature: An environmental appraisal of "haunted houses"'. *Frontiers in Psychology* (2020).

Darwin, Charles. *On the Origins of Species*. London: Penguin, 1985 [1895].

Davies, Owen and Ceri Houlbrook. *Building Magic: Ritual and Re-enchantment in Post-Medieval Structures*. London: Palgrave Macmillan, 2021.

Davis, Caroline Franks. *The Evidential Force of Religious Experience*. Oxford: Oxford University Press, 1989.

Dawkins, Richard. *The Extended Phenotype: The Gene as the Unit of Selection*. Oxford: Oxford University Press, 1982.

deChant, Dell. 'Religion and Ecology in Popular Culture', in *Religion and Popular Culture*, ed. Terry Ray Clark and Dan W. Clanton, Jr., (Abingdon: Routledge, 2012).

de Craemer, Willy. 'A Cross-Cultural Perspective on Personhood'. *The Milbank Memorial Fund Quarterly: Health and Society* 61, no. 1 (1983): pp. 19–34.

Deleuze, Gilles, and Félix Guattari. *A Thousand Plateaus*. London: Bloomsbury, 1999 [1988].

Descartes, René. *Discourse on Method and The Meditations*. London: Penguin, 1968.

Descola, Philippe. *Beyond Nature and Culture*. Chicago: University of Chicago Press, 2005.

Devall, Bill, and George Sessions. 'Deep Ecology', in *Thinking Through the Environment: A Reader*, ed. M.J. Smith, (Abingdon: Routledge, 1999).

Devereux, Paul. *Earth Lights: Towards an Understanding of the UFO Enigma*. Wellingborough: Turnstone Press, 1982.

———. *Re-visioning the Earth: A guide to opening the healing channels between mind and nature*. New York: Atria Books, 1996.

———. *Sacred Geography: Deciphering Hidden Codes in the Landscape*. London: Gaia, 2010.

————, Stanley Krippner, Robert Tartz and Adam Fish. 'A Preliminary Study on English and Welsh Sacred Sites and Home Dream Reports', in *Transpersonal Ecosophy Vol. 1: Theory, Methods and Clinical Assessments*. ed. Mark A. Schroll, (Llanrhaeadrym-Mochnant: Psychoid Books, 2016).

Dickinson, Gordon, and Kevin Murphy. *Ecosystems*. Abingdon: Routledge, 2007.

Digance, Justine. 'Religious and secular pilgrimage: Journeys redolent with meaning', in *Tourism, Religion and Spiritual Journeys*, ed. D.J. Timothy and D.H. Olsen, (Abingdon: Routledge, 2006).

Dillon, Justin, Mark Rickinson, Kelly Teamey, Marian Morris, Mee Young Choi, Dawn Sanders and Pauline Benefield. 'The value of outdoor learning: evidence from research in the UK and elsewhere', in *Towards a Convergence Between Science and Environmental Education*, ed. Justin Dillon, (Abingdon: Routledge, 2016).

Driesch, Hans. *Psychical Research*. London: Collins, 1933.

Duggan, Ian C. 'The cultural history of the garden gnome in New Zealand'. *Studies in the History of Gardens and Designed Landscapes: An International Quarterly* 36, no. 1 (2016): pp. 78–88.

Durkheim, Émile. *The Elementary Forms of the Religious Life*. Oxford: Oxford University Press, 2008.

Egerton, Frank N. 'A History of the Ecological Sciences, Part 1: Early Greek Origins'. *Bulletin of the Ecological Society of America* 82, no. 1 (2001): pp. 93–97.

————. 'History of Ecological Sciences, Part 47: Ernst Haeckel's Ecology'. *Bulletin of the Ecological Society of America* 94, no. 3 (2013): pp. 222–44.

Eliade, Mircea. *Patterns in Comparative Religion*. Lincoln: University of Nebraska Press, 1996.

————. *The Sacred and the Profane: The Nature of Religion*. New York: Harcourt, 1987.

Enns, Anthony. 'Psychic Radio: Sound Technologies, Ether Bodies and Spiritual Vibrations'. *The Senses and Society* 3, no. 2 (2008): pp. 137–52.

Espirito Santo, Diana, and Jack Hunter, *Mattering the Invisible: Technologies, Bodies and the Realm of the Spectral*. Oxford: Berghahn, 2021.

Evans-Pritchard, Edward E. *Witchcraft, Oracles and Magic Among the Azande*. Oxford: Oxford University Press, 1975.

Fichman, Martin. 'Science in Theistic Contexts: A Case Study of Alfred Russel Wallace on Human Evolution', *Osiris* 16 (2001): pp. 227–50.

The Findhorn Foundation. *The Findhorn Garden: Pioneering a New Vision of Humanity and Nature in Cooperation*. Findhorn: Findhorn Press, 1975.

'Forestry Facts and Figures 2021: A summary of statistics about woodland and forestry in the UK'. Forestry Research. https://cdn.forestresearch.gov.uk/ 2021/09/ frfs021_zgb9htp.pdf [accessed 25 February 2023].

Forstmann, Matthias, and Christina Sagioglou. 'Lifetime experience with (classic) psychedelics predicts pro-environmental behavior through an increase in nature relatedness'. *Journal of Psychopharmacology* 31, no. 8 (2017): pp. 975–88.

Fort, Charles. *The Book of the Damned: The Collected Works of Charles Fort*. London: Tarcher Penguin, 2008.

Foster, John B, and Brett Clark. 'The Sociology of Ecology: Ecological Organicism Versus Ecosystem Ecology in the Social Construction of Ecological Science, 1926–1935'. *Organization and Environment* 21, no. 3 (2008): pp. 311–52.

————, and Brett Clark. 'The Sociology of Ecology: Ecological Organicism Versus Ecosystem Ecology in the Social Construction of Ecological Science, 1926–1935'.

Organization and Environment 21, no. 3 (2008): pp. 89–98.

Fox, Warwick. *Toward a Transpersonal Ecology: Developing New Foundations for Environmentalism.* Foxhole: Resurgence Books, 1995.

Frake, Charles O. 'Cultural Ecology and Ethnography'. *American Anthropologist* 64, no. 1 (1962): pp. 53–59.

Freud, Sigmund. *Totem and Taboo.* Abingdon: Routledge, 2007 [1913].

Fuchs, Christopher A. and Asher Peres. 'Quantum Theory Needs No "Interpretation"'. *Physics Today* 53, no. 3 (2000): pp. 70–71.

Fukuoka, Masanobu. *The One-Straw Revolution.* New York: New York Review of Books, 2009.

Gaffin, Dennis. *Running with the Fairies: Towards a Transpersonal Anthropology of Religion.* Newcastle: Cambridge Scholars Press, 2012.

Gagliano, Monica. 'Green symphonies: a call for studies on acoustic communication in plants'. *Behavioural Ecology* 24, no. 4 (2013): pp. 789–96.

———. *Thus Spoke the Plant: A Remarkable Journey of Groundbreaking Scientific Discoveries and Personal Encounters with Plants.* Berkeley: North Atlantic, 2018.

———, M. Grimonprez, M. Depczynski and M. Renton, 'Tuned in: plant roots use sound to locate water', *Oecologia* 184, no. 1 (2017): pp. 151–160.

———, M. Renton, M. Depczynski, and S. Mancuso. 'Experience teaches plants to learn faster and forget slower in environments where it matters'. *Oecologia* 175, no. 1 (2014): pp. 63–72.

Gallagher, James. 'More than half of your body is not human'. BBC News. https://www.bbc.co.uk/news/health-43674270/ [accessed 25 February 2023].

Gamble, Christopher N., Joshua S. Hanan and Thomas Nail. 'What is New Materialism?' *Angelaki: Journal of the Theoretical Humanities* 24, no. 6 (2019): pp. 111–24.

Gandy, Sam, Matthias Forstmann, Robin Carhart-Harris, Chris Timmermann, David Luke and Rosalind Watts. 'The potential synergistic effects between psychedelic administration and nature contact for the improvement of mental health'. *Health Psychology Open* 7, no. 2 (2020): pp. 1–21.

Garuba, Harry Olúdáre. 'On animism, modernity/colonialism and the African order of knowledge: Provisional reflections', in *Contested Ecologies: Dialogues in the South on Nature and Knowledge*, ed. L. Green, (Cape Town: HSRC Press, 2013).

Geertz, Clifford. 'From the native's point of view: On the nature of anthropological understanding'. *Bulletin of the American Academy of Arts and Sciences* 28, no. 1 (1974): pp. 26–45.

Gell, Alfred. 'Technology and Magic'. *Anthropology Today* 4, no. 2 (1988): pp. 6–9.

Gergen, Kenneth J. *Relational Being: Beyond Self and Community.* Oxford: Oxford University Press, 2009.

Gilbert, S.F., and S. Sarkar. 'Embracing complexity: Organicism for the 21st century'. *Developmental Dynamics* 219 (2000): pp. 1–9.

Glikson, Andrew. 'Fire and human evolution: The deep-time blueprints of the Anthropocene'. *Anthropocene* 3 (2013): pp. 89–92.

Godfrey-Smith, Peter. *Other Minds: The Octopus and the Evolution of Intelligence Life.* London: William Collins, 2017.

Goldman, Jason G. 'Lions are the Brainiest of the Big Cats', *Scientific American* (1 December 2016), https://www.scientificamerican.com/article/lions-are-the-brainiest-of-the-big-cats/ [accessed 20 March 2023]

Gomez-Martin, Alex. 'Facing biology's open questions: Rupert Sheldrake's "heretical" hypothesis turns 40'. *Bioessays* 43, no. 6 (2021).

Graham, Fabian. 'Money God Cults in Taiwan: A Paranthropological Approach'. *Paranthropology: Journal of Anthropological Approaches to the Study of the Paranormal* 3, no. 1 (2012): pp. 9–19.

Grahame, Kenneth. *The Wind in the Willows*. London: Methuen and Co., 1936.

Gray, Michael W. 'Lynn Margulis and the endosymbiont hypothesis: 50 years later'. *Molecular Biology of the Cell* 28, no. 10 (2017).

Grieve-Carlson, Timothy. 'The Hidden Predator', in *Greening the Paranormal: Exploring the Ecology of Extraordinary Experience*, ed. Jack Hunter, (Hove: August Night, 2019).

Griffiths, Paul, and Stefan Linquist. 'The Distinction Between Innate and Acquired Characteristics', *The Stanford Encyclopedia of Philosophy* (Spring 2022 Edition). Edited by Edward N. Zalta. https://plato.stanford.edu/archives/spr2022/entries/innate-acquired/.

Grim, John. 'Indigenous Traditions: Religion and Ecology', in *The Oxford Handbook of Religion and Ecology*, ed. R.S. Gottlieb, (Oxford: Oxford University Press, 2006).

Grøn, Øyvind, and Arne Naess. *Einstein's Theory: A Rigorous Introduction for the Mathematically Untrained*. New York: Springer, 2011.

Gunningham, Neil. 'Averting Climate Catastrophe: Environmental activism, Extinction Rebellion and Coalitions of Influence'. *King's Law Journal* 30, no. 2 (2019): pp. 194–202.

Hallowell, Alfred Irving. 'Ojibwa Ontology, Behavior and World View', in *Readings in Indigenous Religions* (London: Continuum, 2002): pp. 17–50.

Haluza-DeLay, Randolph. 'Religion and climate change: varieties in viewpoints and practices'. *Wiley Interdisciplinary Reviews: Climate Change* 5, no. 2 (2014): pp. 261–79.

Harding, Stephan. *Animate Earth: Science, Intuition and Gaia*. Cambridge: Green Books, 2009.

———. 'Nature's Fragile Seminars', in *The Harmony Debates: Exploring a practical philosophy for a sustainable future*, ed. Nicholas Campion, (Lampeter: Sophia Centre Press, 2020), pp. 221–36.

Hancock, Thomas W. 'Llanrhaiadr-yn-Mochnant: Its Parochial History and Antiquities'. *Collections Historical and Archaeological Relating to Montgomeryshire* 6, (1873): pp. 319–20.

Hardy, Alister. *The Divine Flame: Natural History and Religion*. London: Collins, 1966.

———. *The Spiritual Nature of Man*. Lampeter: Religious Experience Research Centre, 1979.

Harms, Daniel. 'Of Fairies: An Excerpt from a Seventeenth-Century Magical Manuscript'. *Folklore* 129, no. 2 (2018): pp. 192–98.

Harraway. Donna. 'Anthropocene, Capitalocene, Plantationocene, Chthulucene: Making Kin', *Environmental Humanities* 6 (2015): pp. 159–65.

Harvey, Graham. *Animism: Respecting the Living World*. London: Hurst & Co., 2005.

———. 'Animism and ecology: Participating in the world community'. *The Ecological Citizen* 3, no. 1 (2019): pp. 79–84.

———. 'If 'Spiritual But Not Religious' People Are Not Religious What Difference Do They Make?'. *Journal for the Study of Spirituality* 6, no. 2 (2016): pp. 128–41.

Hay, David. 'Zoology and Religion'. https://metanexus.net/zoology-and-religion-work-alister-hardy/ [accessed 25 February 2023]

———, and Rebecca Nye, *The Spirit of the Child*. London: Jessica Kingsley, 2006.

Heelas, Paul, Linda Woodhead, Benjamin Seel, Karin Tusting and Bron Szerszynski. *The Spiritual Revolution: Why Religion Is Giving Way to Spirituality*. Oxford: Blackwell, 2005.

Hibbard, Whit. 'Ecopsychology: A Review'. *The Trumpeter* 9, no. 2 (2003): pp. 23–58.

'HVN: a positive approach to voices and visions'. *Hearing Voices Network*. http://www.hearing-voices.org/about-us/hvn-values/ [accessed 26 February 2023].

Hoffman, W., J. Beyea and J.H. Cook. 'Ecology of agricultural monocultures: Some consequences for biodiversity in biomass energy farms'. *Second biomass conference of the Americas: Energy, environment, agriculture, and industry. Proceedings* (1995).

Holmgren, David. *Permaculture: Principles and Pathways Beyond Sustainability*. Hepburn: Holmgren Design Services, 2006.

Holt, James D. 'The Church of Jesus Christ of Latter-Day Saints in the RE classroom'. *Resource* 24, no. 3 (2002): pp. 6–8.

———. 'Jehovah's Witnesses and the RE Classroom', *Resource* 26, no. 2 (2004): pp. 16–19.

———. *Religious Education in the Secondary School*. Abingdon: Routledge, 2014.

Honko, Lauri. 'Memorates and the Study of Folk Beliefs'. *Journal of the Folklore Institute* 1, no. 1/2 (1964): pp. 5–19.

Houghton, R.A. 'Biomass'. in *Encyclopedia of Ecology*, ed. S.E. Jørgensen and B.D. Fath, (Elsevier, 2008).

Howell, Rachel A., and Simon Allen. 'Significant life experiences, motivations and values of climate change educators'. *Environmental Education Research* 25, no. 6 (2019): pp. 813–31.

Hufford, David J. *The Terror That Comes in the Night: An Experience-Centered Study of Supernatural Assault Traditions*. Philadelphia: University of Pennsylvania Press, 1982.

Huggett, Richard J. 'Ecosphere, biosphere, or Gaia? What to call the global ecosystem'. *Global Ecology and Biogeography* 8 (1999): pp. 425–31.

Hughes, Dewi Arwel. 'Mysticism: the perennial philosophy?', in *Mysticisms East and West*, ed. C. Partridge and T. Gabriel, (Cumbria: Paternoster, 2003), pp. 306–24.

Hume, David. *Dialogues Concerning Natural Religion*. Oxford: Oxford University Press, 1993.

Hume, Lynn. 'The dreaming in contemporary Aboriginal Australia', in *Indigenous Religions: A Companion,* ed. Graham Harvey, (London: Cassell, 2000), pp. 125–38.

Humphreys, Aelys M., R. Govaerts, S.Z. Ficinski, E.N. Lughadha and M.S. Vorontsova. 'Global dataset shows geography and life form predict modern plant extinction and rediscovery'. *Nature Ecology and Evolution* 3 (2019): pp. 1043–47.

Hunter, Jack. *Deep Weird: The Varieties of High Strangeness Experience*. Hove: August Night, 2023.

———. *Greening the Paranormal: Exploring the Ecology of Extraordinary Experience*. Hove: August Night, 2019.

———. 'Harmony and Ecology', in *The Harmony Debates: Exploring a practical philosophy for a sustainable future*, ed. Nicholas Campion, (Lampeter: Sophia Centre Press, 2020), pp. 209–20.

———. *Manifesting Spirits: An Anthropological Study of Mediumship and the Paranormal*. London: Aeon Books, 2020.

———. 'Preliminary Report on Extraordinary Experience in Permaculture: Collapsing the Natural/Supernatural Divide'. *Journal of Exceptional Experiences and Psychology* 6, no. 1 (2018): pp. 12–22.

———. 'The MA in Ecology and Spirituality: Background and Interview with Dr. Andy Letcher'. *Journal for the Study of Religious Experience* 7, no. 2 (2021): pp. 140–45.

———. 'Through a Crystal Darkly: Cultural, Experiential and Ontological Reflections on Faery', in *Fairy Films: Wee-Folk on the Big Screen,* ed. Joshua Cutchin, (Educated Dragon Publishing, 2023).

———, and Rachael Ironside, *Folklore, People and Place: International Perspectives on Tourism and Tradition in Storied Places*. Abingdon: Routledge, 2023.

"Concern about climate change reaches record levels with half now 'very concerned'". *Ipsos Mori.* https://www.ipsos.com/en-uk/concern-about-climate-change- reaches-record-levels-half-now-very-concerned [accessed 26 February 2023].

Ironside, Rachael, and Stewart Massie. 'The Folklore-Centric Gaze: A Relational Approach to Landscape, Folklore and Tourism'. *Time and Mind: Journal of Archaeology, Consciousness and Culture* 13, no. 3 (2020): pp. 227–44.

'Islamic Declaration on Global Climate Change'. https://cambridgecentralmosque.org/wp-content/uploads/2020/03/writings-climate-declaration-mwb.pdf [accessed 13 March 2023].

James, Ronald M. 'Knockers, Knackers, and Ghosts: Immigrant Folklore in the Western Mines'. *Western Folklore* 51, no. 2 (1992): pp. 153–77.

James, William. 'Frederic Myers's service to psychology'. *Proceedings of the Society for Psychical Research* 17 (1901): pp. 1–23.

———. *The Varieties of Religious Experience*. New York: Barnes and Noble, 2004.

Jepson, Paul, and Cain Blythe. *Rewilding: The Radical New Science of Ecological Recovery*. London: Icon Books, 2020.

Johnson, Norris Brock. 'Geomancy, sacred geometry, and the idea of a garden: Tenryu-ji temple, Kyoto, Japan'. *The Journal of Garden History* 9, no. 1 (1989): pp. 1–19.

Jones, Alysha, and David Segal. 'Unsettling Ecopsychology: Addressing Settler Colonialism in Ecopsychology Practice'. *Ecopsychology* 10, no. 3 (2018): pp. 127–36.

Jones, Steve, and Jack Hunter. *One School One Planet Vol. 1: Climate. Education. Innovation.* Llanrhaeadr-ym-Mochnant: Psychoid Books, 2018.

———, and Jack Hunter. *One School One Planet Vol. 2: Permaculture, Education and Cultural Change*. Llanrhaeadr-ym-Mochnant: Psychoid Books, 2019.

———, Jack Hunter and Angharad Rees, A. *Small and Slow Solutions: Unleashing the Creativity of the Climate Change Generation*. Llanrhaeadr-ym-Mochnant: Sector39, 2019.

Jung, Carl G. *Psychology and the Occult*. Abingdon: Routledge, 2007.

Kastrup, Bernardo. 'The Universe in Consciousness'. *Journal of Consciousness Studies* 25, no. 5–6 (2018): pp. 125–55.

Kedar, Yafit, Gil Kedar and Ran Barkai. 'Hypoxia in Paleolithic decorated caves: the use of artificial light in deep caves reduces oxygen concentration and produces altered states of consciousness'. *Time and Mind* 14, no. 1 (2021): pp. 1–36.

Keel, John. *Our Haunted Planet*. London: Neville Spearman, 1971.

———. *Strange Creatures from Time and Space*. Greenwich: Fawcett, 1970.

———. *The Eighth Tower: On Ultraterrestrials and the Superspectrum*. Charlottesville: Anomalist Books, 2013.

Kelleher, Colm A., and George Knapp. *Hunt for the Skinwalker: Science Confronts the Unexplained at a Remote Utah Ranch*. New York: Paraview Pocket Books, 2005.

Kerr, Margaret, and David Key. 'The Ouroboros (Part 1): Towards an ontology of connectedness in ecopsychology research'. *European Journal of Ecopsychology* 2 (2011): pp. 48–60.

Keys, Eric. 'Kaqchikel Gardens: Women, Children, and Multiple Roles of Gardens among the Maya of Highland Guatemala'. *Yearbook (Conference of Latin Americanist Geographers)* 25 (1999): pp. 89–100.

Kimmerer, Robin Wall. *Braiding Sweetgrass: Indigenous Wisdom, Scientific Knowledge, and the Teachings of Plants.* Minneapolis: Milkweed, 2013.

———. 'Restoration and Reciprocity: The Contributions of Traditional Ecological Knowledge', in *Human Dimensions of Ecological Restoration: Integrating Science, Nature and Culture*, ed. D. Egan, E.E. Hjerpe & J. Abrams, (Washington, DC: Island Press, 2011): pp. 257–76.

———. '*Mishkos Kenomagwen*, the Lessons of Grass: Restoring Reciprocity with the Good Green Earth', in *Traditional Ecological Knowledge: Learning from Indigenous Practices for Environmental Sustainability*, ed. Melissa K. Nelson and Dan Shilling, (Cambridge: Cambridge University Press, 2018), pp. 31.

———. 'Weaving Traditional Ecological Knowledge into Biological Education: A Call to Action'. *BioScience* 52, no. 5 (2002): pp. 432–38.

Kingsland, Sharon Elizabeth. 'Facts or Fairy Tales? Peter Wohlleben and the Hidden Life of Trees'. *Bulletin of the Ecological Society of America* 99, no. 4 (2018).

Kirchner, James. 'The Gaia Hypotheses: Are They Testable? Are They Useful?', *Philosophical Foundations of Gaia* (1991), pp. 38–46.

Kohn, Eduardo. *How Forests Think: Toward an Anthropology Beyond the Human.* Berkeley: University of California Press, 2013.

Kõivupuu, Marju. 'Tradition in landscape, landscape in tradition: discourse of natural sanctuaries in Estonia'. *Time and Mind* 13, no. 3 (2020): 267–81.

Kripal, Jeffrey J. *Authors of the Impossible: The Paranormal and the Sacred.* Chicago: University of Chicago Press, 2010.

———. *Comparing Religions: Coming to Terms.* Chichester: Wiley Blackwell, 2014.

———. *The Flip: Epiphanies of Mind and the Future of Knowledge.* New York: Bellevue Literary Press, 2019.

Krippner, Stanley. 'Personal Mythology: An Introduction to the Concept'. *The Humanistic Psychologist* 18, no. 2 (1990): pp. 137–42.

Kuhn, Thomas. *The Structure of Scientific Revolutions.* Chicago: University of Chicago Press, 1962.

Laland, Kevin, and William Hoppitt. 'Do Animals Have Culture?' *Evolutionary Anthropology* 12, no. 3 (2003): pp. 150–59.

Lancaster, Brian L. *Approaches to Consciousness: The Marriage of Science and Mysticism.* Basingstoke: Palgrave Macmillan, 2004.

Latour, Bruno. *Facing Gaia: Eight Lectures on the New Climatic Regime.* Cambridge: Polity Press, 2017.

Laughlin, Charles D. 'Communing with the Gods: The Dreaming Brain in Cross-cultural Perspective'. *Time and Mind: Journal of Archaeology, Consciousness and Culture* 4, no. 2 (2011): pp. 155–88.

Laursen, Christopher. 'Plurality through imagination: The emergence of online tulpa communities in the making of new identities', in *Believing in bits: Digital media and the supernatural*, ed. Simone Natale and Diana W. Pasulka, (Oxford: Oxford University Press, 2019), pp. 163–79.

Lecouteux, Claude. *Demons and Spirits of the Land: Ancestral Lore and Practice*. Rochester: Inner Traditions, 2015.

Lenton, Timothy M., and Bruno Latour. 'Gaia 2.0 – Could humans add some level of self-awareness to Earth's self-regulation?' *Science* 361, no. 6407 (2018): pp. 1066–68.

Leopold, Aldo. *A Sand County Almanac: And Sketches Here and There*. Oxford: Oxford University Press, 1949.

Letcher, Andy. 'The Scouring of the Shire: Fairies, Trolls and Pixies in Eco-Protest Culture'. *Folklore* 112 (2001): pp. 147–61.

Lévi-Strauss, Claude. *Structural Anthropology, Volume I*. London: Penguin, 1986.

Lewis, Gareth, and Ben Scambary. 'Sacred Bodies and Ore Bodies: Conflicting Commodification of Landscape by Indigenous Peoples and Miners in Australia's Northern Territory', in *The Right to Protect Sites: Indigenous Heritage Management in the Era of Native Title*, ed. P.F. McGrath, (Canberra: Australian Institute of Aboriginal and Torres Strait Islander Studies, 2016), pp. 221–52.

Lewis, Simon L., and Mark A. Maslin. 'Defining the Anthropocene'. *Nature* 519 (2015): pp. 171–80.

Lioi, Anthony. 'Of Swamp Dragons: Mud, Megalopolis, and a Future for Ecocriticism', in *The Monster Theory Reader,* ed. Jeffrey A. Weinstock, (Minneapolis: University of Minnesota Press, 2020), pp. 439–58.

Loreau, Michel, A. Downing, M. Emmerson, A. Gonzalez, J. Hughes, P. Inchausti, J. Joshi, J. Norberg and O. Sala. 'A New Look at the Relationship Between Diversity and Stability', in *Biodiversity and Ecosystem Functioning*, ed. Michel Loreau, Shahid Naeem and Pablo Inchausti, (Oxford: Oxford University Press, 2002).

Louth, Jonathan. 'From Newton To Newtonianism: Reductionism And The Development Of The Social Sciences'. *Emergence: Complexity and Organization* 13, no. 4 (2011): pp. 63–83.

Lovelock, James. 'A Physical Basis for Life Detection Experiments'. *Nature* 207 (1965): pp. 568–70.

———. 'Atmospheric Fluorine Compounds as Indicators of Air Movements'. *Nature* 230 (1971): p. 379.

———. *Gaia: A New Look at Life on Earth*. Oxford: Oxford University Press, 2000.

———, and Lynn Margulis. 'Atmospheric homeostasis by and for the biosphere: the gaia hypothesis'. *Tellus* 26, nos. 1–2 (1974): pp. 2–10.

Luke, David, and Marios Kittenis. 'A preliminary survey of paranormal experiences with psychoactive drugs'. *Journal of Parapsychology* 69, no. 2 (2005): pp. 305–27.

Lynch, Gordon. *Understanding Theology and Popular Culture*. Oxford: Blackwell, 2005.

Mack, John E. *Abduction: Human Encounters with Aliens*. New York: Ballantine Books, 1995.

Mackinon, Iain, Lewis Williams and Arianna Waller. 'The re-indigenization of humanity to Mother Earth: A learning platform to cultivate social-ecological resilience and challenge the Anthropocene'. *Journal of Sustainability Education* 16 (2017).

MacManaway, Patrick. 'Land Whispering: Practice Applications of Consciousness and Subtle Energy Awareness in Agriculture', in *Subtle Agroecologies: Farming with the Hidden Half of Nature* (Abingdon: CRC Press, 2021), pp. 293–304.

Macy, Joanna. 'Working Through Environmental Despair', in *Ecopsychology: Restoring the earth, healing the mind*, ed. T. Roszak *et al.,* (Sierra Club Books, 1995).

Malinwoski, Bronislaw. *Coral Gardens and their Magic: A Study of the Methods of Tilling Soil and Agricultural Rites in the Trobriand Islands*. Woking: Unwin Brothers, 1935.

Mancuso, Stefano, and Alessandra Viola. *Brilliant Green: The Surprising History and Science of Plant Intelligence*. London: Island Press, 2015.

———. *The Revolutionary Genius of Plants: A New Understanding of Plant Intelligence and Behavior*. New York: Atria Books, 2018.

Mann, Charles. 'Lynn Margulis: Science's unruly Earth Mother'. *Science* 252, no. 5004 (1991): pp. 378–81.

Mann, Janet, and Eric M. Patterson. 'Tool Use by Aquatic Animals'. *Philosophical Transactions of the Royal Society – Biological Sciences* 368, no. 1630 (2013): pp. 1–11.

Mannion, Antoinette. *Global Environmental Change*. Harlow: Longman Scientific and Technical, 1994.

Margulis, Lynn, and Bermudes. 'Symbiosis as a Mechanism of Evolution: Status of Cell Symbios– is Theory'. *Symbiosis* 1 (1985): pp. 101–24.

Markus, Hazel R. and Shinobu Kitayama. 'Culture and the self: Implications for cognition, emotion and motivation'. *Psychological Bulletin* 98, no. 2 (1991): pp. 224–353.

Marsh, Chris. 'Permaculture (and) Religion'. https://www.academia.edu/7131096/Permaculture_and_Religion [accessed 26 February 2023].

Marshall, Paul. *Mystical Encounters with the Natural World: Experiences and Explanations*. Oxford: Oxford University Press, 2005.

Martin. Leanne, M.P. White, A. Hunt, M. Richardson, S. Pahl and J. Burt. 'Nature contact, nature connectedness and associations with health, well-being and pro-environmental behaviours'. *Journal of Environmental Psychology* 68 (2020).

Matthews, Freya. *The Ecological Self*. London: Routledge, 2006.

Mauss, Marcel. 'A Category of the Human Mind: The Notion of Person; The Notion of Self', in *The Category of the Person: Anthropology, Philosophy, History*, ed. M. Carrithers, S. Collins, and S. Lukes, (Cambridge: Cambridge University Press. 1985), pp. 1–26.

Mayer, F. Stephan, and Cynthia McPherson Frantz. 'The Connectedness to Nature Scale: A Measure of Individuals' Feeling in Community with Nature'. *Journal of Environmental Psychology* 24, no. 4 (2004): pp. 503–15.

Mazinegiizhigo-kwe Bédard, Renée E. 'Jiisakiiwigaan: Shaking Tent Ceremony as Sacred Metamorphosis,' in *Deep Weird: The Varieties of High Strangeness Experience*, ed. Jack Hunter, (Hove: August Night, 2023): p. 337.

McCann, Greg. 'Bioregions and Spirit Places: Taking Up Jim Dodge's Long-Lost Suggestion'. *The Trumpeter* 27, no. 3 (2017): pp. 10–26.

McCue, Peter. *Zones of Strangeness: An Examination of Paranormal and UFO Hot Spots*. Bloomington: AuthorHouse, 2012.

McGovern, Sean. 'The Ryôan-ji Zen garden: textual meanings in topographical form'. *Visual Communication* 3, no. 3 (2004): pp. 344–59.

Metzner, Ralph. *Green Psychology: Transforming Our Relationship to the Earth*. Rochester: Park Street Press, 1999.

Mills, Martin. 'Anthropology and Religious Studies', in *The SAGE Handbook of Social Anthropology*, ed. R. Fardon, O. Harris, T.H.J. Marchand, C. Shore, V. Straong, R. Wilson & M. Nuttall (London: Sage, 2012), pp. 183–96.

Mizrach, Steven. 'The Para-Anthropology of UFO Abductions: The Case for the Ultraterrestrial Hypothesis', in *Strange Dimensions: A Paranthropology Anthology*, ed. Jack Hunter, (Llanrhaeadr-ym-Mochnant: Psychoid Books, 2015), pp. 299–336.

Mollison, Bill. *Travel in Dreams: 'One Fat Foot after Another': The Autobiography of Bill Mollison*. Stanley: Tagari Press, 1996.

———, and David Holmgren. *Permaculture One: A Perennial Agriculture for Human Settlements*. Tyalgum: Tagari Publications, 1990.

Molyneaux, Brian Leigh, and Piers Vitebsky. *Sacred Earth, Sacred Stones*. San Diego: Laurel Glen, 2001.

Monbiot, George. *Feral: Rewilding the Land, Sea and Human Life*. London: Penguin, 2014.

Moore, Jason W. 'The Capitalocene, Part I: on the nature and origins of our ecological crisis'. *Journal of Peasant Studies* 44, no 3 (2017): pp. 594–630.

Morrison, Kenneth M. 'The cosmos as intersubjective: Native American other-than-human persons', in *Indigenous Religions: A Companion*, ed. Graham Harvey, (New York: Cassell, 2000).

Morton, Timothy. *Being Ecological*. London: Pelican, 2018.

———. *Hyperobjects: Philosophy and Ecology after the End of the World*. Minneapolis: University of Minnesota Press, 2013.

———. *The Ecological Thought*. Cambridge, MA: Harvard University Press, 2010.

R. B. Myneni, J. Dong, C. J. Tucker, R. K. Kaufmann, P. E. Kauppi, J. Liski, L. Zhou, V. Alexeyev, and M. K. Hughes. 'A large carbon sink in the woody biomass of northern forests'. *Earth, Atmospheric and Planetary Scienes* 98, no. 26 (2001): pp. 14784–89.

Myers, Frederic W. H., *Human Personality and its Survival of Bodily Death*. Norwich: Pelegrin Trust, 1992.

———. 'Multiplex Personality' (1888), https://www.bl.uk/collection-items/multiplex-personality-from-the-nineteenth-century [accessed 26 February 2023].

Naess, Arne, *Ecology of Wisdom*. London: Penguin Books, 2008.

———. 'Intrinsic value: Will the defenders of nature please rise', in *Wisdom in the Open Air*, ed. P. Reed and D. Rothenberg, (Minneapolis: University of Minnesota Press, 1993), pp. 70–82.

———. 'Self-realization: An ecological approach to being in the world', in *Deep ecology for the twenty-first century*, ed. George Sessions, (Boston: Shambhala, 1995).

———. 'The Shallow and the Deep, Long-Range Ecology Movement. A Summary'. *Inquiry* 16, no. 1–4 (1973): pp. 95–100.

Nagel, Thomas. *Mind and Cosmos: Why the Materialist Neo-Darwinian Conception of Nature is Almost Certainly False*. Oxford: Oxford University Press, 2012.

Narby, Jeremy. *Intelligence in Nature: An Inquiry into Knowledge*. New York: Tarcher-perigee, 2006.

Natale, Simone. 'The Invisible Made Visible: X-rays as attraction and visual medium at the end of the nineteenth century'. *Media History* 17, no. 4 (2011): pp. 345–58.

Naydler, Jeremy. *Gardening as Sacred Art*. Edinburgh: Floris Books, 2011.

Nelson, Roger, and Peter Bancel. 'Effects of Mass Consciousness: Changes in Random Data during Global Events'. *Explore: Journal of Science and Healing* 7, no. 6 (2011): pp. 373–83.

Norris, Ken. 'Agriculture and biodiversity conservation: opportunity knocks'. *Conservation Letters*, 1 (2008): pp. 2–11.

Odum, Eugene, *Ecology*. New York: Holt, Rinehart and Winston, 1975.

———. 'The Strategy of Ecosystem Development'. *Science* 164 (1969): pp. 262–70.

Oman, Doug. 'Defining religion and spirituality', in *Handbook of the psychology of religion and spirituality*, ed. R.F. Paloutzian and C.L. Park, (Guildford: The Guildford Press, 2013), pp. 23–47.

Onori, Luciano, and Guido Visconti. 'The GAIA theory: from Lovelock to Margulis. From homeostatic to a cognitive autopoietic worldview'. *Rend. Fis. Acc. Lincei* 23 (2012): p. 376.

Oss, O.T., and O.N. Oeric. *Psilocybin Magic Mushroom Grower's Guide*. Grand Junction: Quick American Archives, 2006.

Otto, Rudolf. *The Idea of the Holy*. Oxford: Oxford University Press, 1958.

Owen, Suzanne. 'The World Religions paradigm: time for a change'. *Arts and Humanities in Higher Education* 10, no. 3 (2011): pp. 253–68.

Pace, Michael L., J.J. Cole, S.R. Carpenter and J.F. Kitchell. 'Trophic cascades revealed in diverse ecosystems'. *Trends in Ecology and Evolution* 14, no. 12 (1999): pp. 483–88.

Paine, Robert T. 'Food Web Complexity and Species Diversity'. *The American Naturalist* 100, no. 910 (1966): pp. 65–75.

Paley, William. *Natural Theology: Or, Evidences of the Existence and Attributes of the Deity, Collected from the Appearances of Nature*. Cambridge: Cambridge University Press, 2009.

Park, Chris. *Sacred Worlds: An Introduction to Geography and Religion*. Abingdon: Routledge, 1994.

Paul, Andrew, Robin Roth and Saw Sha Bwe Moo. 'Relational ontology and more-than-human agency in Indigenous Karen conservation practice'. *Pacific Conservation Biology* 27, no. 4 (2021): pp. 376–90.

Pavord, Anna. *The Naming of Names: The Search for Order in the World of Plants*. London: Bloomsbury, 2005.

Peake, Anthony. *The Hidden Universe: An Investigation into Non-Human Intelligences*. London: Watkins, 2019.

Pearce, Michael Robert. 'Accommodating the discarnate: Thai spirit houses and the phenomenology of place'. *Material Religion* 7, no. 3 (2015): pp. 344–72.

Persinger, Michael A., K.S. Saroka, S.A. Koren, and L.S. St-Pierre. 'The Electromagnetic Induction of Mystical and Altered States within the Laboratory'. *Journal of Consciousness Exploration and Research* 1, no. 7 (2010): pp. 808–30.

Petit, J.R., J. Jouzel, D. Raynaud, N.I. Barkov, J.-M. Barnola, I. Basile, M. Bender, J. Chappellaz, M. Davisk, G. Delaygue, M. Delmotte, V.M. Kotlyakov, M. Legrand, V.Y. Lipenkov, C. Lorius, L. Pépin, C. Ritz, E. Saltzmank and M. Stievenard. 'Climate and atmospheric history of the past 420,000 years from the Vostok ice core, Antarctica'. *Nature* 399 (1999): 429–36.

Phillipson, Garry. 'Panpsychism and Astrology', in *Skylights: Essays in the History and Contemporary Culture of Astrology*, ed. Frances Clynes, (Lampeter: Sophia Centre Press, 2022), pp. 165–86.

Pickard, Catriona, Ben Pickard and Clive Bonsall. 'Autistic Spectrum Disorder in Prehistory'. *Cambridge Archaeological Journal* 21, no. 3 (2011): pp. 357–64.

Pimentel, David, C. Harvey, P. Resosudarmo, K. Sinclair, D. Kurz, M. McNair, S. Crist, L. Shpritz, L. Fitton, R. Saffouri and R. Blair. 'Environmental and Economic Costs of Soil Erosion and Conservation Benefits'. *Science* 267 (1995): 1117–23.

Plato. *Timaeus*, translated by R.G. Bury. Cambridge, MA: Harvard University Press,

1931.

Platvoet, Jan G. 'Does God have a Body? On the Materiality of Akan Spirituality', in *New Paths in the Study of Religions: Festschrift in Honour of Michael Pye on his 65th Birthday,* ed. C. Kleine, M. Schrimpf and K. Triplett, (Munich: Biblion Verlag, 2004), pp. 175–205.

Plumwood, Val. 'Nature in the Active Voice'. *Australian Humanities Review* 46 (2010): pp. 113–29.

———. 'Surviving a Crocodile Attack'. https://www.utne.com/arts/being-prey/ [accessed 31 December 2022].

Polkey, Angie. 'The Permaculture Path to Harmony: a study of personal emergence', in *The Harmony Debates: Exploring a practical philosophy for a sustainable future,* ed. Nicholas Campion, (Lampeter: Sophia Centre Press, 2020), pp. 411–16.

Pope Francis, Laudato Si. https://www.vatican.va/content/dam/francesco/pdf/encyclicals/documents/papa-francesco_20150524_enciclica-laudato-si_en.pdf [accessed 25 February 2023].

Possamai, Adam, and Murray Lee. 'Hyper-real religions: Fear, anxiety and late-modern religious innovation'. *Journal of Sociology* 47, no. 3 (2011): pp. 227–42.

Price-Williams, David, and Rosslyn Gaines. 'The Dreamtime and Dreams of Northern Australian Aboriginal Artists'. *Ethos* 22, no. 3 (1994): pp. 373–88.

'Project Hessdalen'. http://www.hessdalen.org/index_e.shtml [accessed 14 March 2023].

Purewal, Navtej K., and Virinder S. Kalwa. 'Women's "popular" practices as critique: Vernacular religion in Indian and Pakistani Punjab'. *Women's Studies International Forum* 33 (2010): pp. 383–89.

Radin, Dean, Leena Michel, Karla Galdamez, Paul Wendland, Robert Rickenbach and Arnaud Delorme. 'Consciousness and the double-slit interference pattern: Six experiments'. *Physics Essays* 25, no. 2 (2012): pp. 157–71.

Randall, John L. *Parapsychology and the Nature of Life.* London: Souvenir Press, 1975.

Rappaport, Roy A. *Ecology, Meaning, and Religion.* Berkeley: North Atlantic, 1979.

Restall, Brian, and Elisabeth Conrad. 'A literature review of connectedness to nature and its potential for environmental management'. *Journal of Environmental Management* 159 (2015): pp. 1–15.

Rhodes, Christopher J. 'Permaculture: Regenerative – not merely sustainable'. *Science Progress* 98, no. 4 (2014): pp. 403–12.

Richet, Charles. *Thirty Years of Psychical Research: A Treatise on Metapsychics.* London: Macmillan, 1923.

Ring, Kenneth, and Evelyn Elsaesser Valarino. *Lessons from the light: What we can learn from the Near-Death Experience.* Needham: Moment Point Press, 2006.

Robichaud, Paul. *Pan: The Great God's Modern Return.* London: Reaktion Books, 2021.

Rockström ,Johann, O. Gaffney, J. Rogelj, M. Meinshausen, N. Nakicenovic and Schellnhuber. 'A Roadmap for Rapid Decarbonization'. *Science* 355, no. 6331 (2017): pp. 1269–71.

Roney-Dougal, Serena. *Where Science and Magic Meet.* Glastonbury: Green Magic, 2002.

Rootes, Christopher. 'Environmental movements: From the local to the global'. *Environmental Politics* 8, no. 1 (1999): pp. 1–12.

Rosa, Claudio D., C. C. Profice and S. Collado. 'Nature Experiences and Adults' Self-Reported Pro-environmental Behaviors: The Role of Connectedness to Nature and

Childhood Nature Experiences'. *Frontiers in Psychology* 9, no. 1055 (2018): pp. 1–10.

Roszak, Theodore. *The Voice of the Earth: An Exploration of Ecopsychology.* New York: Bantam, 1993.

Royal Society for the Protection of Birds. 'Starling Murmurations'. https://www.rspb. org.uk/birds-and-wildlife/wildlife-guides/bird-a-z/starling/starling-murmurations/ [accessed 20 March 2023].

Rummukainen, Markku. 'Changes in climate and weather extremes in the 21st century'. *Wiley Interdisciplinary Reviews: Climate Change* 3, no. 2 (2012): pp. 115–29.

Rumsey, Alan. 'The Dreaming, Human Agency and Inscriptive Practice'. *Oceania* 65 (1994): pp. 116–30.

Sauven, John. 'Harmony and the Climate Crisis', in *The Harmony Debates: Exploring a practical philosophy for a sustainable future*, ed. Nicholas Campion, (Lampeter: Sophia Centre Press, 2020), pp. 439–43.

Scheuerman, William E. 'Political Disobedience and the Climate Emergency'. *Philosophy and Social Criticism* 48, no. 6 (2022).

Schmidt, Bettina. *The Study of Religious Experience: Approaches and Methodologies.* Sheffield: Equinox, 2016.

Schroll, Mark A. *Ecology, Cosmos and Consciousness: Comic-Book Lore, Dreams and Inquiries into Various Other Transpersonal Ecosophical States.* Llanrhaeadr-ym-Mochnant: Psychoid Books, 2018.

———. *Transpersonal Ecosophy Vol. 1: Theory, Methods and Clinical Assessments.* Llanrhaeadr-ym-Mochnant: Psychoid Books, 2016.

Seed, John, Joanna Macy, Pat Fleming and Arne Naess, A. *Thinking Like A Mountain: Towards a Council of All Beings.* Gabriola Island: New Catalyst Books, 2007.

Sewall, Laura, and Thomas L. Fleischner. 'Why Ecopsychology Needs Natural History'. *Ecopsychology* 11, no. 2 (2019): pp. 78–80.

Shamdasani, Sonu. 'Introduction', in *From India to the Planet Mars: A Case of Multiple Personality with Imaginary Languages*, Theodore Flournoy, (Princeton: Princeton University Press,1994).

Sheaffer, Robert. 'Do Fairies Exist?'. *The Zetetic* (Fall/Winter, 1977): pp. 46–52.

Sheldrake, Merlin. *Entangled Life: How Fungi Make Our Worlds, Change Our Minds, and Shape Or Futures.* London: Vintage, 2020.

Sheldrake, Rupert. *A New Science of Life.* London: Icon Books, 2009.

———. 'Harmony, Science and Spirituality', in *The Harmony Debates: Exploring a practical philosophy for a sustainable future*, ed. Nicholas Campion, (Lampeter: Sophia Centre Press, 2020), pp. 237–45.

———. 'Is the Sun Conscious?' *Journal of Consciousness Studies* 28, no. 3–4 (2021): pp. 8–28.

———. *The Science Delusion.* London: Coronet, 2012.

Shilling, Daniel. 'The Soul of Sustainability', in *Traditional Ecological Knowledge: Learning from Indigenous Practices for Environmental Sustainability*, ed. M.K. Nelson & D. Schilling, (Cambridge: Cambridge University Press, 2018), pp. 3–14.

Sikes, Wirt. *British Goblins: Welsh Folklore, Fairy Mythology, Legends and Traditions.* Cockatrice Books, 2020 [1880].

Simard, Suzanne W., K.J. Beiler, M.A. Bingham, J.R. Deslippe, L.J. Philip and F.P. Teste. 'Mycorrhizal networks: Mechanisms, ecology and modelling'. *Fungal Biology Reviews* 26 (2012): pp. 39–60.

Simberloff, Daniel. 'A Succession of Paradigms in Ecology: Essentialism to Materialism and Probabilism'. *Synthese* 43, no. 1 (1980): pp. 3–39.

Sinclair, Upton. *Mental Radio*. Charlottesville: Hampton Roads, 2001.

Sjöstedt-Hughes, Peter. 'The Philosophy of Organism'. *Philosophy Now* (June/July, 2016): pp. 14–15.

———. *Modes of Sentience: Psychedelics, Metaphysics, Panpsychism*. Falmouth: Psychedelic Press, 2022).

Skeie, Geir. 'Transforming local places into learning spaces in religious education: Revisiting a collaborative research project', in *Location, Space and Place in Religious Education*, ed. Martin Rothgangel, Kerstin von Bromssen, Hans-Gunter Heimbrock and Geir Skeie, (Munster: Waxmann, 2017), pp. 115–30.

Smith, Caroline. 'The Getting of Hope: Personal Empowerment Through Permaculture'. *Proceedings of the Sixth International Permaculture Conference September-October 1996, Perth, Western Australia* (1996).

Smith. Linda Tuhiwai. *Decolonizing Methodologies: Research and Indigenous Peoples*. London: Zed Books, 2012.

'Society for Psychical Research'. SPR. https://www.spr.ac.uk [accessed 2 March 2023].

Solomon, Susan, G-K. Plattner, R. Knutti and P. Friedlingstein. 'Irreversible climate damage due to carbon dioxide emissions', *PNSA* 106, no. 6 (2008): pp. 1704–9.

Solomon, Olga. 'Sense and the Sense: Anthropology and the Study of Autism'. *Annual Review of Anthropology* 39, no. 1 (2010): pp. 241–59.

Sommer, Andreas. 'Tackling Taboos—From Psychopathia Sexualis to the Materialisation of Dreams: Albert von Schrenck-Notzing (1862–1929)'. *Journal of Scientific Exploration* 23, no. 3 (2009): pp. 299–322.

Spikins. Penny. 'Autism, the Integrations of "Difference" and the Origins of Modern Human Behaviour'. *Cambridge Archaeological Journal* 19, no. 2 (2009): pp. 179–201.

Stace, Walter T. *Mysticism and Philosophy*. London: Macmillan, 1960.

Stamets, Paul. *Mycelium Running: How Mushrooms Can Help Save the World*. Berkeley: Ten Speed Press, 2005.

Stauffer, Robert C. 'Haeckel, Darwin, and Ecology'. *The Quarterly Review of Biology*, 32 no. 2 (1957): pp. 138–44.

Steiner, Rudolf. *Agriculture Course: The Birth of the Biodynamic Method*. Forest Row: Rudolf Steiner Press, 2004.

Stocking Jr., George W. *Race, Culture, and Evolution: Essays in the History of Anthropology*. Chicago: University of Chicago Press, 1982.

Stolow. Jeremy. 'Techno-Religious Imaginaries: On the Spiritual Telegraph and the Circum-Atlantic World of the 19th Century'. Institute on Globalization and the Human Condition, McMaster University, Working Paper Series (2006).

Surin, Kenneth. 'Marxism and religion'. *Critical Research on Religion* 1, no. 1 (2013): pp. 9–14.

Swamy, P.S., M. Kumar and S.M. Sundarpandian. 'Spirituality and ecology of sacred groves in Tamil Nadu, India'. *Unasylva* 54, no. 213 (2003): pp. 53–58.

Swanson, Heather, Anna Tsing, Nils Bubandt and Elaine Gan. 'Introduction', in *Arts of Living on a Damaged Planet*, ed. A. Tsing, H. Swanson, E. Gan and N. Bubandt, (Minneapolis: University of Minnesota Press, 2017).

Taitimu, Melissa. 'Ngā whakawhitinga: standing at the crossroads: Māori ways of understanding extra-ordinary experiences and schizophrenia'. PhD Thesis, University of Auckland, 2008.

Taves, Ann. 'Religious Experience and the Divisible Self: William James (and Frederic Myers) as Theorist(s) of Religion', *Journal of the American Academy of Religion* 71, no. 2 (2003): pp. 306–11.

Taylor, Bron. *Avatar and Nature Spirituality*. Waterloo: Wilfrid Laurier University Press, 2013.

———. *Dark Green Religion*. Chicago: University of Chicago Press, 2010.

———, Gretel Van Wieren and Bernard Daley Zaleha. 'Review: Lynn White Jr. and the greening of religion hypothesis'. *Conservation Biology* 30, no. 5 (2016): pp. 1000–9.

Taylor, Charles. *A Secular Age*. Cambridge, MA: Harvard University Press, 2007.

Taylor, Greg. 'Michael Persinger Defends the "God Helmet", says Richard Dawkins Was Affected by Alcohol When He Tried It'. *The Daily Grail*. https://www.dailygrail. com/2015/11/michael-persinger-defends-the-god-helmet-says-richard-dawkins-was-affected-by-alcohol-when-he-tried-it/ [accessed 3 March 2023].

Thorley, Anthony. 'Sacred Geography: a conceptual work in progress'. *SPICA: Postgraduate Journal for Cosmology in Culture* 4, no. 2 (2016): pp. 4–8.

———, and Celia M. Gunn. *Sacred Sites: An Overview*. London: The Gaia Foundation, 2008.

Thunberg, Greta. *No One Is Too Small to Make a Difference*. London: Penguin, 2019.

Tilley, Christopher. *Phenomenology of Landscape*. Oxford: Berg, 1994.

Tompkins, Peter, and Christopher Bird. *The Secret Life of Plants*. New York: Harper, 2002.

Trigwell, Jasmine L., Andrew J. P. Francis and Kathleen L. Bagot. 'Nature Connectedness and Eudaimonic Well-Being: Spirituality as a Potential Mediator'. *Ecopsychology* 6, no. 4 (2014): pp. 241–51.

Turinek, M., S. Grobelnik-Mlakar, M. Bavec and F. Bavec. 'Biodynamic agriculture research progress and priorities'. *Renewable Agriculture and Food Systems* 24, no. 2 (2009): pp. 146–54.

Turner, Edith. *Experiencing Ritual: A New Interpretation of African Healing*. Philadelphia: University of Pennsylvania Press, 1998.

———. 'The reality of spirits: A tabooed or permitted field of study?'. *Anthropology of Consciousness* 4, no. 1 (1993): pp. 9–12.

Turner, Victor. 'Liminality and Communitas', in *Readings in the Anthropology of Religion*, ed. Michael Lambek, (Oxford: Blackwell, 2004), pp. 358–74.

Tylor, Edward Burnett. *Anthropology: An Introduction to the Study of Man and Civilization*. London: C. A. Watts, 1930.

'Emissions Gap Report 2022'. UNEP. https://www.unep.org/re- sources/emissions-gap-report-2022 [accessed 28 December 2022].

'World is off track to meet Paris Agreement climate targets'. UNEP. https://unepccc.org/world-is-off-track-to-meet-paris-agreement-climate-targets/ [accessed 27 February 2023].

'Plant for the Planet: The Billion Tree Campaign'. UNEP. https://www.unep.org/resources/publication/plant-planet-billion-tree-campaign [accessed 28 February 2023].

'Backgrounder - Traditional Ecological Knowledge'. UN Permanent Forum on Indigenous Issues. https://www.un.org/development/desa/indigenouspeoples/wp-content/uploads/sites/19/2019/04/Traditional-Knowledge-backgrounder-FINAL.pdf [accessed 4 March 2023].

'The Water in You: Water and the Human Body'. USGS. https://www.usgs.gov/special-topics/water-science-school/science/water-you-water-and-human-body   [accessed 28 February 2023].

Van de Kooij, Jacomijn C., Doret J. de Ruyter and Siebren Miedema, 'The Merits of Using "Worldview" in Religious Education', *Religious Education* 112, no. 2 (2016): pp. 172–84.

Van Gennep, Arnold, *The Rites of Passage* (Chicago: University of Chicago Press, 1961).

Vaughan-Lee, Llewellyn, *Spiritual Ecology: The Cry of the Earth* (Point Reyes: The Golden Sufi Center, 2019).

Velmans, Max, 'The Co-evolution of Matter and Consciousness', *Synthesis Philosophica* 22, no. 44 (2007): pp. 273–82.

Viveiros de Castro, Eduardo, 'Cosmological Deixis and Amerindian Perspectivism', in *A Reader in the Anthropology of Religion,* ed. Michael Lambek (Oxford: Blackwell, 2006), pp. 307–8.

Voss, Angela, and William Rowlandson, *Daimonic Imagination: Uncanny Intelligence* (Newcastle: Cambridge Scholars Press, 2013).

———, and Simon Wilson, *Re-Enchanting the Academy* (Auckland: Rubedo Press, 2017).

Walker, Lawrence R., David A. Wardle, Richar D. Bardgett and Bruce D. Clarkson. 'The use of chronosequences in studies of ecological succession and soil development'. *Journal of Ecology* 98 (2010): pp. 725–36.

Walters, Holly. *Shaligram Pilgrimage in the Nepal Himalayas.* Amsterdam: Amsterdam University Press, 2020.

Warburg, Margit. 'Graduation in Denmark: Secular Ritual and Civil Religion'. *Journal of Ritual Studies* 23, no. 2 (2009): pp. 31–42.

Watson, Lyall. *Supernature: A Natural History of the Supernatural.* London: Hodder and Stoughton, 1973.

Way, Twigs. *Garden Gnomes: A History.* Oxford: Shire Publications, 2009.

Weaver, Zofia, 'The Mystery of Ectoplasm: Where Biology and Imagination Meet', in *Deep Weird: The Varieties of High Strangeness Experience*, ed. Jack Hunter, (Hove: August Night, 2023).

Weber, Max. *The Sociology of Religion.* London: Methuen, 1965.

Weikart, Richard. 'Progress through Racial Extermination: Social Darwinism, Eugenics, and Pacifism in Germany, 1860-1918'. *German Studies Review* 26, no. 2 (2003): pp. 273–94.

Weinstock. Jeffrey A. *The Monster Theory Reader.* Minneapolis: University of Minnesota Press, 2020.

West, Donald. 'Society for Psychical Research'. https://psi-encyclopedia.spr.ac.uk/articles/society-psychical-research [accessed 25 February 2023].

White Jr., Lynn. 'The Historical Roots of Our Ecologic Crisis'. *Science* 155, no. 3767 (1967): pp. 1203–7.

Whitehead, Amy. 'A method of "things": a relational theory of objects as persons in lived religious practice'. *Journal of Contemporary Religion* 30, no. 2 (2020): 231–50.

Whiteley, Aliya. *The Secret Life of Fungi: Discoveries from a Hidden World.* London: Elliott and Thompson, 2020.

'Whitewashed Hope: A Message from 10+ Indigenous Leaders and Organisations: regenerative agriculture and permaculture offer narrow solutions to climate crisis'. https://www.culturalsurvival.org/news/whitewashed-hope-message-10-indigenous-leaders-and-organizations [accessed 6 March 2023].

Wildman, Wesley J. 'An Introduction to Relational Ontology', in *The Trinity and an*

Entangled World: Relationality in Physical Science and Theology, ed. John Polkinghorn, (Michigan: Wm B. Eerdmans, 2010).

Williams, Dilafruz R., and Jonathan Brown. *Learning Gardens and Sustainability Education: Bringing Life to Schools and Schools to Life*. Abingdon: Routledge, 2012.

Willmer, Gareth. 'Bats have different song cultures and chatter about food, sleep, sex and other bats'. https://ec.europa.eu/research-and-innovation/en/horizon-magazine/bats-have-different-song-cultures-and-chatter-about-food-sleep-sex-and-other-bats [accessed 25 February 2023].

Wilson, Edward O. 'Biophilia and the Conservation Ethic'. in *Evolutionary Perspectives on Environmental Problems*, ed. Dustin J. Penn and Iver Mysterud, (Abingdon: Routledge, 2007).

Winterhalder, Bruce. 'The behavioural ecology of hunter gatherers', in *Hunter-Gatherers: An Interdisciplinary Perspective*, ed. C. Panter-Brick, R. H. Layton and P. A. Rowley-Conwy (Cambridge: Cambridge University Press, 2001), pp. 13–38.

Wohlleben, Peter. *The Hidden Life of Trees: What they Feel, How they Communicate —Discoveries from a Secret World*. London: William Collins, 2016.

Wright, Julia. *Subtle Agroecologies: Farming with the Hidden Half of Nature*. Abingdon: CRC Press, 2021.

'Our Living Planet Report'. WWF. https://wwf.panda.org/knowl- edge_hub/all_publications/living_planet_report_2018/ [accessed 23 January 2020].

Wystrach, Antoine. 'We've Been Looking at Ant Intelligence the Wrong Way'. *The Conversation*, 30 August 2013, https://theconversation.com/weve-been-looking-at-ant-intelligence-the-wrong-way-17619 [accessed 20 March 2023].

Xu, Ping. 'An Interdisciplinary Study: Rock Worship in Chinese Classical Gardens'. *International Journal of Arts and Sciences* 7, no. 5 (2014): pp. 547–58.

Yachi, Shigeo, and Michel Loreau. 'Biodiversity and ecosystem productivity in a fluctuating environment: The insurance hypothesis'. *PNAS* 96, no. 4 (1999): pp. 1463–68.

Yaden, David Bryce, Jonathan Haidt, Ralph W. Hood Jr., David R. Vago and Andrew B. Newberg. 'The Varieties of Self-Transcendent Experience'. *Review of General Psychology* 21, no. 2 (2017): pp. 1–18.

Yilkoski, Petri, 'Micro, Macro and Mechanism,' in *The Oxford Handbook of Philosophy of Social Science*, ed. Harold Kincaid, (Oxford: Oxford University Press, 2012): pp. 21–45.

Young, David, and Michiko Young. *The Art of the Japanese Garden: History, Culture, Design*. Rutland: Tuttle, 2019.

Young, Simon. 'The Fairy Census'. 2014–2017. http://www.fairyist.com/wp-content/uploads/2014/10/The-Fairy-Census-2014-2017-1.pdf [accessed 22 July 2019].

———. 'Children Who See Fairies'. *Journal for the Study of Religious Experience* 4, no. 1 (2018): pp. 81–98.

Yunkaporta, Tyson. *Sand Talk: How Indigenous Thinking Can Save the World*. Melbourne: The Text Publishing Company, 2019.

Zaehner, Robert C. *Mysticism Sacred and Profane*. Oxford: Oxford University Press, 1957.

Zelko, Frank. 'Scaling Greenpeace: From Local Activism to Global Governance'. *Historical Social Research* 42 (2017): pp. 318–42.

Zylstra, Matthew J., Andrew T. Knight, Karen J. Eslier and Lessley L. L. Le Grange. 'Connectedness as a Core Conservation Concern: An Interdisciplinary Review of Theory and a Call for Practice'. *Springer Science Reviews* 2 (2014): pp. 119–43.

INDEX

ABOUT THE AUTHOR

Jack Hunter, PhD, is an Honorary Research Fellow with the Alister Hardy Religious Experience Research Centre, and a tutor with the Sophia Centre for the Study of Cosmology in Culture, University of Wales Trinity Saint David, where he is lead tutor on the MA in Ecology and Spirituality and teaches on the MA in Cultural Astronomy and Astrology. He also teaches on the 'Approaches to Consciousness' module of the Alef Trust's MSc in Consciousness, Spirituality and Transpersonal Psychology. His doctoral research took the form of an ethnographic study of contemporary trance and physical mediumship in Bristol. He is the author of *Manifesting Spirits: An Anthropological Study of Mediumship and the Paranormal* (2020), and *Spirits, Gods and Magic: An Introduction to the Anthropology of the Supernatural* (2020). He is the editor of *Deep Weird: The Varieties of High Strangeness Experience* (2023), *Greening the Paranormal: Exploring the Ecology of Extraordinary Experience* (2019), *Damned Facts: Fortean Essays on Religion, Folklore and the Paranormal* (2016), and is co-editor with Dr. Rachael Ironside of *Folklore, People and Place: International Perspectives on Tourism and Tradition in Storied Places* (2023), and with Dr. Diana Espirito Santo of *Mattering the Invisible: Technologies, Bodies and the Realm of the Spectral* (2021). He is also a musician and lives in the hills of mid-Wales with his family.

Milton Keynes UK
Ingram Content Group UK Ltd.
UKHW052315060924
447982UK00019B/236

9 781907 767234